REASONING, MEANING, AND MIND

Reasoning, Meaning and Mind

GILBERT HARMAN

CLARENDON PRESS · OXFORD
1999

Oxford University Press, Great Clarendon Street, Oxford OX2 6DP

Oxford New York

Athens Auckland Bangkok Bogotá Buenos Aires Calcutta
Cape Town Chennai Dar es Salaam Delhi Florence Hong Kong Istanbul
Karachi Kuala Lumpur Madrid Melbourne Mexico City Mumbai
Nairobi Paris São Paulo Singapore Taipei Tokyo Toronto Warsaw

and associated companies in
Berlin Ibadan

Oxford is a registered trade mark of Oxford University Press

Published in the United States
by Oxford University Press Inc., New York

British Library Cataloguing in Publication Data
Data available

Library of Congress Cataloging in Publication Data
Harman, Gilbert.
Reasoning, meaning, and mind / Gilbert Harman.
Includes bibliographical references.
1. Reasoning. 2. Meaning (Philosophy) 3. Philosophy of mind.
I. Title.
BC177.H375 1999 128'.33—dc21 98-50498
ISBN 0–19–823803–7
ISBN 0–19–823802–9 (pbk.)

1 3 5 7 9 10 8 6 4 2

Typeset by Invisible Ink
Printed in Great Britain
on acid-free paper by
Biddles Ltd, Guildford and King's Lynn

For Lucy

ACKNOWLEDGEMENTS

Preparation of some of the material in this book was supported in part by grants to Princeton University from the James S. McDonnell Foundation and the National Science Foundation. I am also grateful to the publishers of the original versions of the essays in this book for permission to reprint them.

'Rationality', in E. E. Smith and D. N. Osherson (eds.), *Thinking: Invitation to Cognitive Science*, vol. iii (Cambridge, Mass.: MIT Press, 1995), 175–211.

'Practical Reasoning', *Review of Metaphysics*, 29 (1976), 431–63.

'Simplicity as a Pragmatic Criterion for Deciding what Hypotheses to Take Seriously', in Douglas Stalker (ed.), *Grue: The New Riddle of Induction* (Peru, Ill.: Open Court, 1994), 153–71.

'Pragmatism and Reasons for Belief', in C. B. Kulp (ed.), *Realism/ Antirealism and Epistemology* (Lanham, Md.: Rowman & Littlefield, 1997), 123–47.

'The Death of Meaning' originally appeared as 'Quine on Meaning and Existence, I: The Death of Meaning', *Review of Metaphysics*, 21 (1967), 124–51.

'Doubts about Conceptual Analysis', in M. Michael and J. O'Leary-Hawthorne (eds.), *Philosophy in Mind: The Place of Philosophy in the Study of Mind* (Dordrecht: Kluwer, 1994), 43–8.

'Analyticity Regained?', *Nous*, 30 (1996), 392–400.

'Three Levels of Meaning', *Journal of Philosophy*, 65 (1968), 590–602.

'Language Learning', *Nous*, 4 (1970), 33–43.

'Meaning and Semantics', in Milton K. Munitz and Peter K. Unger (eds.), *Semantics and Philosophy* (New York: New York University Press, 1974), 1–16.

'Language, Thought, and Communication', in Keith Gunderson (ed.), *Language, Mind, and Knowledge: Minnesota Studies in the Philosophy of Science*, vol. vii (Minneapolis, Minn.: University of Minnesota Press, 1975), 279–98.

'(Nonsolipsistic) Conceptual Role Semantics', in Ernest LePore (ed.), *New Directions in Semantics* (London: Academic Press, 1987), 55–81.

'Wide Functionalism', in Stephen Schiffer and Susan Steele (eds.),

Cognition and Representation (Boulder, Colo.: Westview Press, 1988), 11–20.

'The Intrinsic Quality of Experience', *Philosophical Perspectives*, 4 (1990), 31–52.

'Immanent and Transcendent Approaches to Meaning and Mind' originally appeared as 'Immanent and Transcendent Approaches to the Theory of Meaning', in Roger Gibson and Robert B. Barrett (eds.), *Perspectives on Quine* (Oxford: Blackwell, 1990), 144–57.

CONTENTS

INTRODUCTION

These essays have all been previously published. I have edited them substantially, putting them into a uniform format, reducing repetition, removing some errors, and tinkering with wording.

In general, many themes are negative. There is no a priori knowledge or analytic truth. Logic is not a theory of reasoning. A theory of truth conditions is not a theory of meaning. A purely objective account of meaning or mind cannot say what words mean or what it is like to see things in colour.

Other themes are positive. Theoretical reasoning has important practical aspects. Meaning depends on how words are used to think with, that is, on how concepts function in reasoning, perception, and action. The relevant uses or functions relate concepts to aspects of the environment and other things in the world. Translation plays a central role in any adequate account of mind or meaning.

Although the essays are highly interrelated, I have somewhat arbitrarily divided them into four groups, on (1) reasoning and rationality, (2) analyticity, (3) meaning, and (4) mind. Here are brief summaries of the essays.

The first four are concerned with basic principles of reasoning and rationality.

In Essay 1, 'Rationality', I sharply distinguish logic from the theory of reasoning, reject special foundationalism in favour of general epistemological conservatism, and discuss the role in reasoning of coherence and simplicity. (Simplicity is the main topic of Essay 3.) Throughout Essay 1 I am concerned with the difference between theoretical and practical reasoning and with the role that practical considerations play in theoretical reasoning, an issue addressed further in Essay 4.

In Essay 2, 'Practical Reasoning', I argue for several conclusions. Intentions are distinct real psychological states, not mere constructs out of beliefs and desires. One intends to do something only if one believes one will do it. The various things one intends to do should be consistent with each other and with one's beliefs in the same way that one's beliefs should be consistent with each other. There is no similar consistency requirement on desires. Practical reasoning can lead one to the intention to do something only if one is justified in thinking that one's intention will lead to one's doing it. This is so for positive intentions, anyway, which are to be distinguished from negative and conditional intentions. All intentions are self-referential and are to be distinguished from beliefs by means of differences between theoretical reasoning, which directly modifies beliefs, and practical reasoning, which directly modifies intentions.

I discuss when conclusions are to be reached via practical reasoning and when they are to be reached via theoretical reasoning and make two further points. One can sometimes adopt intrinsic desires at will. One sometimes pursues a plan in order to give significance to earlier acts.

Essay 3, 'Simplicity as a Pragmatic Criterion for Deciding what Hypotheses to Take Seriously', begins by discussing curve fitting and Goodman's 'new riddle of induction'. Taking the simplicity of a hypothesis to depend entirely on the simplicity of the way it is represented does not work because simplicity of representation is too dependent on the method of representation, and any hypothesis can be represented simply. An alternative 'semantic' theory also has problems. I am led to propose a 'computational' theory that considers how easy it is to use a hypothesis to get answers in which one is interested. (This leads to issues about pragmatism that are addressed at length in the following essay.) I also discuss the use of calculators and tables in getting such answers and I compare (bad) parasitical theories with (good) idealizations in science.

In Essay 4, 'Pragmatism and Reasons for Belief', I consider how to explain the distinction between epistemic and nonepistemic reasons while allowing epistemic reasons to be affected by pragmatic considerations of simplicity, coherence, and conservatism. I discuss various sorts of practical reasons to believe things and argue that it is sometimes possible to decide to believe something on the basis of practical considerations. After noting difficulties with trying to explain epistemic reasons in terms of connections with truth or the goal of believing what is true, I discuss certain issues in the foundations of probability theory, suggesting that epistemic reasons connect with conditional probability in a way that nonepistemic reasons do not.

Essays 5–7 argue against the once popular philosophical idea that certain claims are true by virtue of meaning and knowable by virtue of meaning.

The original version of Essay 5, 'The Death of Meaning', was the first part of a two-part essay on W. V. Quine's early philosophical views. The essay begins by noting that the analytic–synthetic distinction presupposes an explanatory claim. I describe Quine's argument that logic cannot be true by convention but only by convention plus logic. In any event, the relevant 'conventions' are merely postulates. We can conceive of them failing to hold just as we can conceive of any other postulates failing to hold. Failing to hold is not the same as having a false negation. It may be that certain terminology must be rejected as committing one to false presuppositions. Analyticity is often explained in terms of synonymy, but this requires an explained technical notion of synonymy, not the more ordinary notion. Some philosophers have been tempted by a paradigm case argument for analyticity: we can teach students how to use the term 'analytic', so there must be analytic truths. A similar argument would show that there really were witches in Salem. The philosophical use of these notions depends upon a proposed explanation of the difficulty some people have at imagining certain things. As one's imagination improves, it becomes more difficult to accept the analytic–synthetic distinction.

I go on in Essay 5 to discuss the postulation of language-independent meanings and other intensional objects. I discuss Quine's thesis of the indeterminacy of radical translation, using the example of various ways to translate number theory to set theory. (However, I argue against indeterminacy of radical translation in Essay 10.) Finally, I discuss the positive Quinean theory of meaning, which puts weight on translation, where translation is a similarity relation, not a strict equivalence relation.

Essay 6, 'Doubts about Conceptual Analysis', is a brief response to a paper by Frank Jackson. Although philosophers sometimes defend certain 'analyses' as analytic or a priori truths, I point out that such analyses are far from obviously true and are defended inductively. Jackson says that the rejection of the analytic–synthetic distinction rests on biased samples of hard cases. That is just wrong. The historical rejection of analyticity was based on consideration of central cases. After making these points I go on to summarize a few of the arguments against analyticity of Essay 5.

In Essay 7, 'Analyticity Regained?', I comment on a defence of analyticity by Paul Boghossian.

The next five essays are directly concerned with meaning.

Essay 8, 'Three Levels of Meaning', distinguishes three conceptions of meaning—meaning as conceptual role, meaning as communicated thought, and meaning as speech-act potential. At one time, these were conceived as competing conceptions, but it is better to see them as potentially compatible theories that are concerned with different aspects or levels of meaning.

Essays 9 and 10 discuss the idea that a natural language like English is in the first instance incorporated into the system of representation with which one thinks. This 'incorporation' view is compared with a translation or 'decoding' view of communication. Essay 9, 'Language, Thought, and Communication', develops the basic argument, and argues that compositional semantics only makes sense given the implausible decoding view. Essay 10, 'Language Learning', discusses what it might be for thoughts to include instances of sentences of a language and notes that children can understand more than they can themselves say. Essay 10 ends by arguing that, even though Quine's thesis of the indeterminacy of radical translation should be rejected, considerations of translation do not argue against the incorporation view.

Essay 11, 'Meaning and Semantics', critically examines the popular suggestion that a theory of meaning ought to take the form of a theory of truth. After rejecting several arguments of the suggestion, I sketch a conceptual role semantics in which the meanings of logical constants are determined in large part by implications involving those logical constants, where implication is to be explained in terms of truth. Although truth conditions are sometimes relevant to meaning, this is only the case for the meanings of logical constants.

Essay 12, '(Nonsolipsistic) Conceptual Role Semantics', further elaborates the suggested approach to meaning. I distinguish the use of symbols in calculation and other thinking from the use of symbols in communication. I note that Grice's analysis of speaker meaning fails for certain uses of symbols in calculation. Following Ryle, I note that words and concepts have uses, but sentences or whole thoughts do not. I sketch some of the uses or functional roles of concepts—in perception, inference, and practical reasoning. I discuss issues of indeterminacy and what it is for aspects of a description of functional role to correspond to reality. I stress that functional roles must be understood in terms of ways an organism functions in relation to a presumed normal environment, applying the point to discussions of Twin Earth and inverted qualia.

The final three essays (13–15) are more directly concerned with the nature of mind, although they carry on themes developed in the previous essays.

Essay 13, 'Wide Functionalism', argues that psychological explanation is a kind of functional explanation, like some biological explanation, where the relevant functions tend to have to do with perceiving and acting in relation to the environment. Pain serves as a kind of alarm system; perception allows an organism to get information about the environment; and so on. Although there are defenders of a narrow, more solipsistic psychological functionalism, I offer a brief history of the subject that indicates that the dominant trend has involved the wider version. In any event, the wider functionalism is clearly more plausible, and methodological solipsism in psychology is actually incoherent.

Essay 14, 'The Intrinsic Quality of Experience', discusses three related arguments against the sort of functionalism I have been defending. The first argument says that we are directly aware of intrinsic features of our experience and points out that there is no way to account for such an awareness in a purely functional view. The second claims that a person blind from birth can know all about the functional role of visual experience without knowing what it is like to see something red. The third holds that functionalism cannot account for the possibility of an inverted spectrum. I argue that all three arguments can be defused by distinguishing properties of the object of experience from properties of the experience of an object.

The final essay, 'Immanent and Transcendent Approaches to Meaning and Mind', distinguishes two approaches to the understanding of the experiences and uses of language of others. One emphasizes *Verstehen* or translation. The other restricts itself to an objective description of use and function. I argue that each approach by itself must leave something out. We need both approaches.

PART I

Reasoning

1

Rationality

INTRODUCTION

What is it for someone to be rational or reasonable, as opposed to being irrational or unreasonable? Think of some examples in which someone is being rational or reasonable as well as examples in which someone is being irrational or unreasonable. What do you think makes the difference? Think also of some examples in which someone makes a mistake but is not therefore irrational or unreasonable.

1.1.1 *Some Examples*

Here is one kind of example:

> *Giving in to temptation*
> Jane very much wants to do well in history. There is a crucial test tomorrow and she needs to study tonight if she is to do well in the test. Jane's friends are all going to a party for Bill tonight. Jane knows that if she goes to the party, she will really regret it. But she goes to the party anyway.

It is irrational for Jane to go to the party, even if it is understandable. The rational thing for her to do is to stay home and study.

Many examples of giving in to temptation involve a bit of irrationality. For example, smoking cigarettes while knowing of the health hazards involved is at least somewhat irrational. The rational thing to do is to give up smoking.

Here is a different sort of example:

> *Refusing to take a remedial course*
> Bob, a college freshman, takes a test designed to indicate whether students should take a useful remedial writing course. Students do not write their names in their examination booklets but write an identifying number instead, so that graders will not know the identity of

the students whose answers they are grading. Bob does poorly in the test and is told he should take a remedial writing course. He objects to this advice, attributing his poor score on the test to bias on the part of the grader against his ethnic group, and does not take the remedial writing course.

Bob's belief that his score is the result of bias is irrational. It would be more rational for Bob to conclude that he got a poor score because he did poorly on the test.

Refusing a reasonable proposal

Three students, Sally, Ellie, and Louise, have been assigned to a set of rooms consisting of a study room, a small single bedroom, and another small bedroom with a two-person bunk bed. Sally has arrived first and has moved into the single. The other two room-mates propose that they take turns living in the single, each getting the single for one-third of the school year. Sally refuses to consider this proposal and insists on keeping the single for herself the whole year.

Sally's room-mates say she is being unreasonable. (Is she?)

Confusing two philosophers

Frieda is having trouble in her introductory philosophy course. Because of a similarity in their names, she confuses the medieval philosopher Thomas Aquinas with the twentieth-century American philosopher W. V. Quine.

This is a mistake but does not necessarily exhibit irrationality or unreasonableness (although it may).

Failing to distinguish twins

Harry has trouble distinguishing the twins Connie and Laura. Sometimes he mistakes one for the other.

That by itself is not irrational or unreasonable, although it would be unreasonable for Harry to be over-confident in the judgement that he is talking to Connie, given his past mistakes.

Adding mistake

Sam makes an adding mistake when he tries to balance his chequebook.

A mistake in addition need not involve any irrationality or unreasonableness.

Consider mistakes about probability. Under certain conditions some people assign a higher probability to Linda's being a feminist and a bank teller than to her merely being a bank teller. The probabilities that people assign to certain situations can depend on how the situation is described, even though the descriptions are logically equivalent. Are mistakes of this sort always irrational or unreasonable? Are some of them more like mistakes in addition?

What is the difference between the sort of mistake involved in being irrational or unreasonable and other mistakes that do not involve being irrational or unreasonable? Does it matter what the difference is?

Do you think it is irrational or unreasonable to believe in astrology? To be superstitious? To believe in God? To believe in science? To be moral? To think that other people have mental experiences like your own? To suppose that the future will resemble the past? These questions increasingly raise a question of scepticism. A sceptic about X is someone who takes it to be irrational or unreasonable to believe in X. Is scepticism sometimes itself irrational or unreasonable?

1.1.2 *Rationality and Cognitive Science*

Issues about rationality have significance for cognitive science. For example, one strategy for dealing with cognition is to start with the assumption that people think and act rationally, and then investigate what can be explained on that basis. Classical economic theory seeks to explain market behaviour as the result of interactions among completely rational agents following their own interests. Similarly, psychologists sometimes explain 'person perception', the judgements that one makes about others, by taking these judgements to be the result of reasonable causal inferences from the way others behave in one's presence. In ordinary life, we often base predictions on the assumption that other people will act rationally (Dennett, 1971), as we do when we assume that other drivers will act rationally in traffic.

Such strategies require assumptions about rationality. Economics assumes that the rational agent maximizes expected utility (for example, von Neumann and Morgenstern, 1944). Classical attribution theory identifies rationality with the scientific method (for example, Kelley, 1967). It is less clear how we identify what is rational in our ordinary thinking. (One possibility is that each person asks what he or she would do in the other person's shoes and identifies that imagined response as the rational one.)

Some research has been interpreted as showing that people often depart systematically from the ideal economic agent, or the ideal scientist. People often ignore background frequencies, tend to look for confirming evidence rather than disconfirming evidence, take the conjunction of two claims to have a higher probability than one of the claims by itself, and so on.

There is more than one way to try to explain (away) these apparent departures from ideal rationality. One type of explanation points to resource limits.

Resource limits

Reasoning uses resources and there are limits to the available resources. Reasoners have limited attention spans, limited memories, and limited time. Ideal rationality is not always possible for limited beings: because of our limits, we may make use of strategies and heuristics, rules of thumb that work or seem to work most of the time, but not always. It is rational for us to use such rules, if we have nothing better that will give us reasonable answers in the light of our limited resources.

A second way to explain apparent departures from rationality is to challenge the view of rationality according to which these are departures even from ideal rationality. If people depart from what is rational according to a particular theory, that may be either because they are departing from rationality or because that particular theory of rationality is incorrect.

Some of the cases in which people appear to depart from ideal rationality are cases in which people appear to be inconsistent in what they accept. They make logical mistakes or violate principles of probability that they also seem to accept. How could these cases not be cases of irrationality?

Two ways have been suggested. First, it may be that people are not actually being inconsistent in their judgements.

Different concepts

People may be using concepts in a different way from the experimenter. When people judge that Linda is more likely to be a feminist bank teller than a bank teller, they may be using 'more likely' to mean something like 'more representative'. When people make apparent mistakes in logic, that may be because they mean by 'if' what the experimenter means by 'if and only if'. Given what they mean by their words, they may not be as inconsistent as they appear to be (Cohen, 1981).

Second, even if people are sometimes inconsistent, that does not show they are being irrational.

Reasonable inconsistency

It is not always irrational or unreasonable to be inconsistent (Pollock, 1991; Nozick, 1993).

It is an important question just what connection there is between being inconsistent and being unreasonable or irrational.

In this essay, I look more closely at rationality and reasonableness. I consider both actions and beliefs. What is it to act rationally or reasonably and what is it to act irrationally or unreasonably? What is it to have rational or reasonable beliefs and what is it to have irrational or unreasonable beliefs?

1.2 BACKGROUND

1.2.1 *Theoretical and Practical Rationality*

Let us begin by contrasting two of the examples mentioned above, 'Giving in to temptation' and 'Refusing to take a remedial course'. Jane goes to a party knowing she should instead study for tomorrow's exam. Bob thinks his grade on the writing placement exam is due to prejudice against his ethnic group even though he knows the grader does not have any way to discover the ethnic backgrounds of those taking the exam. One obvious difference is that Jane's irrationality is manifested in a decision to do something, namely, to go to the party, whereas Bob's irrationality is manifested in his belief, whether or not he acts on that belief. Bob does go on to make an irrational decision to refuse to take the writing course that he needs, but the source of that irrational decision is Bob's irrational belief. The source of Jane's irrational decision is not an irrational belief. Jane knows very well that she should stay home and study.

In deciding to go to the party knowing she should instead study for tomorrow's exam, Jane exhibits a defect in practical rationality. In believing that his grade on the writing placement exam is due to prejudice against his ethnic group, Bob exhibits a defect in theoretical rationality. Theoretical rationality is rationality in belief; practical rationality is rationality in action, or perhaps in plans and intentions.

Just as we can distinguish theoretical from practical rationality, we can distinguish theoretical reasoning, which most directly affects beliefs, from practical reasoning, which most directly affects plans and intentions. The upshot of theoretical reasoning is either a change in beliefs or no change, whereas the upshot of practical reasoning is either a change in plans and intentions or no change. Bob's irrationality arises from a problem with his theoretical reasoning. There may be nothing wrong with his practical reasoning apart from that. Jane's irrationality arises entirely from a defect in practical reasoning and not at all from anything in her theoretical reasoning.

Theoretical and practical reasoning are similar in certain respects, but there are important differences. One important difference has to do with the rationality of arbitrary choices.

> *Arbitrary belief*
> Jane is trying to decide which route Albert took to work this morning. She knows that in the past Albert has taken Route A about half the time and Route B about half the time. Her other evidence does not support one of these conclusions over the other. So, Jane arbitrarily decides to believe that Albert took Route A.

Clearly, Jane should suspend judgement and neither believe that Albert took Route A nor believe that he took Route B. It is irrational or unreasonable for her to adopt one of these beliefs in the absence of further evidence distinguishing the two possibilities.

On the other hand, consider the practical analogue.

> *Arbitrary intention*
> Albert is trying to decide how to get to work this morning. He could take either Route A or Route B. Taking either of these routes will get him to work at about the same time and the balance of reasons does not favour going one way over going the other way. So, Albert arbitrarily forms the intention of taking Route A.

This arbitrary decision is quite reasonable. In fact, it would be quite irrational or unreasonable for Albert not to decide on one route rather than the other, even though his decision in the case must be completely arbitrary. Someone who was unable to make an arbitrary choice of routes would suffer from a serious defect in practical rationality! Arbitrary choices of what to intend can be practically rational in a way that arbitrary choices of what to believe are not theoretically rational.

Another difference between theoretical and practical rationality has to do with the rationality or irrationality of wishful thinking. Wishful thinking is theoretically unreasonable, but practically reasonable. Wishes and desires are relevant to practical reasoning in a way that they are not relevant to theoretical reasoning.

> *Wishful practical thinking*
> Jane's desire to get a good grade on the final exam leads her to study

for the exam in order to try to make it true that she will get a good grade on the final exam.

It is rational for Jane to let her desires influence her practical reasoning in this way. But consider the analogous theoretical case.

Wishful theoretical thinking
After Jane has taken the exam and before she has learned what her grade is, her desire to get a good grade on the exam leads her to conclude that she did get a good grade.

This sort of wishful thinking does not by itself give Jane a reason to believe that she got a good grade. To believe that something is so merely because she wants it to be so is theoretically unreasonable, whereas to decide to try to make something so because she wants it to be so is reasonable practical thinking. Desires can rationally influence the conclusions of practical reasoning in a way that they cannot rationally influence the conclusions of theoretical thinking.

This point has to be carefully formulated. Consider the following case in which desires do rationally influence what theoretical conclusions someone reaches.

Goal-directed theoretical reasoning
There are various conclusions that Jack could reach right now. He could try to figure out what Albert had for breakfast this morning. He could solve some arithmetical problems. He could work on today's crossword puzzle. He could try to resolve a philosophical paradox that Sam told him the other day. But, at the moment, Jack is locked out of his house and really ought to try to figure out where he left his keys. If Jack thinks about where he left his keys, however, he won't be able at the same time to resolve the philosophical paradox or solve the arithmetical puzzles. Because he wants very much to get into his house, he devotes his attention to figuring out where his keys must be.

Jack's goals can therefore be relevant to what conclusions he reaches. So, it is over-simple to say that your desires cannot rationally affect what conclusions you can legitimately reach in theoretical reasoning. Your desires can rationally affect your theoretical conclusions by affecting what questions you use theoretical reasoning to answer. The right statement of the constraint on theoretical wishful thinking therefore seems to be something like this: given what question you are using theoretical reasoning to answer, your desires cannot rationally affect what answer to that question you reach. In practical reasoning, on the other hand, your desires can rationally influence not just the questions you consider but also the practical answers you give to those questions.

1.2.1.1 Practical Reasons for Belief

However, there are complications. Although wishful theoretical thinking is normally irrational, it is possible to have good practical reasons to believe something.

> *The power of positive thinking*
> Jonathan is sick. He has just read a study showing that people tend to recover more quickly if they believe that they will recover quickly. So Jonathan takes himself to have a practical reason to believe he will recover quickly.
>
> *Loyalty*
> Mary has been accused of stealing a book from the library. It would be disloyal for her best friend, Fran, to believe the charge against Mary. So Fran has a practical reason, loyalty, to believe that Mary is innocent.
>
> *Group think*
> Karen has been trying to decide what she thinks about capital punishment. She has noticed that the in-crowd at her school all believe that capital punishment for murder is justified and she has also noticed that members of the in-crowd do not like people who disagree with them about such things. Karen wants very much to be liked by members of the in-crowd. So she takes herself to have a practical reason to believe that capital punishment for murder is justified.

What do you think about this last example? Is there something wrong with Karen if she adapts her opinions to people she wants to please? How does that compare with Fran's belief in Mary's innocence based on loyalty to Mary?

Here are two further examples:

> *Advertising account*
> Landon would like very much to get the RST Tobacco advertising account. The RST Tobacco Company will hire only advertisers who believe that cigarette smoking is a healthy pastime. So Landon takes himself to have a practical reason to believe that cigarette smoking is a healthy pastime.

Pascal's argument for belief in God

Pascal (1995) reasons as follows. 'Either there is a God or there is not, and either I believe in God or I do not. So there are four possibilities with the following payoffs: (I) If I believe in God and there is a God, then I go to heaven and have infinite bliss. (II) If I believe in God and there is no God, then my costs are whatever is involved in believing in God. (III) If I do not believe in God and there is a God, then I go to hell and suffer the torments of the damned for eternity. (IV) If I do not believe in God and there is no God, then I have no costs and no gains. Now, the expected value of belief in God is the value of infinite bliss multiplied by the probability that there is a God minus the costs of belief in God multiplied by the probability that there is no God; and the expected value of not believing in God is the negative value of an eternity in hell multiplied by the probability that there is a God. No matter how small the likelihood that God exists, the expected value of belief is infinitely greater than the expected value of disbelief. Therefore, I should believe in God.'

Here we have what purport to be good practical reasons to believe one thing or another. This conclusion suggests that the difference between practical reasons and theoretical reasons is not just a matter of what they are reasons for, intentions *versus* beliefs.

1.2.1.2 Epistemic versus nonepistemic reasons for belief

All but the first of the examples in the preceding section have this feature: the examples mention a reason to believe something that does not make it more likely that the belief is true. Such reasons are sometimes called (for example, by Foley, 1987) 'nonepistemic reasons' for belief, in contrast with the more usual epistemic reasons for belief that do make the belief more likely to be true.

Epistemic reason for belief
R is an epistemic reason to believe P only if the probability of P given R is greater than the probability of P given not-R.

Nonepistemic reason for belief
R is a nonepistemic reason to believe P if R is a reason to believe P over and above the extent to which the probability of P given R is greater than the probability of P given not-R.

These definitions leave open the important question whether all practical reasons for belief are nonepistemic reasons, a question we come back to below.

1.2.2 *Inference and Reasoning versus Implication and Consistency*

Issues about inference and reasoning need to be distinguished from issues about implication and consistency.

Inference and reasoning are psychological processes leading to possible changes in belief (theoretical reasoning) or possible changes in plans and intentions (practical reasoning). Implication is most directly a relation among propositions. Certain propositions imply another proposition when and only when, if the former propositions are true, so too is the latter proposition.

It is one thing to say

(1) A, B, C imply D.

It is quite another thing to say

(2) If you believe A, B, C, you should (or may) infer D.

Statement (1) is a remark about implication; (2) is a remark about inference. Statement (1) says nothing special about belief or any other psychological state (unless one of A, B, C has psychological content), nor does (1) say anything normative about what anyone 'should' or 'may' do (Goldman, 1986).

Statement (1) can be true without (2) being true.

> *Rationality versus genius*
> A, B, C imply D. Sam believes A, B, and C. But Sam does not realize that A, B, C imply D. In fact, it would take a genius to recognize that A, B, C imply D. And Sam, although a rational man, is far from a genius.

Here Sam has no reason at all to believe D. Consider also:

> *Discovering a contradiction*
> Sally believes A, B, C and has just come to recognize that A, B, C imply D. Unfortunately, she also believes for very good reasons that D is false. So she now has a reason to stop believing A, B, or C, rather than a reason to believe D.

> *Clutter avoidance*
> Jane believes A, B, C, she recognizes that A, B, C imply D, she does not

believe that D is false, and she has no reason to think that D is false. She is also completely uninterested in whether D is true or false and has no reason to be interested. D is the proposition that either $2 + 2 = 4$ or the moon is made of green cheese. There are many, many trivial consequences like this of her beliefs that she has no reason to infer. She has no reason to clutter her mind with trivial consequences of her beliefs just because they follow from things she believes.

Such examples indicate that, if implication is relevant to what it is reasonable to believe, the connection has to be fairly complex. (We discuss below how implication might be relevant to what it is reasonable to believe.)

Just as issues about implication have to be distinguished from issues about reasonable inference, issues about consistency have to be distinguished from issues about rationality and irrationality. Consistency and inconsistency are in the first instance relations among propositions and only indirectly relations among propositional attitudes. Propositions are consistent when and only when it is possible for them all to be true together. Propositions are inconsistent when and only when it is not possible for them all to be true together.

So, it is one thing to say,

> (3) Propositions A, B, C are inconsistent with each other.

It is quite another to say,

> (4) It is irrational (or unreasonable) to believe A, B, C.

The first remark, (3), unlike (4), says nothing special about belief or other psychological states, nor does it say anything normative. Hence, (3) can be true without (4) being true. Even if A, B, C are actually inconsistent, the inconsistency may have gone unnoticed and may be very difficult to discover. And even if you notice that A, B, C are inconsistent, there may still be reasons to accept each and it may be quite unclear which should be given up. You may not have the time or the ability to work out which should be given up or you may have more urgent matters to attend to before trying to figure out which to give up of A, B, C. In the meantime, it may very well be rational for you to continue to believe all three.

Age of the earth

In the nineteenth century, Kelvin's calculation of the age of the earth using principles of thermodynamics gave a result that was too small to allow for what was calculated to be the time needed for evolution (Gould, 1985). One scientific response was to continue to accept all the relevant principles, despite their leading to this contradiction, while waiting for someone to figure out what was going wrong.

This would seem to have been a rational response to the difficulty. (Kelvin's calculations depended on assumptions about sources of energy. The discovery of radioactivity revealed a source he had not allowed for.)

Someone may show you a paradoxical argument leading to the conclusion that $3 = 1$, or a proof that a certain claim, which says of itself that it is not a true claim, is both a true claim and not a true claim.

> *Proof that $3 = 1$.*
> Let $n = 1$.
> Then $2n = 2$.
> $n^2 + 2n = n^2 + 2$ [adding n^2 to both sides].
> $n^2 = n^2 - 2n + 2$ [subtracting $2n$ from both sides].
> $n^2 - 1 = n^2 - 2n + 1$ [subtracting 1 from both sides].
> $(n + 1)(n - 1) = (n - 1)(n - 1)$ [factoring].
> $n + 1 = n - 1$ [eliminating common factor from both sides].
> $n + 2 = n$ [adding 1 to both sides].
> $3 = 1$ [replacing n with its value, 1].

> 'Liar paradox'
> Let (L) be the claim *that (L) is not true.*
> The claim *that (L) is not true* is true if and only if (L) is not true
>   [meaning of 'true'].
> (L) is true if and only if (L) is not true [substituting].
> But that is impossible [logic].

Someone can see that certain assumptions lead to paradox without being able to figure out which assumptions are most plausibly abandoned. In that situation, it may be rational to continue to accept the assumptions in question, trying to avoid the paradoxical patterns of argument.

1.2.3 *The Relevance of Goals and Interests*

The examples above called 'Goal-directed reasoning' and 'Clutter avoidance' indicate that what it is rational or reasonable for you to believe can depend upon your needs, goals, and interests in various ways. This is part of what lies behind the

> *General principle of clutter avoidance*
> It is not reasonable or rational to fill your mind with trivial conse-

quences of your beliefs, when you have better things to do with your time, as you often do.

If you spend all your time deriving trivial logical implications, for example, you will fail to attend to more important things, like finding food and drink and a place to spend the night.

More generally, whether it is rational to reach a particular conclusion will always depend in part on what questions you want to answer or have reasons to answer. If you need your keys to get into the house and you have data from which you could figure out where your keys are, then you have a reason to use those data to reach a conclusion about where your keys are. If it is urgent that you get into the house, it is not rational for you to spend your time drawing conclusions that do not promise to help you in this task. It is not rational for you to infer trivial consequences of your beliefs, as in '1 + 1 = 2; so either 1 + 1 = 2 or the moon is made of green cheese', even though the disjunctive proposition 'Either 1 + 1 = 2, or the moon is made of green cheese' has to be true if its first disjunct, '1 + 1 = 2' is true.

There is a practical aspect to all reasoning, including theoretical reasoning. What theoretical inferences it is reasonable for you to make depend in part on your needs and goals, because the inferences it is reasonable for you to make depend on what questions you have reasons to answer, and what those questions are depends on your needs and goals.

Of course, that is not to say that merely wanting P to be true can give you a reason to believe P (wishful theoretical thinking), although it may give you a reason to find out whether P is true, and it may give you a reason to make P true (wishful practical reasoning).

1.2.4 *Ideal Reasoners?*

Another point already mentioned is also behind the principle of clutter avoidance. Reasoning is subject to 'resource limits' of attention, memory, and time. So, it is not rational to fill your time inferring trivial consequences of your beliefs when you have more important things to attend to. Some theories of rationality (Stalnaker, 1984; Gärdenfors, 1988) begin by abstracting away from these limits. Theories of ideal rationality are concerned with an 'ideally rational agent' whose beliefs are always consistent and 'closed under logical implication'.

Deductive closure
An ideal agent's beliefs are deductively closed, or closed under logical

implication, if, and only if, any proposition logically implied by some of those beliefs is itself also believed.

Other theorists argue that such an idealization appears to confuse rationality, ideal or otherwise, with logical genius or even divinity! And, as we shall see, it is unclear how to relate such an ideal to actual finite human beings, with their resource-limited rationality.

We have already seen that ordinary rationality requires neither deductive closure nor consistency. It does not require deductive closure, because it is not always rational to believe D simply because D is implied by your beliefs in A, B, C. Rationality does not require consistency, because you can be rational even though there are undetected inconsistencies in your beliefs, and because it is not always rational to respond to the discovery of inconsistency by dropping everything else in favour of eliminating that inconsistency.

Now consider an ideal agent with no limitations on memory, attention span, or time, with instantaneous and cost-free computational abilities. It is not obvious whether such an agent would have a reason to infer all the trivial consequences of his or her beliefs. True, it would not cost anything for the agent to draw all those consequences, even all infinitely many of them, let us suppose. But there would also be no need to draw any of those consequences in the absence of a reason to be interested in them, for the agent can effortlessly compute any consequence whenever it may later be needed.

Could an ideal agent's beliefs be inconsistent? If these beliefs were also deductively closed, the agent would then believe everything, because everything follows from inconsistency.

> *Inconsistency implies everything*
> An inconsistent deductively closed agent believes both P and not-P.
> Consider any arbitrary proposition Q.
> P implies (P or Q), so the agent believes (P or Q).
> Not-P and (P or Q) imply Q, so the agent believes Q.
> So an inconsistent deductively closed agent believes every proposition Q.

Now consider rational recovery from inconsistent beliefs.

> *Ordinary recovery from inconsistency*
> An ordinary non-ideal rational agent, Tamara, believes that Bill is in his office, but when she looks into the office, no one is there. At least for a moment, Tamara has inconsistent beliefs, believing both that

Bill is in his office and that no one is in Bill's office. Tamara quickly and painlessly recovers from this inconsistency by dropping her belief that Bill is in his office, concluding that he must have stepped out for a moment.

Ordinary rational agents deal with this sort of momentary inconsistency all the time, whenever something surprising happens. You are surprised when you believe P but discover Q, realizing that P and Q cannot both be true.

But consider the implications of surprise for an ideal deductively closed agent.

> *A deductively closed agent is unable to recover from inconsistency!*
> If the beliefs of such an agent were even momentarily inconsistent, the agent could never rationally recover, for there would be no trace in the agent's beliefs of how the agent had acquired inconsistent beliefs. Because rational recovery from inconsistency can appeal only to present beliefs, and, because the deductively closed agent has exactly the same beliefs no matter how he or she got into inconsistency, there is no way in which the deductively closed agent could use temporal criteria in retreating from inconsistency—the agent would have to recover in exactly the same way, no matter where he or she had started.

It is unclear how ideal rational agents might deal with ordinary surprise. Various possibilities suggest themselves, but we need not explore them here. In what follows, we will be directly concerned with real rather than ideal rational agents.

That is enough background. We now turn to some less obvious and more controversial aspects of rationality.

1.3 CONSERVATISM

The first less obvious aspect of rationality is that ordinary rationality is generally conservative in the following sense. You start from where you are, with your present beliefs and intentions. Rationality or reasonableness then consists in trying to make improvements in your view. Your initial beliefs and intentions have a privileged position in the sense that you begin with them rather than with nothing at all or with a special privileged part of those beliefs and intentions serving as data. So, for example, an ordinary rational person continues to believe something that he or she starts out believing in the absence of a special reason to doubt it.

1.3.1 *Special Foundations: Rejection of General Conservatism*

An alternative conception of rationality going back at least to Descartes (1637) might be called 'special foundationalism'. In this view, your beliefs are to be associated with your reasons or justifications for them. These justifications appeal to other beliefs of yours, themselves to be associated with justifications, and so on. Circular justifications of belief are ruled out, so the process of justification ultimately rests on special foundational beliefs that are self-justifying and need no further justification. Special foundational beliefs include beliefs about immediate experience, such as headaches and perceptual experiences, obvious logical and mathematical axioms, and similar beliefs. In other words, you start from your evidence: those things that are evident to you. Rationality or reasonableness then consists in accepting only what can be justified from your evidence, on this view.

> *Ted's justification for believing that this is a piece of paper*
> It is thin, flexible, and white, with printing on it; it has the feel of paper rather than plastic. This evidence is best explained on the supposition that it is a piece of paper. Ted's justification for believing it is white is that it looks white to him and the circumstances of perception are such that something's looking white is best explained by the supposition that it is white. Ted needs no justification for believing that this looks white, because that is a foundational belief . . .

According to recent versions of special foundationalism (for example, Foley, 1987; Alston, 1989; Chisholm, 1982), foundational beliefs do not have to be guaranteed to be true. In the absence of specific challenges to them, they are justified, but their initial justified status might be overridden by special reasons to doubt them.

> *Defeating a foundational belief*
> Omar is terrified as he sits in the dentist's chair about to have a tooth drilled. When the dentist begins, Omar yells. The dentist stops and asks what's wrong. 'That hurt!' exclaims Omar, quite sincerely. 'But I haven't yet touched the drill to your teeth,' says the dentist. 'Oh!' says Omar after a pause, 'I guess I was confusing my anticipation of pain with actual pain.' Omar's initial foundational belief that he feels pain

is overridden by the further consideration that nothing had happened that could have caused pain. Beliefs about pain are foundational, but can be overridden by special reasons.

There are similar examples involving seemingly obvious logical or definitional truths.

> *Defeating a definitional belief*
> Paula is quite confident that all women are female, something she takes to be true by definition. Quinn objects, 'Wasn't a woman disqualified by the Olympic Committee for having the wrong chromosomes? Didn't they decide that she was not female?' Paula is set back by this question. 'I don't remember that case, but now that you mention that possibility, I can see that there could be a woman who is not, strictly speaking, female.'

Paula's confidence that she has intuited a definitional truth is shaken by the awareness of a possibility she had not previously considered. Seemingly obvious axioms or definitions are foundational but their justification can be overridden by special considerations.

We can describe each of the competing theories (foundationalism, conservatism) in the terminology of the other theory. So, we can say that the special foundations theory is conservative only about foundational beliefs. And we can say that general conservatism treats all beliefs as foundational.

1.3.2 *Objections to Special Foundationalism as a Theory of Rationality*

One problem for special foundationalism is to explain why special foundational beliefs should have special status. What distinguishes foundational beliefs from others that would justify applying conservatism to the foundational beliefs but not other beliefs?

A second, and perhaps more serious problem is that people tend not to keep track of their reasons for their nonfoundational beliefs. But, according to special foundationalism, if you don't associate a complete enough justification with a nonfoundational belief, then it is not rational or reasonable for you to continue to believe it. This realization may undermine a great many of your beliefs.

> *General beliefs with forgotten justifications*
> *Foundationalist:* What country is Athens in?
> *Maureen:* That's easy—Greece. Everyone knows that!
> *F:* But what reason do you have for thinking Athens is in Greece? Can

you remember a specific occasion on which you learned that infor-
mation?
M: Well, no; but I'm sure if you just ask anyone . . .
F: But what grounds do you have now before you ask someone else?
M: I can't put my finger on anything specific, but I am sure.
F: If you don't have a justification that goes beyond the mere fact that
you believe it, you are not justified in continuing to believe it.
M: Oh dear!

Specific beliefs originally based on perception
Foundationalist: Was Paul at the meeting yesterday?
Maureen: Yes, he was, although he didn't say anything.
F: Can you remember your perceptual evidence for thinking he was there?
M: Well, I remember seeing him.
F: Was he wearing a tie?
M: I don't recall.
F: Can you remember what he looked like?
M: Not in detail, but I do remember seeing him there.
F: If you no longer recall the sensory evidence on which that conclu-
sion is based, you should abandon it.
M: That's ridiculous!

Originally, Maureen's belief was based on the evidence of her senses. But
she almost immediately lost track of exactly what her sensory evidence
was. Now she has at best the memory (another belief) that her belief was
justified, without any special justification for it that would distinguish it
from her other nonfoundational beliefs.

Special foundationalism implies that she should abandon such a belief
as no longer justified. Because most of her nonfoundational beliefs are in
the same position with respect to justification, almost all her nonfoundational beliefs should be abandoned as unjustified, according to special
foundationalism. Special foundationalism implies that it is not reasonable
or rational for her to continue to believe most of the things she currently
believes! Some foundationalists are happy to endorse that sort of sceptical
conclusion, but it is an extreme one and we will try to avoid such extremes
in our discussion.

1.3.3 *The Burden of Proof*

The issue between general conservatism and special foundationalism
amounts to a question about the burden of proof, or (better) the burden

of justification. According to special foundationalism, the burden of justification falls on continuing to believe something, at least for nonfoundational beliefs. Any nonfoundational belief requires special justification. Foundational beliefs do not require special justification. For them, what requires justification is failing to continue to believe them. Sometimes there is a reason to abandon a foundational belief, but such abandonment requires such a special reason.

According to general conservatism, the burden of justification is always on changing beliefs or intentions. You start with certain beliefs and intentions and any change in them requires some special reason. Any sort of change in belief or intention requires special justification. Merely continuing to believe what you believe or intend requires no special justification in the absence of a specific challenge to that belief or intention.

Which of these views, general conservatism or special foundationalism, best fits ordinary judgements about rationality and irrationality? (What do you think?) Not special foundationalism, for that view implies that it is irrational or unreasonable to continue to believe most of what you believe. So general conservatism fits better.

We now turn to a different issue, the relation between deduction and induction.

1.4 INDUCTION AND DEDUCTION

It is important to notice that deduction and induction are not two kinds of reasoning. In fact, induction and deduction are not two kinds of anything. Deduction is concerned with certain relations among propositions, especially relations of implication and consistency. Induction is not concerned with those or any similar sort of relation among propositions. Induction is a kind of reasoning. But, as we will see, deduction is not a kind of reasoning.

1.4.1 *Induction and Deduction as Two Kinds of Reasoning*

Consider this misleading account (based on Black, 1958*b*) of the relation between induction and deduction.

> *Deductive model of inference*
> Deductive logic is presented via a certain notion of 'proof' or 'argument'. A proof or argument has premises, intermediate steps, and a

final conclusion. Each step must follow logically from prior steps in accordance with one or another specific rule, sometimes called a 'rule of inference'. Such a proof or argument is an instance of 'deductive reasoning'. Deductive reasoning in this sense is contrasted with 'inductive reasoning', which is said to take a similar form, with premises, maybe intermediate steps, and final conclusion, but with the following difference: deductive steps are always truth-preserving, whereas inductive steps are not.

This picture is very misleading. First, consider the reasoning that goes into the construction of a deductive proof or argument. Except in the simplest cases, the best strategy is not to expect to start with the premises, figure out the first intermediate step of the proof, then the second, and so on until the conclusion is reached. Often it is useful to start from the proposition to be proved and work backward. It is useful to consider what intermediate results might be useful.

The so-called deductive rules of inference are not rules that you follow in constructing the proof. They are rules that the proof must satisfy in order to be a proof.

In other words, there is a difference between reasoning that may involve the construction of a proof which must satisfy certain rules and reasoning that proceeds temporally in the same pattern as the proof in accordance with those rules. You do not reason deductively in the sense that your reasoning has the pattern of a proof. You can reason about a deductive proof, just as you can reason about anything else. But your reasoning is not well represented by anything like a proof or argument in the sense above.

1.4.2 *Implication and Consistency: Deduction*

Deduction is not a kind of inference or reasoning, although you can reason about deductions. Deduction is implication. A deduction or proof or argument exhibits an implication by showing intermediate steps.

Logic, the theory of deduction, is not by itself a theory of reasoning. In other words, it is not by itself a theory about what to believe (or intend); it is not a theory concerning how to change your view.

It is true that deductions, proofs, arguments do seem relevant to reasoning. It is not just that you sometimes reason about deductions in the way you reason about the weather or how much tax you owe. It is an interesting and nontrivial problem to say just how deductions are relevant to reasoning, a problem that is hidden by talk of deductive and inductive reasoning, as if it is obvious that some reasoning follows deductive principles.

The answer must be that it is often useful to construct deductions in reasoning about ordinary matters, and not just when you are explicitly reasoning about deductions or proofs. But why should it be useful to construct deductions? What role do they play in our reasoning?

Sometimes we do accept a conclusion because we have constructed a proof of it from other things we accept. But there are other cases in which we construct a proof of something we already accept in order to see what assumptions might account for it. In such a case, the conclusion that we accept might be a premise of the proof. The connection between proofs and reasoning is complex.

1.4.3 *Kinds of Induction*

The term 'induction' is sometimes restricted to 'enumerative induction'.

> *Enumerative induction*
> Given that all observed Fs are Gs, you infer that all Fs are Gs, or at least that the next F is a G.

But often the term 'induction' is used more widely so as to include also inference to the best explanation of the evidence.

> *Inference to the best explanation*
> Holmes infers the best explanation for the footprints, the absence of barking, the broken window: 'The butler wears size 10 shoes, is known to the dog, broke the window to make it look like a burglary ...'

> *Scientific hypothetic induction*
> Scientists infer that Brownian motion is caused by the movement of invisible molecules.

What makes one hypothesis better than another for this purpose is something we must discuss later.

1.4.4 *Problem of Induction*

It is sometimes said that there is a 'problem of induction' (Bonjour, 1992).

> *(Alleged) problem of induction*
> When your beliefs logically imply the conclusion you come to accept, your conclusion cannot be wrong unless your premises are. Your premises guarantee your conclusion. This is not so in inductive

reasoning, where your prior beliefs do not logically imply your conclusion. A question therefore arises whether you can be justified in drawing a conclusion that is not guaranteed by your premises.

But it is not clear what the problem of induction is supposed to be. Premises in an argument are to be distinguished from the starting points in reasoning, as we have already observed. The conclusion of an argument is not to be identified with the conclusion of reasoning in the sense of what you end up with or 'conclude' after reasoning. Even when reasoning culminates in the construction of an argument, the conclusion of the *argument* may be something you started off believing, and the conclusion of your *reasoning* may be to accept something that is a premise of an explanatory argument constructed as a result of inference to the best explanation.

Clearly, it would be stupid—indeed, highly irrational—not to engage in inductive reasoning. You would no longer be able to learn from experience. You would have no basis for any expectations at all about the future, for your evidence entirely concerns the past.

So, it would seem that the 'problem of induction' is a creation of confusion about induction and deduction, arising out of the deductive model of inference. Again, it is important to see that there are not two mutually exclusive kinds of reasoning, deductive and inductive. Deduction has to do with implication and consistency and is only indirectly relevant to what you should believe.

1.4.5 *Nonmonotonic Reasoning*

Unclarity about the relation between deduction and induction may be responsible for the occasional description of induction as 'nonmonotonic reasoning' in alleged contrast with deduction, which is described as 'monotonic'.

The terms 'monotonic' and 'nonmonotonic' are borrowed from mathematics.

> *Monotonic function*
> A monotonic (or 'monotonically nondecreasing') function $f(x)$ is a function whose value does not decrease as x increases. (A monotonic nonincreasing function is one whose value does not increase as x increases.) A nonmonotonic function is one whose value sometimes increases as x increases and sometimes decreases as x increases.

Deductive implication is monotonic in this sense:

Deductive implication is monotonic
Everything deductively implied by a set of propositions is also
implied when additional propositions are added to a set. So, the
deductive implications of a set of premises do not decrease in any
respect as new premises are added. If A and B logically imply Z, so do
A, B, and C, and so do A, B, C, and D, and so on.

On the other hand, reasoning is nonmonotonic in this sense:

Reasoning is nonmonotonic
Conclusions that are reasonable on the basis of specific information
can become unreasonable if further information is added. Given the
announced schedule for your course, your experience of the last few
weeks, and that today is Monday, it may be reasonable for you to
believe that your course will meet at 11:00 this morning. But if you
are also given the further information that there is a sign on the classroom door saying that the 11:00 meeting of the course is cancelled
today because your professor is ill, it is no longer reasonable for you
to believe that your course will meet at 11:00 a.m. Now it is reasonable for you to believe that your course will not meet at 11:00 a.m.
And, given the further information that the sign on the classroom
door is a hoax by a student, it will be no longer reasonable to believe
your course will not meet. New information can make old conclusions unreasonable, whereas additional premises in a deductive argument do not affect what conclusions follow deductively.

This aspect of inductive reasoning has been described in various ways. For
example, it is sometimes said that inductive reasoning is 'defeasible'.
Considerations that support a given conclusion can be defeated by additional information.

Sometimes this is described as 'default' reasoning. Given your original
information, your default assumption is that the course will meet on
Monday at 11:00 a.m. Additional information can override that default.

Default assumptions need not even be the usual case, as long as you can
expect to find out when they do not hold. A default assumption might
therefore take the form, 'Assume P, unless you hear otherwise.'

One use of default assumptions is sometimes called 'negation from failure'.

Negation from failure
The idea is to assume that something is not so unless you find information that it is so. Suppose, for example, you are interested in

whether there are any direct flights from Newark, New Jersey, to Lincoln, Nebraska. You do a computer search trying to locate such flights. When the computer does not find any, you conclude that there are none. The failure to find positive information leads you to accept a negative conclusion.

A number of attempts have been made to develop 'nonmonotonic logics' to capture these aspects of reasoning. Results have been fairly limited (Ginsberg, 1987). Some of these attempts are due to thinking of induction and deduction as two things of the same sort, the thought being that, because we have a deductive logic for deductive reasoning, we should develop an inductive logic for inductive reasoning. We have already seen what is wrong with this idea, namely, that deductive logic is concerned with deductive implication, not deductive reasoning. All reasoning is inductive.

It will be useful to develop an inductive or nonmonotonic logic only as an account of a kind of implication: default implication. Whether this development leads to any results that are useful to a theory of reasoning is still unclear.

There has been some discussion of the logic of conditionals, that is, statements of the form, 'If A, B'. At least some conditionals have the following sort of nonmonotonic property. 'If A, B' can be true, when 'If C and A, B' is not true.

> *Nonmonotonic conditionals*
> 'If you turn the key, the engine will start' can be true even though 'If I disconnect the battery and you turn the key, the engine will start' is not true.

Horty and Thomason (1991) observe that research on the logic of conditionals comes together with research in nonmonotonic logic if we associate 'A default implies B' with 'If A, B'.

1.5 COHERENCE

The nonmonotonic aspect of inductive reasoning means that everything you believe is at least potentially relevant to the conclusions you can reasonably draw. Rationality is a matter of your overall view, including your beliefs and your intentions.

If it is reasonable to change your view in a certain way, let us say that your view would be more rationally 'coherent' if changed in that way. We can then describe principles of rationality as principles of rational coherence.

Adopting this terminology, we can (following Pollock, 1979) distinguish two sorts of coherence, positive and negative.

1.5.1 *Negative Coherence*

Negative coherence is the absence of incoherence. Beliefs and intentions are incoherent to the extent that they clash with each other, for instance, through being inconsistent. Incoherence is something to be avoided, if possible, although we have seen that it is not always possible to avoid incoherence. Your beliefs might be inconsistent without your knowing that they are. And even if you are aware of inconsistency, you may not know of a sufficiently easy way to get rid of it.

> *Principle of negative coherence*
> To the extent that you are aware of incoherence in your view, you have a reason to modify it in order to get rid of the incoherence, if you can do so without too much expense.

Here is one way in which deductive logic is relevant to the theory of rationality, through providing an account of (one kind of) incoherence or inconsistency.

1.5.2 *Positive Coherence*

There is positive coherence among your beliefs (and intentions) to the extent that they are connected in ways that allow them to support each other. We can only speculate about what provides positive coherence. Some of the factors that seem relevant are the following.

> *Explanatory connections*
> A set of unrelated beliefs seems to be less coherent than a tightly organized conceptual scheme that contains explanatory and other principles that make sense out of most of your beliefs. This is why inference to the best explanation is an attractive pattern of inference.

Causal connections are a special case of coherence giving explanatory connections.

> *Causal connections*
> Belief in two events seems to be more coherent if one is seen as a cause

of the other. When the lights go out in one room in her house, it makes more sense for Zelda to conclude that the fuse for that room has blown than to suppose that the fuse in a neighbour's house has blown. She easily envisages a causal connection between the fuse for that room blowing and the lights in the room going out. She does not as easily envisage a causal connection between the fuse in her neighbour's house blowing and the lights in her room going out.

To be sure, Zelda can envisage a complex causal connection between the fuse in her neighbour's house and the lights in her room. But to believe in that complicated connection would presumably offend against conservatism, which would seem to favour minimal changes in belief in order to obtain explanatory coherence. Also, without evidence of such complication, adding a belief in such a complication would actually decrease the overall coherence of her view.

Causation is not the only thing that would seem to bring explanatory coherence. Connecting generalization is another.

Coherence from connecting generalizations

All the emeralds Steve has observed are green. Steve infers that emeralds tend to be green, or even that all emeralds are green. This is an instance of enumerative induction.

We might think of enumerative induction as inference to the best explanation, taking the generalization to explain its instances. But then we must recognize that this is a different kind of explanation from causal explanation. A general correlation does not cause its instances!

Implication is an important kind of connector among beliefs.

Coherence from implication

Teri believes that Jack is either in his office or at home. She finds that his office is empty. She concludes that he is at home. This conclusion is implied by her prior beliefs.

Here is a second way in which deductive logic can be relevant to rationality. It is relevant to implication, and implication is a coherence-giving connection.

In trying to develop an account of rational coherence, we might try to reduce some of the factors mentioned to others in a substantive way. One idea would be to try to treat all factors as special cases of explanatory coherence. That idea is not very plausible for many cases like the last one, in which a conclusion is accepted because it is implied by other beliefs. What is the relevant explanation in that case? One might say that the premises of Teri's argument explain why its conclusion is true. But that seems to stretch the notion of explanation.

Another idea would be to try to reduce all coherence to that involved in implication. That has some plausibility for certain explanations. And strict generalizations are related to their instances by implication. Often explanations in physics work via implication. Recognition of this fact gave rise to the so-called deductive nomological model of explanation (Hempel, 1965*a*), which works for many scientific explanations, but not for all.

One class of exceptions appeals to default principles that hold, other things being equal.

Explanation without implication

A certain substance dissolved in a certain liquid because it is sugar placed in water, and sugar normally dissolves in water. We have to say 'normally' because sugar does not always dissolve in water. It does not dissolve if there is already a supersaturated solution in the water, or if there is wax covering the outside of the sugar, or indefinitely many other things have occurred.

Here a general default principle helps to explain the dissolving in this case without guaranteeing that the sugar will dissolve. So, this explanatory connection is not based on strict implication.

1.6 SIMPLICITY

In trying to explain some data, it is reasonable to consider a very limited range of the infinitely many logically possible explanations. The rational inquirer restricts attention to the set of relatively simple hypotheses that might account for most of the data.

This is not to say very much, for it amounts to using the term 'simple' for whatever the relevant factors are that restrict rational attention to a certain few hypotheses. Furthermore, we are concerned with *relative* simplicity in this sense. A hypothesis that is too complicated, as compared with other available hypotheses at one time, can have a different status at another time if those other hypotheses have been eliminated. The first hypothesis might then be among the simplest of available hypotheses.

So, to say that the rational inquirer is concerned to find a simple hypothesis is not to say that the rational inquirer is committed to believing that 'reality is simple', whatever that might mean.

Let us now try to say more about simplicity in this sense, understanding that our discussion must be even more speculative than what has gone before. First, let us see how the relevant kind of simplicity might be involved in a famous philosophical 'riddle'.

1.6.1 *Goodman's 'New Riddle of Induction'*

Goodman (1965) discusses the following example. Suppose that Fran has a test for emeralds that does not depend on colour, she has examined various emeralds for colour, and she has found that each was green at least when she examined it. This evidence rationally supports the hypothesis

(H1) All emeralds are green.

Using the terminology of the preceding section, the evidence supports (H1) because it consists of instances of (H1) that are made more coherent if (H1) is true.

But there are many other hypotheses that are generalizations of the evidence, where the evidence consists of instances of each of these hypotheses. For example,

(H2) All emeralds are: either green if first examined before AD 2000 or blue if not first examined before AD 2000.

Goodman suitably defines the term 'grue' to stand for the predicate after the colon in (H2), so that the hypothesis can be abbreviated as follows:

(H2) All emeralds are grue.

Notice that (H2) conflicts with (H1) for any emeralds not first examined by AD 2000. According to (H1) those emeralds are green. According to (H2) they are blue.

Goodman points out that hypotheses like (H2) are not taken seriously. His 'new riddle of induction' asks what the difference is between (H1) and (H2).

Clearly, there is a sense in which Fran's (and our) preference for (H1) is due to its being a much simpler hypothesis than (H2). But what sort of simplicity is in question and why is it relevant?

1.6.2 *Using Simplicity to Decide among Hypotheses that are Taken Seriously*

It is very important to see that using simplicity to rule hypotheses out of consideration is to be distinguished from using simplicity as an explicit consideration in theory choice. Sometimes a scientist will say that a particular theory is better than another because the first theory assumes the existence of fewer objects, fewer basic principles, or whatever. When a scientist argues in some such way he or she is arguing in favour of one rather than another hypothesis that is being taken seriously. As Sober (1988) observes, such appeals to simplicity are often quite controversial. That is, it is controversial whether simplicity in one or another respect is a relevant consideration in choosing among hypotheses.

But, even where there are deep controversies in a subject, reasonable disputants will still take seriously only a very few of the infinitely many possible hypotheses. We are concerned with whatever it is that leads reasonable people to disregard most of the hypotheses as too 'silly' to be considered.

(To repeat an earlier point, silliness is a relative matter. Hypothesis (H2) is silly because (H1) has not been ruled out. We can imagine a situation in which (H2) becomes acceptable.)

Let's call the sort of simplicity we are concerned with 'basic simplicity'. Because the phenomenon of ruling out crazy or silly hypotheses occurs in all domains, let us assume that there is a single domain-independent notion of simplicity for this purpose.

1.6.3 *Speculation: Basic Simplicity Has to Do with How Easy it is to Use Hypotheses*

The basic simplicity of a hypothesis seems to have something to do with the simplicity of its representation. But it is always possible to represent any hypothesis simply, so the matter is a bit more complex.

> *Simple representation of a complex hypothesis*
> We have already seen that the complex hypothesis (H2), 'All emeralds are: either green if first examined before AD 2000 or blue if not first examined before AD 2000', can be given a much simpler representation, if a suitable predicate is defined: 'all emeralds are grue.'

In fact, any hypothesis can be abbreviated by a single symbol, so simplicity of representation cannot be taken at face value.

Now, if a hypothesis like 'All emeralds are grue' is used to explain the data, it has to be expanded to its more complex form, 'All emeralds are: either green if first examined before AD 2000 or blue if not first examined before AD 2000.' This expansion is required on the assumption that we are more interested in accounting for the colours of objects, like whether they are blue or green, as opposed to their 'cholers', like whether they are grue or bleen. If instead we were more interested in explaining why emeralds were grue, we could use the hypothesis 'All emeralds are grue' without having to expand it, and the hypothesis 'All emeralds are green' would require elaboration in terms of 'grue' and 'bleen' in order to provide the desired explanation.

So, perhaps the thing to look at is not so much the mere statement of the hypothesis but also how complicated it is to use the hypothesis to explain the data and predict new observations of a sort in which we are interested. (Here again theoretical rationality would depend on practical concerns.)

> *Simplicity as ease of use*
> In considering possible explanations of given data, it is rational and reasonable to ignore hypotheses that are much harder to use in explanation and prediction than other available hypotheses that in other respects account equally well for the data.

1.6.4 *Parasitic Theories*

A parasitic theory says that, as far as evidence goes, it is as if some other theory were true.

> *Descartes's demon hypothesis*
> Your sensory experience is the result of a powerful evil demon, giving you experiences as if of a world of physical objects.

> *Scientific instrumentalism*
> Scientific theories can be used as devices for calculating observations, but should not be treated as saying anything about the real nature of the world. All that can be rationally believed is that it is as if this or that scientific theory holds (van Fraassen, 1989).

In the classroom, it may be unclear how you can reject Descartes's demon hypothesis. But it would be crazy to take that hypothesis seriously in ordinary life. Similarly, outside the philosophy classroom it makes sense to take scientific instrumentalism seriously only when a theory can be accepted as no more than an instrument; for example, when the theory is known not to be wholly true. In that case, it makes sense to consider instrumentalist hypotheses.

> *Newton's laws as instruments*
> Relativity theory tells us that Newton's laws are not completely accurate, but they hold as good approximations at speeds much less than

the speed of light. Under those conditions, it is as if Newton's laws were correct.

We do not take parasitic theories seriously unless we have reason to reject the theories on which they are parasitic. In other words, parasitic theories are treated as 'less simple' than the theories on which they are parasitic.

This result fits our tentative suggestion that simplicity should be measured by how easy it is to use a hypothesis to explain data and make new predictions. A parasitic theory is normally more complicated according to this suggestion than is the theory on which it is parasitic, because to use the parasitic theory you have to do everything you do when using the nonparasitic theory and you have to do something more. You first calculate what is to be expected on theory T, then use the principle that what will happen is what is expected according to theory T. So, there is an additional step to the use of the parasitic theory that is not part of the original theory T.

> *Nonparasitic explanation*
> Why does E occur? Because of initial conditions C and laws L. Given C and L and the following calculation . . ., we expect E.

> *Parasitic explanation*
> Why does E occur? According to theory T, it is because of initial conditions C, and laws L. Given C and L and the following calculation …, we would on theory T expect E. Our theory is that things will occur as if T is true. So, we expect E also.

The explanation of E from the nonparasitic explanation occurs as a part of the parasitic explanation. So, the parasitic explanation has to be somewhat more complicated than the nonparasitic explanation.

1.7 PRACTICAL RATIONALITY AND REASONABLENESS

So far, all that has been said about practical rationality is that your goals play a role in practical rationality that they do not play in theoretical rationality. The negative part of this remark, concerning theoretical rationality, may require qualification, given the apparent role of simplicity and conservatism in theoretical rationality, if these factors have a practical justification. We will discuss the possible need for such a qualification in the next section. In the present section, we say something more about the way in which goals are relevant to practical rationality.

One issue is whether there is a single category of goal, or perhaps a single measure of 'utility', as opposed to a variety of functionally different things: desires, values, goals, intentions, commitments, principles, rules, and so on. A related issue is whether we need to allow for a structure within goals in which some goals depend on others.

But let us begin with a few remarks about the mathematical decision theory that is often used as a model of rationality in economics.

1.7.1 *Decision Theory*

In its simplest form (for example, von Neumann and Morgenstern, 1944), mathematical decision theory applies when you are faced with a decision between two or more exclusive acts. Each act has one or more possible outcomes to which you assign certain values or 'utilities'. Let us use $u(A)$ to represent the utility of act A. You also assign conditional probabilities, $p(O,A)$, to each possible outcome O in relation to a given act A. Then the 'expected gain' of a given outcome O of an act A is $u(O) \times p(O,A)$. The 'expected utility' of each act A is the sum of the expected gains of each possible consequence of that act. Finally, the theory holds that rationality requires doing either the act with the highest expected utility or, if there is a tie for highest, one of the acts with highest expected utility.

The principles of decision theory are like principles of logic in being principles of consistency or coherence. It would be a mistake to identify decision theory with a full theory of practical rationality, just as it is a mistake to identify the theory of theoretical rationality with logic.

Some decision theorists argue that it is useful for individuals faced with hard practical problems to think of them in decision-theoretic terms. Such individuals are advised to consider carefully what their possible acts are, what possible consequences each act might have, what utility they assign to each possible consequence, and how likely they think a given act would be to have a given consequence. They should then calculate expected utilities and choose that act with the highest calculated expected utility.

Is that good advice? That is an empirical question: do people do better using such a method or not? The suggested method is not obviously good advice. Given a poor enough assignment of utilities and probabilities, you could be led very wrong by your calculation.

1.7.2 *Derivative Goals*

Some goals are derivative from others in a way that is important for practical rationality. You want A. B is a means to A. So you want B. That is, you want B as a means to A. If you get A in some other way, you no longer have the same reason to want B. Or if you discover that B is not going to lead to A you no longer have the same reason to want B. It is irrational to continue to pursue an instrumental goal after your reason for wanting it has lapsed.

Also, consider the problem of deciding what to do when you have several goals. If you do A, you will satisfy goals G1, G2, and G3. If you do B, you will satisfy goals G4, G5, and G6. It is not easy to say how a rational person reaches an overall evaluation of acts A and B by combining his or her evaluation of the outcomes of each act. One idea (Franklin, 1817) is to try to reduce the lists by trying to match outcomes of A with equivalent outcomes of B, cancelling these equivalent goals out, and then considering only the remaining advantages of each course of action. That can still leave difficult choices.

But one thing can be said: do not count the satisfaction of two goals as distinct advantages of an act if your only reason for one of the goals is that it will enable you to attain the other.

> *Choosing a career*
> Mabel is trying to decide between a career in business and a career in teaching. These careers are associated with different lifestyles, and she considers which lifestyle she would prefer. She also considers the difference in income and wealth associated with the two choices, forgetting that income and wealth are means to the lifestyles associated with the choices.

Mabel is irrationally counting the same consideration (style of life) twice when she treats income as a separate consideration.

1.7.3 *Nonultimate, Noninstrumental Desires*

You can care about things that are neither ultimate ends nor instrumental toward getting other things you want.

> *Good news*
> Jack has been tested to see whether he has a fatal disease D. The test is quite reliable. Jack desperately wants the results of the test to be negative, indicating that he does not have the disease. Jack's desire is not an ultimate end of his, nor is it a desire for something that might be instrumental in obtaining something else that Jack desires. He desires a negative result because of what it indicates about him, not because of what it might lead to.

Notice that Jack's desire in this case is not for something that he could rationally treat as a goal. It would be irrational for Jack to bribe a lab technician to guarantee that the test yields a negative result. That wouldn't have any effect on whether Jack has disease D, which is (after all) what Jack is basically concerned with.

1.7.4 *Intentions*

Does a rational person always reason directly from current goals, always figuring out the best ways to maximize satisfaction of current goals? That would resemble special foundationalism with respect to theoretical reasoning.

It ignores the role of long-term intentions. Such intentions record the decisions already made. These decisions are not irrevocable, but they carry considerable weight and should not be frivolously discarded. A person incapable of maintaining long-term intentions would be incapable of long-term planning and would have at best only a low level of rationality (Bratman, 1987).

Intentions are not reducible to desires and beliefs, but put constraints on current planning of a special kind. A person's actual goals, as contrasted with things merely valued or desired, might be identified with what that person intends.

Intentions are directly related to action in ways not fully understood. Some authors think there are special intentions to do something now, constituting acts of will or volitions serving as the immediate causes of action.

1.7.5 *Strength of Will*

Our initial example of irrationality was an example of practical irrationality: Jane goes to the party rather than study for her exam. She finds the immediate pleasure of an evening more attractive than the longer-term considerations involved in doing well in her history course.

It is not that Jane temporarily overvalues the immediate pleasure of the party and undervalues the longer-term gains of study. She remains aware of the relative importance of these things. Her desires conflict with her evaluations.

In such a case, rationality requires sticking with her previously formed intentions, staying with her principles and resisting temptation.

1.7.6 *Reasonable Cooperation*

Finally, consider our earlier example of unreasonable negotiation, which I repeat:

> *Refusing a reasonable proposal*
> Three students, Sally, Ellie, and Louise, have been assigned to a set of rooms consisting of a study room, a small single bedroom, and another small bedroom with a two-person bunk bed. They discuss the proposal that they should take turns, each getting the single for one-third of the school year. Sally refuses to consider this proposal and insists on keeping the single for herself the whole year.

When her room-mates say that Sally is being unreasonable, they seem to be making a moral judgement about Sally. She is not being 'fair' (R. W. Miller, 1992).

Notice that her room-mates say that Sally is being 'unreasonable' and would not say that she is being 'irrational'. Similarly, a teenager asking for permission to use the family car might plead with his mother by saying, 'Be reasonable, Mom!' and not by saying, 'Be rational, Mom!'

1.8 THEORETICAL RATIONALITY AND PHILOSOPHICAL PRAGMATISM

Earlier I said that goals are relevant to practical rationality in a way in which they are not relevant to theoretical rationality. Although your goals are relevant to what questions it is rational for you to be interested in answering, they are not relevant to determining the answer you should accept through theoretical reasoning in the way in which your goals can be relevant to determining what it is rational for you to decide to do through practical reasoning. Wishful thinking is theoretically irrational even as it is practically okay.

We mentioned the possibility of good practical reasons to believe certain things and were therefore led to distinguish epistemic or theoretical reasons to believe something from nonepistemic practical reasons to believe something. Evidence that John was elsewhere at the time of the crime is an epistemic or theoretical reason to believe him innocent. On the other hand, loyalty to John provides a nonepistemic, practical reason to believe him innocent.

The possibility of philosophical pragmatism complicates this picture.

Everyone can agree that practical considerations are relevant to the choice of a notation for developing a theory.

> *Roman numerals*
> It would be hard to balance your bank account if you had to use roman numerals rather than the more standard arabic decimal notation. There are good practical reasons to use the one notation rather than the other.

Philosophical pragmatism argues against any sharp distinction between choice of theoretical hypothesis and choice of notation (Quine, 1960*a*). Pragmatists stress such practical features as we have already mentioned— simplicity, ease of use, and conservatism, for example—in deciding what to believe about any subject.

But then what happens to the distinction between theoretical and practical reasoning or, more precisely, the distinction between epistemic and nonepistemic reasons?

Pragmatists can still allow for this last distinction, defined as we defined it earlier.

> *Epistemic reason for belief*
> R is an epistemic reason to believe P only if the probability of P given R is greater than the probability of P given not-R.

> *Nonepistemic reason for belief*
> R is a nonepistemic reason to believe P if R is a reason to believe P over and above the extent to which the probability of P given R is greater than the probability of P given not-R.

Considerations of simplicity and conservatism are reflected in our probability judgements in a way that more specific practical considerations are not. For example, of the hypotheses that explain the evidence, we treat the simpler hypotheses as more likely to be true than the less simple hypotheses, given that evidence. On the other hand, a rational advertising agent should not suppose that it would be evidence that cigarettes do not cause cancer (in the sense of making that conclusion more likely to be true) if a tobacco company were willing to give advertising accounts only to agents who believe that smoking cigarettes does not cause cancer, even though that consideration might provide the rational advertising agent with a reason to have that belief.

So pragmatism seems to be compatible with distinguishing epistemic from nonepistemic reasons, allowing some practical considerations to fall on the epistemic side of this distinction.

1.9 CONCLUDING REMARKS

Despite the clear intuitive distinction we must make between theoretical and practical reasoning, theoretical and practical considerations are rationally intertwined in more than one way. Theoretical reasoning is goal-directed in the sense that goals are relevant to the questions to be considered theoretically and there are practical reasons behind the role of conservatism and simplicity in reasoning.

At present, there is no mathematically elegant account of all aspects of rationality. Formal theories of implication and consistency are possible, but these are only part of the subject. Conservatism, simplicity, and coherence are important aspects of rationality, with explanation, implication, and consistency being relevant to coherence. Our ordinary judgements about rationality and reasonableness are often sensitive to these considerations, but also to strength of will and even fairness.

Logic and probability theory are not directly theories of rationality and reasonableness and, furthermore, it is a misuse of language to say that violations of principles of logic and probability theory are indications of irrationality or unreasonableness. We do not normally consider someone to be 'irrational' or 'unreasonable' simply because of a mistake in arithmetic, or probability theory, or logic. Instead we use the words 'irrational' and 'unreasonable' in a rather different way; for example, for those who refuse to accept 'obvious' inductions, or for those who jump to conclusions on insufficient evidence, or for those who act knowing that they are frustrating their own purposes, or for those who are uncooperative.

These issues are considered further in the next three essays. Essay 2 discusses practical reasoning in more detail. Essay 3 says more about simplicity. Essay 4 takes up the distinction between practical and epistemic reasons for belief.

2

Practical Reasoning

Reasoning is here taken to be distinguished from proof or argument in a logician's sense. Reasoning is a process of modifying antecedent beliefs and intentions, perhaps by adding some new ones, perhaps by deleting some of the original ones— normally by adding some and deleting others. An argument or proof is sometimes relevant to reasoning in this sense but is never an instance of it. An argument or proof is more like an explanation than an instance of reasoning. It has premises, intermediate steps, and a conclusion. Reasoning has no premises and no conclusion, unless we are to say that the 'premises' comprise all of the antecedent beliefs and intentions and that the 'conclusion' is the resulting set. But that way of speaking might be misleading, since reasoning often leads to abandoning some 'premises'.

The theory of reasoning is not the same as logic, which is a theory of argument or proof. Logic is relevant to reasoning only because there is a connection between reasoning and explanation and explanation often takes the form of an argument. But logic is not directly a theory of reasoning. There is deductive logic but no such thing as deductive reasoning; given a deductive argument, one can always abandon a premise rather than accept the conclusion. There is inductive reasoning (perhaps better called theoretical reasoning) but no such thing as inductive logic. Again, there is practical reasoning, but no such thing as a practical logic and no such thing as the practical syllogism.

Let us distinguish practical reasoning from theoretical reasoning in the traditional way: practical reasoning is concerned with what to intend, whereas theoretical reasoning is concerned with what to believe. Theoretical or inductive reasoning is an attempt to improve one's overall view of the world by increasing its explanatory coherence. The present essay argues, among other things, that similar considerations are relevant to practical reasoning.

An important aspect of the view of practical reasoning defended here is that intentions are taken seriously as psychological states on a par with beliefs. Intentions are, therefore, treated as primitive in the sense that they are not to be analysed away in terms of reasons, beliefs, desires, and behavior. A great deal will be said below about the nature of intentions, because we must understand what intentions are if we are to understand practical reasoning.

2.1 INTENTIONS

It is essential to distinguish intentions from desires, wishes, hopes, and aims. One important difference, which I will now discuss, is that intention involves belief in a way that these other attitudes do not. If one intends to do something, it follows that one believes that one will do it; such a belief is not similarly involved in wanting to do something, wishing to do it, hoping to do it, or aiming at doing it.

It is true, of course, that the future is always uncertain and that anything can happen. Knowing that, one may still have definite intentions as to what one is going to do, which may seem to indicate that intention does not always involve belief. But one may also have beliefs about what one is going to do, despite knowing that anything can happen. Does that show that belief does not involve belief? Surely not. The point, then, is that intention involves belief only in the way in which belief involves belief.

To take a specific instance of the point: Albert intends to be in Rome next summer, although he does not believe that he will be there no matter what. He believes, for example, that he will not be there if he changes his mind and he will admit that he might change his mind. This may seem to indicate that, although Albert now intends to be in Rome next summer, he does not believe without qualification that he will be in Rome next summer. But he does not intend without qualification to be in Rome next summer, either. A description of his intention that is accurate for one context must not be compared with a description of his belief that is accurate only for a different context. In as much as it is true that Albert now intends to be in Rome next summer, although he admits that there is a chance that he may not be there, it is also true that Albert now believes that he will be in Rome next summer, although he admits that there is a chance that he may not be there. In as much as it is true that Albert does not flatly believe that he will be in Rome next summer but believes only that he will be in Rome next summer provided that he does not change his mind, it is also true that Albert does not intend flatly to be in Rome next summer but intends only to be there provided that nothing happens that would give him a sufficient reason to change his mind. Either way, intention involves belief (Grice, 1972).

It might be objected that someone may intend to do something without being sure of success. A sniper shoots at a soldier from a distance, trying to kill him, knowing that the chances of success are slim. Does he not intend to kill the soldier, even though he does not positively believe that he will kill him? If he succeeds, despite the odds, the sniper kills the soldier intentionally and, if he kills him intentionally, must he not intend to kill him?

The answer to this objection is that, in the case described, the sniper does not flatly intend to kill the soldier, although, if he succeeds, he does kill him intentionally. It is a mistake to suppose that whenever someone does something intentionally, he intends to do it. Things someone does as foreseen but unintended consequences of what he intends are sometimes things he does intentionally. In firing his gun, the sniper knowingly alerts the enemy to his presence. He does this intentionally, thinking that the gain is worth the possible cost. But he certainly does not intend to alert the enemy to his presence. Similarly, if someone tries to do something and succeeds, he sometimes does it intentionally, even if, not being sure of success, he does not, flatly, intend to do what he succeeds in doing. Our sniper is again a case in point.

In order to see this, consider apparently similar cases in which one tries and succeeds but does not do something intentionally. Henry tries to win a game of chess and succeeds. Does Henry win intentionally? Only if it was up to him whether he would win. Similarly, it would be true to say that the winner of a lottery wins intentionally only if he had rigged things so that he would win. In the more normal case a winner does not win intentionally, even though he tries to win and succeeds. Again, at the firing range the sniper intentionally shoots a bull's-eye only if that is something he can do at will. If it is just a lucky shot, he does not intentionally shoot a bull's-eye.

The reason why we say that the sniper intentionally kills the soldier but do not say that he intentionally shoots a bull's-eye is that we think that there is something wrong with killing and nothing wrong with shooting a bull's-eye. If the sniper is part of a group of snipers engaged in a sniping contest, they will look at things differently. From their point of view, the sniper simply makes a lucky shot when he kills the soldier and cannot be said to kill him intentionally.

The same sort of consideration leads us to say that, in firing his gun, the sniper intentionally alerts the enemy to his presence. We say this because the sniper acts in the face of a reason not to alert the enemy to his presence. On the other hand, we will not say in any normal case that the sniper intentionally heats the barrel of his gun, even though in firing his gun he know-ingly does heat the barrel, because there is no reason for the sniper not to heat the barrel of his gun. One can do something intentionally even though one does not intend to do it, if one does it in the face of what ought to be a reason not to do it, and either one tries to do it, or one does it as a fore-seen consequence of something else that one intends to do.

If we are to appeal to facts about when someone does something inten-tionally in order to support claims about what someone intends to do, we must restrict our attention to intentional actions that the agent has no rea-son not to do—actions like winning at chess or shooting a bull's-eye rather than actions like killing a soldier or alerting the enemy to your presence. But consideration of such actions indicates that intention involves belief. As we have seen, one intentionally wins at chess or intentionally shoots a bull's-eye only if it is up to oneself whether one will do it, only if one can do it at will, only if it is something that one knows that one can do if one chooses to do it. One intentionally wins a chess game or shoots a bull's-eye only if one does so knowing that one is going to do so. But knowing involves believing. In such cases, then, one intends to win or to shoot a bull's-eye only if one also believes that one will win or shoot a bull's-eye.

This thesis, that intention involves belief, helps to explain certain simi-larities between theoretical and practical reasoning. Recall that we have defined the distinction between theoretical and practical reasoning as a distinction between reasoning concerned with what to believe and reason-ing concerned with what to intend or desire. So defined, the distinction cannot be a sharp one, given that intention involves belief. Practical rea-soning that affects intentions must in that case also have an effect on beliefs. Similarly, theoretical reasoning must often have an effect on inten-tions since, if one concludes that one will not be able to do what one has been intending to do, that conclusion must change one's intention. Since intention involves belief, theoretical and practical reasoning overlap.

In theoretical reasoning, one seeks to increase the coherence of one's overall view of the world (see the previous essay). Since intention involves belief, and theoretical and practical reasoning overlap, coherence must be relevant to any sort of reasoning about the future, theoretical or practical. One's conception of the future therefore consists in both plans and pre-dictions; and, in reasoning about the future, one must seek to make one's total conception of the future coherent with itself and with one's other beliefs and desires, where the coherence aimed at is, at least partly, explana-tory coherence. Other things being equal, a given conception of the future, containing plans as well as predictions, is more coherent than another to the extent that the first leaves less unexplained than the second. As this point applies to theoretical reasoning, it is reflected in the slogan 'Inference is inference to the best explanation'. As it applies to practical reasoning, it is reflected in the slogan 'To will the end is to will the means'. The point is the same in both cases. If intentions or predictions involve doing something, one's total system of intentions and predictions will be more coherent, other things being equal, if it also includes an explanation of one's doing that thing. When what one is going to do is something intended, such as winning at cards, and the explanation cites one's means, for example, cheating, one's reason for accepting the explanation is not different in kind from one's reason when what one is going to do is not something intended, such as falling down, and the explanation, for example, that someone will pull on the rug, does not cite one's means.

The thesis that intention involves belief associates practical reasoning about means and ends with theoretical reasoning. It brings these two sorts of reasoning under a single principle. And it does this in a way that illustrates an important difference between intentions and, say, desires. The various things that one intends to do should be consistent with each other. If, for example, one has a choice between doing A, B, or C, knowing that only one of these things can be done, then it would be inconsistent to intend to do A and, at the same time, to intend to do B, just as it would be inconsistent to believe both that one was going to do A and that one was going to do B. The analogous point does not hold for desires. One can, in the situation described, want to do A and also want to do B, without inconsistency. This is easy to understand, given that intention involves belief in a way that desire does not. For this means that intentions, but not desires, are subject to the same demands of joint consistency to which beliefs are subject.

Intention involves desire as well as belief. If one intends to do something, there is a sense in which one must want to do it, even if there is also another sense in which one may not want to do it. So, practical reasoning that affects intentions also affects desires.

Now, even if there is nothing one can do about a situation, the belief that a given event would promote a desired end can lead one to desire that event. How can we account for this fact about the way in which practical reasoning can affect desires?

In order to answer this question we must distinguish intrinsic desires from others. Intrinsic desires are basic in the following sense. When planning what to do, one's plan should be not only internally coherent but should also, as far as possible, promote one's intrinsic desires. Other desires, let us call them extrinsic desires, are derived from or motivated by intrinsic desires, just as intentions are. To say that one's plan should promote extrinsic desires as well as intrinsic desires would be to encourage one to count certain intrinsic desires several times, which would be misleading. Furthermore, if one learns that an event extrinsically desired is not, after all, going to promote intrinsic desires, one should ordinarily abandon one's extrinsic desire for that event rather than one's intrinsic desire for the end that had been previously thought to promote the event. The two types of desire are, then, in a sense really two different attitudes, even though both are called desires.

Now, it would seem that intentions are primitive in the sense that they are not to be analysed away in terms of reasons, beliefs, desires, and behaviour. Similarly, beliefs and intrinsic desires are primitive, unanalysable attitudes. However, extrinsic desires, unlike the other attitudes mentioned, are usefully treated not as primitive attitudes but as analysable in terms of intentions and dispositions to intend. An extrinsic desire is a disposition to choose; more exactly, it is an intention or a disposition to intend. This would explain why something like means–ends reasoning can affect extrinsic desires. Such reasoning can affect intentions and dispositions to intend, which is what extrinsic desires are. This sort of practical reasoning, as it affects extrinsic desires, can in this way be brought under the same principle that connects means–ends reasoning as it affects intentions and inference to the best explanation as it affects beliefs. This can be done, furthermore, in such a way that desires are not made subject to the same demands of joint consistency to which intentions and beliefs are subject. To want A, in other words, to have an extrinsic desire for A, is to be disposed to choose A, in other words, to be disposed to intend to take A, given a choice between getting A or not. Knowing that one cannot have both A and B, one may still want A and want B in the sense that one would choose A, given a choice between getting A or not, and would also choose B, given a choice between getting B or not.

It is unclear what to say about hopes. Unlike desires, hopes seem to be subject to the same requirements of joint consistency as intentions and beliefs. If one knows that one cannot have both A and B, it is irrational to hope for A and at the same time to hope for B. This cannot be because hope involves belief in the way that intention does, for hope does not involve belief at all; in fact, hope apparently excludes belief. It is not clear what the explanation of this requirement on hopes is. It is not even clear whether hopes are basic primitive attitudes that play a role in the causal order, like beliefs, intentions, and intrinsic desires, or are constructs analysable in terms of other attitudes and dispositions, in the way that extrinsic desires are.

This ends my discussion of the thesis that intention involves belief. No real proof of the thesis has been given, but certain objections have been answered and some indication has been given concerning how the thesis might account for a similarity between theoretical and practical reasoning. The discussion that follows will assume that the thesis is true. Indeed, it is unclear how the following argument could be given without such an appeal to the thesis that intention involves belief. The resulting theory, therefore, supports this thesis to the extent that the theory is independently plausible and to the extent to which the argument really does depend on this thesis.

2.2 INTENTIONS AS MEANS TO THEIR OWN SATISFACTION

The next thing to be shown is that forming an intention is something one does, which, like other things one does, can be done for a reason, can have a purpose, and can serve as a means to one's ends. In particular, forming the intention to do A settles in one's mind the question whether one is going to do A. It can be useful to settle that question because, having done so, one will no longer need to consider whether or not to do A and one can turn one's mind to other issues. Furthermore, in any additional theoretical or practical reasoning, one will be able to take it for granted that one will be doing A. Sometimes one forms the intention to do A simply to settle what it is one is going to do; settling that question is one's reason for forming the intention. Forming that intention is, moreover, one's means of settling that question and of enabling oneself to think about other matters while taking it for granted that one is going to do A.

There is also a second way in which forming an intention can serve as a means to one's ends. Judy is going to a party. Should she go by subway or by cab? Should she walk to the nearby cabstand or walk in the other direction to the subway entrance? After brief thought, she decides to take a cab rather than the subway. In other words, she forms the intention of walking to the cabstand. Now, forming that intention is something she does and, furthermore, something she does for a reason. She does it in order to get to the party in the quickest and most convenient way. She supposes that, because of having formed that intention, she will walk to the cabstand where she will be provided with the needed transportation. Forming the intention to take a cab is therefore part of her means of getting to the party.

It is something that she does because she thinks that it will lead to her actually taking a cab and obtaining a ride to the party. She supposes that if she did not form that intention she would not take a cab and would not get to the party that way.

In fact, forming the intention to take a cab is also her means of getting herself to take a cab, although that sounds odd and suggests that forming that intention is something like making an effort of will. Forming an intention to hail a cab is certainly not the same thing as making an effort of will; nevertheless, it is for Judy her means of getting herself to take a cab. For she supposes in this case that she must form that intention if she is to take a cab and she supposes that, if she does form the intention, she will take a cab, and will do so because of that intention. Therefore, there is a sense in which she views her intention as a means to what she intends.

A similar thing is true of Judy's original intention to go to the party. In forming the intention to go to the party tonight, she supposed that she would arrive at the party at an appropriate time because of her intention. She supposed that she would not be going to the party except for having intended to go. Furthermore, she foresaw that, because of her intention, she would leave home and be guided in an appropriate route to the relevant place. Her intention helps to get her to the party by guiding her actions in such a way that she arrives at the party when the time comes. So there is a sense in which her intention to go to the party is part of her means of getting to the party.

On the other hand, if Judy had decided to stay home tonight and not go to the party, she would then have intended to stay home but, normally, she would not have supposed that she was going to stay home because of her intention. (Here I am indebted to Judith Jarvis Thomson.) She would not have thought of her intention as leading her to stay home or as guiding her actions or nonactions in such a way that she stayed home—at least not in any normal case. Her intention to stay home would not have been part of her means of staying home unless she would have gone to the party except for that intention—for example, if, being continually assailed by the temptation to go to the party, she had firmly resolved that she would resist temptation and stay home. Normally, though, she would stay home even if she did not intend to stay home, as long as she did not intend to do something else. Normally, therefore, her staying home would not have been a consequence of her intending to stay home; at best it would have been a consequence of her not intending to go out.

Now, although Judy's intention to stay home is not normally part of her means of staying home, it is her means of doing something else—namely, guaranteeing that she will stay home. She forms the intention of staying home because she does not take it to be otherwise certain that she will stay home. She forms the intention in order to eliminate the possibility that she will not stay home, to settle the issue, so that she can think about other things and can rely in her later deliberations on her presence at home this evening.

The 'act' of forming an intention is always a means to an end. It is always a means of guaranteeing that one will do what one intends to do. Sometimes it is also a means of actually doing what one intends to do, as when Judy intends to go to the party. Let us call such an intention a 'positive intention'. Sometimes, on the other hand, one's intention is only a conditional means to doing what one intends. Judy intends, for example, to go to the party if Harry calls. If Harry then calls, her intention will become operative in getting her to the party. If Harry does not call, her intention will remain inoperative. Let us call this sort of intention a 'conditional intention'. Sometimes, finally, one's intention is not so much a means or conditional means to doing what one intends to do, as it is a means of ensuring that one will not do something else, as when Judy forms the intention of staying home, which then settles that question and keeps her from the further consideration that might conceivably lead her to form the intention of going out. Let us call this last sort of intention a 'negative intention'. All three sorts of intention are at least means of guaranteeing that one will do what one intends.

Forming an intention is something one does as a means of doing something else. So, forming an intention is itself something one does intentionally. This does not, however, give rise to an infinite regress (contrary to Prichard, 1949; Sellars, 1966; and Grice, 1972). When one forms the intention to do A, one intends to intend to do A; but these are not distinct intentions. The intentions are inseparable. One cannot intend to do A without intending to intend to do A. So the intention to do A contains the intention of intending to do A. Intentions are self-referential.

The intention to do A is in part the intention that one have that very intention. The intention to do A is the intention that, because of that very intention, it is guaranteed that one will do A. More specifically, a positive intention to do A is also the intention that, because of that very intention, one will do A. A conditional intention to do A, if C, is also the intention that, if C, one will, because of that very intention, do A. And a negative intention to do A is also the intention that it, that very intention to do A, will ensure that one will not decide to do something other than A.

It might be wrongly objected, by the way, that a child can intend to do something before it has the concept of an intention and, therefore, before it can have self-referential intentions. But there is no reason why the child must have a theoretically adequate concept of intention before it can have self-referential intentions. Which of us has a theoretically adequate concept of intention? Furthermore, it is not clear what the test is for saying that the child has a concept of intention. If the test is whether the child knows how to use the word 'intend' or some equivalent word, then to be sure it would seem that the child can intend to do things before it has the concept of intention. But how does that show that the child does not have self-referential intentions? If the test is whether the child does things that require the use of the concept of intention, and if the child can have self-referential intentions only if it uses the concept of intention, and if intentions are self-referential, the child who intends to do something already has the concept of intention.

The second thesis, then, is that intentions are self-referential. It is now time to present reasons for thinking that this thesis is true. The argument that follows will proceed by stages and will concentrate on positive intentions.

First, it is clear that in the normal case a successful positive intention to do A is in fact instrumental in one's doing A. It leads one to do A and is part of the explanation of one's doing A. This can be denied only if intentions are not taken seriously as real attitudes and are treated as epiphenomenal constructs to be analysed away in terms of desires, beliefs, and behaviour. But no plausible analysis of this sort has ever been suggested, and it is much more reasonable to take intentions to be a real part of the causal and explanatory order. Indeed, it seems quite obvious that actions cannot be explained in terms of beliefs and desires alone; these attitudes must be translated into intentions before one can act. And, if intentions have the sorts of effect we normally suppose they have, a successful positive intention will normally be instrumental in one's doing what one intends to do.

Furthermore, one can rationally form a positive intention to do A only if one can at the same time justifiably conclude that one's intention will be instrumental in one's doing A. For, as has already been argued, one's intention to do A involves the belief that one will do A. One can rationally form that intention, therefore, only if one can rationally form the corresponding belief. Since one's intention is a positive intention, moreover, one cannot rationally believe that one is going to do A whether or not one intends to. One can rationally believe that one will do A, therefore, only if one can rationally believe that one intends to do A and that this intention will lead to one's doing A. It follows that one can rationally form a positive intention to do A only if one can rationally conclude that one's intention will be instrumental in leading one to do A.

The same point can be put another way. As the result of practical reasoning, one forms the positive intention of doing A. It has been noted above that practical reasoning and theoretical reasoning overlap and that considerations of explanatory coherence are relevant to both sorts of reasoning. Furthermore, one's intention to do A involves the belief that one will do A. Since one's intention is a positive intention, one's practical conclusion has explanatory coherence only if it involves the supposition that one's intention to do A will lead to one's doing A. Without that supposition, one has no reason to think that one will do A. So, for reasons of explanatory coherence, one can form the positive intention to do A only if one can also conclude that one's intention will be instrumental in one's doing A.

None of this needs to be conscious. Reasoning is not the conscious rehearsal of argument; it is a process in which antecedent beliefs and intentions are minimally modified, by addition and subtraction, in the interests of explanatory coherence and the satisfaction of intrinsic desires. One is not ordinarily aware of all of the relevant beliefs, desires, and intentions— nor is one ordinarily aware of the details of the change that reasoning brings about. One may not even be conscious that any reasoning at all has occurred.

So far, then, we have seen that one can form the positive intention of doing A only if one can also conclude that this intention will be instrumental in one's doing A. The next thing to see is that one must also draw a conclusion about *how* one's intention will lead one to do A. This is true even in the limiting case in which A is something immediately within one's power. In such a case, the intention to do A (now) will, without further ado, lead one to do A. Let us call the way in which one's intention produces one's action in such a case the 'normal simple way'. For example, Ludwig forms the simple intention of raising his arm that leads him to flex his arm muscles in such a way that he raises his arm. Now, in order rationally to form this simple intention, Ludwig must conclude not only (as has been previously argued) that his intention will be instrumental in getting him to raise his arm, but also that it will do so in the normal simple way. Otherwise Ludwig's conception of the immediate future will lack explanatory coherence. If he cannot conclude that his simple intention will in the normal simple way lead him to raise his arm, he cannot coherently form the simple intention of raising his arm. If he sees, for example, that Alice is holding his arm down, he must adopt either a weaker intention, for instance to try to raise his arm, or a more complex intention, for instance to push Alice away and then raise his arm. Even if A is immediately within one's power, therefore, one can coherently form the positive intention of doing A (now) only if one has some idea about how one's intention will lead to one's doing A.

If A is not immediately within one's power, one may develop a plan of more or less complexity for doing A. Or one may simply rely on one's ability at a later time to plan accordingly and take whatever steps will be necessary to do A. More will be said about this below. The present point is that, even though one can intend to do A without having yet planned in detail how it is to be done, one can in that case coherently form the positive intention to do A only if one can now conclude that one's intention will later lead one to make plans and take appropriate steps. Even in such a case, therefore, one can coherently intend to do A only if one has some idea about how one's intention will lead one to do A—namely, that it will lead one at some later time to make plans and take whatever steps are necessary to do A.

But to have a more or less definite idea of this sort about how one's present intention to do A will lead to doing it is to have a more or less definite plan about how one is going to do A. A positive intention to do A includes a more or less definite plan concerning how the intention is (or is going to be) instrumental in doing A. One's plan is that one's intention will lead in such and such a way to one's doing A. Furthermore, one's plan says what one intends to do. Whenever one has a positive intention to do A, therefore, one intends that one's intention will lead in such and such a way to one's doing A. This means, as has already been said, that one's positive intention to do A must be the self-referential intention that it, that very intention, will lead (in such and such a way) to one's doing A; otherwise, there would be an infinite regress.

This conclusion is further supported by consideration of the conditions under which someone does something intentionally. We have already seen that one can do something intentionally even if one does not intend to do it, if one has a reason not to do it, and either one tries to do it and succeeds, or one foresees that one will do it in consequence of doing something else that one intends to do. There are also cases in which one intends to do something and does it, but not intentionally.

For example, Mabel intends to drive to Ted's house, to find him, and to kill him. By chance, Ted happens to walk by as Mabel backs out of her driveway and she runs him down without even seeing him. She intends to kill him and does kill him, but she does not kill him intentionally.

The difficulty in this case is clearly that Mabel does not kill Ted in anything like the way in which she intended to kill him. But it will not be enough simply to say that one kills someone intentionally if one intends to kill him, does kill him, and does so in the way in which one intends. That is too vague. For perhaps Mabel's intention was to bring Ted back to her driveway where she was going to run over him. Then she does kill him in the way in which she intends to kill him, namely by running over him in her driveway, but she still does not kill him intentionally.

The point is that, even though she intends to kill him by running over him and does kill him in that way, she does not do what she intends. One kills someone intentionally if one intends to kill him, does kill him, and thereby does what one intends; but in this case Mabel does not do what she intends. Her intention is not simply 'to kill Ted' or 'to kill Ted by running over him'. It also includes a plan specifying how that intention will lead her to do what she intends to do. She does not do what she intends, because what she does differs significantly from the plan that is part of her intention.

This illustrates a way in which positive intentions differ from desires and hopes. Mabel can want and hope simply to kill someone, but she cannot in the same simple way intend simply to kill someone. Her intention must be the intention that the very intention will lead in a certain way to her killing the person in question. Her intention to kill him cannot be separated from her intention that her intention will lead in a certain way to her killing him. Desires and hopes are different. Mabel's desire or hope that she will kill Ted can easily be separated from a desire or hope that her hope or desire will lead in a certain way to her killing him. That is why it is appropriate to say that in running Ted down Mabel gets what she wants and what she hopes for but does not do what she intends, even though she wants, hopes, and intends to run Ted down.

Here is another example. Betty intends to kill someone. She aims her gun and, at the crucial moment, a noise startles her, leading her to contract her finger so that she shoots and kills him—but not intentionally. Although she intends to kill him and does kill him, she does not do what she intends. For her intention to kill him is the intention that the very intention will lead her to pull the trigger at the crucial moment; and that does not happen. So she does not kill him intentionally. Notice, furthermore, that her intention must lead in the normal simple way to her pulling the trigger. If Betty's intention makes her nervous and nervousness causes her to pull the trigger, her intention leads her to pull the trigger but not in the intended way; so she does not do what she intends and does not kill him intentionally (Davidson, 1973*a*).

All these examples confirm the claim that a positive intention to do something is the intention that it, that very intention, will lead in a more or less explicitly specified way to one's doing the thing in question. An additional reason for accepting this claim is that such a claim is needed in order to distinguish intentions from predictions. But discussion of that point must be deferred until the next part of this essay. First, more must be said about the ways in which intentions incorporate plans.

Now, intentions typically have more than a momentary existence; it is often essential to an intention that it be conceived as existing for a period of time. If Carol intends to meet Jim for lunch, she intends that her present intention will lead her to do so. She envisages herself as arriving at the appointed place and time because of her present intention to do so; and typically she would envisage this happening because she envisages herself as continuing to have the intention to meet Jim at that place and time. Exceptional cases can be imagined; she might now arrange to have herself taken by force to Jim at the appropriate time. In that case, her intention to meet Jim for lunch would not involve the assumption that she would continue to have that intention. But, in the more normal case, an intention does involve the assumption that one will continue to have it.

Intentions often involve planning and coordination. If Carol intends to meet Jim in St. Louis and she is now in New York, she must envisage some way of getting from New York to St. Louis. She cannot wait until the last minute. She may, for example, decide to fly to St. Louis. Then she must plan to order tickets and she must plan to pick up her tickets when they are ready. She must arrange to get to the airport. And so forth. She envisages an intention or plan that will exist over a period of time which will be responsible for various things when they become appropriate: ordering the tickets, picking them up, arranging for a taxi, and so forth.

Typically, Carol's plan is not spelled out in detail from the beginning. She may, for example, accept an invitation to read a paper to some economists in St. Louis in a year's time. She decides that she will read a paper at their meeting; she now intends to read a paper there. Her participation in the meeting will involve a number of things. She must write the paper, perhaps revise it, send a copy to her commentator, purchase plane tickets, reserve a hotel room, and so forth. At first, little of this is settled. She will not have decided yet what hotel to stay at or exactly when she will want to arrive in St. Louis. She may not even know where she will be coming from. She may not know who will be the commentator to whom a copy of her paper must be sent. Indeed, she may not have decided what she will say in her paper or even what the general topic of the paper will be.

This vagueness in her plans is not an objectionable incoherence in them if she can rely on her ability to add to her plans and modify them as appropriate. In planning to read a paper in St. Louis at next year's meeting she sees her plan developing in a natural way. She conceives her plan as existing for a period of time and as changing over time by becoming more specific in ways that have the result that she reads a paper at next year's meeting in St. Louis. If she could not count on that, for example if she could not count on her ability to develop in the time available a more detailed idea of the paper she must write, she could not now intend to read a paper at the St. Louis meeting. Intention involves belief.

This is still oversimplified in at least two important respects. First, what is relevant is not just a single plan evolving over time towards a single final goal, but an evolving system of plans aiming at various goals. In reasoning one must coordinate different plans with each other, and, in intending, one relies on one's ability to be able to continue to do this. For example, when Carol intends to read a paper at next year's meeting, she relies on her ability to coordinate her system of plans and intentions in such a way that she will read a paper in St. Louis next year. If she intends to read several different papers at several different places next year, she counts on being able to plan the writing of each in a way that leaves time and thought for the writing of the others; she counts on her ability to coordinate her travel plans so that she will arrive at the right place at the right time. In one respect, then, the unit of intention is not a momentary attitude or even a growing plan aimed at a single goal; it is the whole evolving system. (Of course, in another respect, the unit of intention is not one's whole evolving system of intentions, since one can intend to do something, do what one intends, and thereby do something intentionally, without having to do everything that one intends in one's whole system of intentions.)

A second complication is that one's system of plans change, not just by becoming more detailed and explicit in response to new information and approaching deadlines, but also through the forming of new plans and intentions in order to satisfy new desires. Becoming hungry, one forms the intention of eating; desiring entertainment, one decides to go to the movies or to play chess; asked to read a paper in Chicago, Carol decides to do that in addition to the paper for St. Louis; and so forth. One's changing system of plans is constituted by one's present intentions along with the relatively routine ways one has of adapting one's plans to deadlines, to new information, and to new desires. Carol's intention to read a paper to the St. Louis meeting is part of her system of plans and routines, and it involves the supposition that she will end up reading a paper there because of that system.

2.3 DISTINGUISHING INTENTIONS FROM PREDICTIONS

Let us return now to the problem of distinguishing intentions from predictions. As we have seen, a positive intention differs from most predictions in virtue of being a self-referential conception that something is going to happen as a result of that very conception. Now, it is possible that some predictions should take the same form. An insomniac may find that the belief that he is going to stay awake is a self-fulfilling belief, which may lead to his being able to make the self-referential prediction that he will stay awake because of that very prediction, although he does not intend to stay awake. (I owe this point to Derek Parfit.) The insomniac concludes that he will stay awake because of his having reached that very conclusion. Someone who intends to stay awake has reached a similar self-referential conclusion. What is the difference?

One difference is that the person who intends to stay awake does so because he wants to stay awake, while the insomniac does not in the same way base his prediction on a desire to stay awake. We might say, then, that intentions and practical reasoning aim at satisfying desires in a way that predictions and theoretical reasoning do not.

In saying this, however, there is a danger of circularity since we have been assuming that extrinsic desires are to be explained in terms of intentions and dispositions to form intentions. To intend to do something is, in a sense, to want to do it. But it would be circular to appeal to this fact in order to distinguish intentions from mere predictions.

On the other hand, intrinsic desires are basic unanalysable attitudes in their own right. Intrinsic desires, unlike extrinsic desires, are not to be explained in terms of intentions and dispositions to intend. It is true that whenever one has an intrinsic desire for something, E, one will be disposed to intend to take E if given that choice. But one's intrinsic desire cannot be identified with that particular disposition, since one's intrinsic desire has implications for one's whole system of intentions and practical reasoning. A new intrinsic desire will bring about many new dispositions to form intentions and cannot be identified with any of them. Intrinsic desires are real attitudes that are part of the causal and explanatory order. They are not constructs out of intentions and dispositions to form intentions. Intrinsic desires like hunger and thirst come and go in ways that are not to be explained by changes in one's beliefs, intentions, and dispositions to form intentions. On the contrary, changes in intentions and in dispositions to form intentions are themselves to be explained by changes in such intrinsic desires. The intrinsic desire for E explains, for example, the disposition to take E if given the choice. That particular disposition is also identifiable as an extrinsic desire for E: it is the limiting case of extrinsic desire. Whenever one has an intrinsic desire, one will also have a disposition to choose, a disposition which constitutes a corresponding extrinsic desire, but the intrinsic desire explains the corresponding extrinsic desire and is not to be identified with it.

We have been trying to say what distinguishes intentions from mere predictions. Self-reference is not enough because some predictions are self-referential in the way that intentions are. Nor is it enough to say simply that intentions aim at satisfying desires in a way that predictions do not, since the relevant desires might be extrinsic desires which are themselves to be explained in terms of intentions. We must limit the relevant desires to intrinsic desires and say that intentions and practical reasoning aim at satisfying intrinsic desires in a way that predictions and theoretical reasoning do not.

What does it mean to say that intentions aim at satisfying intrinsic desires? Someone can intend to stay awake without wanting to stay awake for its own sake. He may want to stay awake only because he needs to stay awake in order to finish an essay that he is writing. In that case, he intends to stay awake but does not have an intrinsic desire to stay awake. So, we cannot say that intentions always aim at satisfying an intrinsic desire to do the intended thing.

Can we say that intentions aim at satisfying some intrinsic desires in the sense that, whenever someone intends to do something, he intends to do it either because he intrinsically wants to do it or because he thinks that doing it may contribute to his getting something that he intrinsically desires? We cannot say exactly this. Sometimes one forms the intention of doing something, not because doing that thing may contribute to the satisfaction of intrinsic desires, but because forming that intention may contribute to the satisfaction of intrinsic desires. Judy forms the intention of staying home tonight, not because staying home will serve her purposes, but because forming that intention will serve her purposes by allowing her to turn to other issues, taking this issue as settled.

Can we say, then, that intentions aim at satisfying intrinsic desires in the sense that whenever someone intends to do something, he intends to do it because he thinks that intending to do it may contribute to getting something that he intrinsically desires? That is almost right, but it leaves out the fact that the system of intentions has an inertia that keeps it going when desire fades. One may form certain intentions because of one's intrinsic desires and retain those intentions even when one no longer has the desires, as long as retaining those intentions does not interfere with the satisfaction of intrinsic desires one now has. The retained intentions will specify ends that do not correspond to any of one's current intrinsic desires, and means–ends reasoning may lead one to form new intentions on the basis of those ends. So it is not even true that whenever someone forms an intention, he does so because he thinks that doing so may contribute to the satisfaction of his current intrinsic desires.

The connection between intention and desire is indirect. Intentions arise from practical reasoning, predictions from theoretical reasoning, and intrinsic desires are relevant to practical reasoning in a way that they are not relevant to theoretical reasoning. In theoretical reasoning one attempts to improve the explanatory coherence of one's beliefs. Explanatory coherence is also relevant to practical reasoning, but so is coherence with intrinsic desires. Sometimes this involves forming an intention to do something that one intrinsically wants to do or that one thinks may contribute to getting something one intrinsically desires; but there are also the other cases mentioned above. Sometimes it involves forming an intention that contributes to the satisfaction of one's intrinsic desires, although doing what one intends does not, and sometimes it involves retaining an intention even though one no longer has the desires that were originally responsible for that intention.

In other words, one thing that distinguishes an intention from a prediction is the kind of reason one has for intending to do something as compared with the kind of reason one normally has for predicting. An intention is an idea of the future for which one has one sort of reason; a prediction is normally an idea for which one has a different sort of reason. This is simply to say that an intention is an idea arrived at and maintained by practical reasoning, whereas a prediction is normally an idea arrived at and maintained by theoretical reasoning; reasons are specified by reasoning. To say how desire is relevant to reasons for intentions, but not to reasons for predictions, is to say how coherence with intrinsic desires is a factor in practical but not in theoretical reasoning.

This point is not by itself sufficient to distinguish intentions from mere beliefs. It is necessary also to add that when someone intends that something will happen he thinks of his intention as guaranteeing that it will happen. One cannot intend that something will happen if one thinks that whether it will happen or not is entirely outside of one's control. It is necessary to add this point because it may be possible for someone to adopt mere beliefs for practical reasons. Pascal argued that this is true of belief in

God. He argued that there is a good practical reason to believe that God exists, namely that, if God exists, he will reward believers, and if God does not exist, little has been lost. As a result of this reasoning, Pascal undertook to get himself to believe in God. His resulting belief was not an intention, however, even though his reasons for it were practical rather than theoretical.

Now, Pascal's belief in God was not itself part of the conclusion of his practical reasoning nor of any reasoning at all; it was the consequence of a course of action he undertook as a result of his practical reasoning. But suppose (perhaps impossibly) that he had been able simply to believe at will that God exists, in the way that he could at will intend to do one thing or another, so that no elaborate process of conditioning was needed in order to get himself to believe in God. Although his practical reasoning would then have led immediately to his believing in God, that belief would still not be an intention that God exists. For Pascal certainly did not suppose that God's existence could depend in any way on what he, Pascal, thought about it, so he could not think of his belief as in any sense guaranteeing that God exists. His belief would therefore not be an intention.

To see how this makes a difference, let us suppose that Pascal already believes in God and believes that God will send him to heaven if he (Pascal) believes that God will. Pascal therefore has a strong practical reason to get himself to believe that he will go to heaven. Let us suppose, furthermore, that Pascal can form this belief at will and that he does so as the result of his practical reasoning. In this case, his belief is not distinct from the intention to go to heaven, since he forms his belief with that intention and the intention already involves the belief. For Pascal to intend to go to heaven by forming the belief that he will go is for him already to believe that he will go to heaven. In this case, then, the question whether Pascal can at will come to believe that he will go to heaven is not to be distinguished from the question whether he can simply decide to go to heaven.

Contrast that example with a slightly different one in which Pascal believes merely that God is more likely to send him to heaven if he believes that God will do so than if he does not believe it. Again Pascal has a practical reason to get himself to believe that he will go to heaven, but this time his belief can be distinguished from his intention. His intention is, perhaps, to try to go to heaven by forming the belief that he will go to heaven. That intention does not by itself involve the belief that he will go to heaven; it involves only the belief that he will try to go. Pascal then forms the belief that he will go to heaven as the result of his practical reasoning. But, since in this case Pascal does not suppose that his forming that belief guarantees that he will go to heaven, that belief cannot be identified with an intention to go to heaven.

Returning now to an earlier example, the insomniac believes that he will, as the result of that very belief, stay awake. His belief is that his belief guarantees that he will stay awake. But his belief is not an intention, because it is not a conclusion of practical reasoning.

This suggests that an intention is a conclusion of practical reasoning that says that the very conclusion itself guarantees that something will happen.

Let us apply this suggestion to the problem of distinguishing intended means to ends from merely foreseen consequences of actions. This will also enable us to note two important requirements on reasoning.

Recall that reasoning is often a combination of theoretical and practical reasoning, resulting in both intentions and predictions. The sniper decides to try to kill the soldier by shooting at him now, so he decides to pull the trigger now, even though he foresees that this will have certain consequences, namely, that he will heat the barrel of his gun and will alert the enemy to his presence. He therefore concludes that he will do a number of things. He will try to kill the soldier, he will pull the trigger, he will shoot his gun, he will heat the barrel of the gun, he will alert the enemy to his presence. Some of these conclusions are intentions, others are predictions. What is the difference?

Here there is an apparent difficulty here for our suggestion concerning the difference between intentions and predictions. The sniper has an intention which he supposes will lead him to pull the trigger and therefore to shoot and therefore to alert the enemy to his presence. As a result of his practical reasoning, he concludes that his conclusion will lead him to alert the enemy. He does not, however, intend to alert the enemy. How, then, can it be suggested that an intention is a conclusion of practical reasoning that says that it, the very conclusion itself, guarantees that something will happen? This suggestion would seem to imply, falsely, that the sniper intends to alert the enemy to his presence.

In order to save the suggestion it is necessary to suppose that the sniper reaches two conclusions, one practical, the other theoretical.

(1) This conclusion (1) will lead me to try to kill the soldier by pulling the trigger of my gun, thereby shooting at him. (Practical conclusion)
(2) Because the conclusion (1) will lead me to shoot, it will lead me to alert the enemy and to heat the barrel of my gun. (Theoretical conclusion)

The theoretical conclusion (2) is not self-referential and does not count as an intention, according to our suggestion. Given this analysis of the sniper's conclusions, our suggestion does not imply that the sniper intends to alert the enemy.

But this analysis merely pushes the problem back one step. Why does the sniper have to draw conclusions (1) and (2)? Why doesn't his practical reasoning lead him to the following single conclusion?

  (3) This conclusion (3) will lead me to try to kill the soldier by pulling the trigger and therefore shooting at him, thereby heating the barrel of my gun and alerting the enemy to my presence. (Practical conclusion)

Our suggestion implies that he does not reach this conclusion, for then he would be intending to alert the enemy and to heat the barrel of his gun, which he is not intending. But why does he not reach this conclusion?

In order to answer this question, we must assume that there is a requirement on reasoning that favours theoretical reasoning over practical reasoning. If a conclusion can be reached by theoretical reasoning alone, it is not to be reached instead as a conclusion of practical reasoning. Let us call this the minimality requirement on practical reasoning. Because of the minimality requirement, the sniper must reach conclusions (1) and (2) rather than conclusion (3). As much of his total conclusion as possible is to be on the theoretical side of that conclusion rather than on the practical side.

There is one exception to the minimality requirement, or, if not an exception, at least a complementary principle which favours practical reasoning over theoretical reasoning in certain cases. Given a choice between reaching a particular practical conclusion or reaching the theoretical conclusion that one will reach that practical conclusion in that way and will therefore do what one's practical conclusion says one will do, one should reach the practical conclusion directly. Let me call this the requirement of not predicting decisions that one can make instead. Because of the requirement of not predicting decisions, the sniper must form the intention of trying to kill the soldier and cannot simply predict that he will intend to try to kill the soldier. For he can predict that he will try only if he can predict that he will intend to try; and he is required actually to form that intention if he can now do so as a consequence of practical reasoning, rather than simply predict that he will do so.

This last requirement does not rule out all mere predictions of one's decisions. It only rules out predicting decisions that one could now make.

More specifically, it rules out reaching the theoretical conclusion that one will reach a certain practical conclusion for certain reasons, if one could instead now reach that practical conclusion directly for those reasons. It is probably an instance of a more general principle that would rule out any conclusion to the effect that one will reach another conclusion, theoretical or practical, on the basis of certain specified reasoning, if one could now instead reach the latter conclusion directly on the basis of that reasoning.

These two requirements, of minimality and of not predicting decisions, lead the sniper to draw conclusions (1) and (2) rather than, say, the following two conclusions.

(4) This conclusion (4) will lead me to try to kill the enemy soldier. (Practical conclusion)
(5) The conclusion (4) will lead me to pull the trigger and therefore to shoot and therefore to heat the barrel of my gun and alert the enemy to my position. (Theoretical conclusion)

For reasons of explanatory coherence, the sniper can suppose that his conclusion (4) will lead him to pull the trigger only if he also supposes that his conclusion (4) will lead him to form the intention of pulling the trigger, which will in the normal simple way lead him to pull the trigger. For the sniper to reach conclusions (4) and (5) would, therefore, be for him to violate the requirement of not predicting decisions.

Now consider what keeps the sniper from drawing the following conclusions.

(6) This conclusion (6) will lead me to try to kill the soldier by pulling the trigger of my gun. (Practical conclusion)
(7) Because the conclusion (6) will lead me to pull the trigger, it will lead me to shoot and therefore to heat the barrel of my gun and alert the enemy to my presence. (Theoretical conclusion)

Given our suggestion about how to distinguish intentions from mere beliefs, the sniper cannot draw these conclusions, since it would then follow that he would not be intending to shoot and would merely foresee that he was going to shoot. Since he must in this example intend to shoot, he cannot draw conclusions (6) and (7). It would, however, be circular to assert that these conclusions violate the requirement of not predicting decisions, because what is now at issue is why the sniper must decide to shoot at all. Why can he not see his shooting as a foreseen but unintended consequence of his pulling the trigger?

The answer must be that, given his intention of trying to kill the soldier, practical reasoning can lead him to form the intention to pull the trigger of his gun only as part of the intention to shoot the gun. Pulling the trigger would not by itself count as trying to kill the soldier. It counts as trying to kill the soldier only on the assumption that it is required in order to shoot the gun. If the sniper were to suppose that the trigger was not connected to the firing pin so that pulling the trigger would not be a way of shooting the gun, he could not and would not suppose that pulling the trigger was a way of trying to kill the soldier.

In other words, the sniper's practical reasoning cannot lead him simply to the conclusion (6). He begins with the intention of trying to kill the soldier. He then has a practical reason to form the intention of shooting at the soldier. For reasons of coherence, he can form that intention only if he also includes an intention to pull the trigger of his gun. Because of the requirement of not predicting decisions, furthermore, he reaches the practical conclusion (1) rather than a theoretical conclusion saying merely that he will form that intention. Considerations of explanatory coherence along with the minimality requirement, moreover, lead him to reach the theoretical conclusion (2) rather than adding to his practical conclusion intentions to alert the enemy and heat the barrel of his gun. That is why the sniper reaches conclusions (1) and (2) rather than any of the other possibilities mentioned.

Now, many philosophers (e.g. Hampshire, 1959) have suggested on intuitive grounds that there is something like the requirement of not predicting decisions. The minimality requirement is less familiar, although it is also intuitively plausible. What is striking about the present argument is that it shows that there is a reason to accept such requirements which is not simply an appeal to intuition. Such requirements are needed in order to distinguish what is intended from what is not intended.

2.4 PSYCHOLOGICAL HEDONISM OVERCOME

According to psychological hedonism, the source of motivation is always desire for pleasure and the absence of pain. This theory has seemed plausible to many psychologists and others who have thought about the development of motivation. For it seems fairly evident that a newborn baby is a selfish pleasure-seeking hedonist, and it is not clear how, from that beginning, a person could develop any nonselfish ends which are not, ultimately, based on his desire for pleasure and the absence of pain.

On the other hand, psychological hedonism seems quite implausible as a description of adults in society. People often seem to want things to happen that cannot bring them pleasure. The clearest examples involve desires concerning what will happen after the death of a person who does not believe in survival after death. Such a person may make a will because he wants his property to be distributed in a certain way after he dies even though he supposes that he will not be around to enjoy that distribution. Similarly, most people, including those who do not believe in any sort of afterlife, desperately hope that they will be remembered after they are gone, although again they will not get any pleasure out of being remembered. Various heroic sacrifices might also be mentioned in this connection.

It is, however, not very helpful to point to the implausibility of psychological hedonism unless we can also show how desires could have arisen that are not ultimately desires for pleasure or the satisfaction of bodily needs. In the absence of an alternative theory, a psychological hedonist will be justified in reinterpreting the data. He will be justified in saying that the person who makes the will does so in order to get pleasure from showing the will to others or from looking at it himself, and that, even if in some sense people believe that they will not survive their own death, when they imagine what the future will be like they illegitimately imagine themselves as hidden spectators reacting to what happens. So, in order to evaluate psychological hedonism, it is not enough simply to assert that an adult has acquired ends that are not ultimately based on his desires for pleasure and the absence of pain. Some account of how this can happen is needed.

Nor is it enough simply to deny the hedonistic premise that a baby is a selfish pleasure-seeking hedonist. Perhaps it can be argued that the child's desire to eat is not a desire for the pleasure of eating or for the absence of the pains of hunger, and similarly for thirst, etc. But this is quibbling. It is, for one thing, by no means obvious how we could decide whether the child's desire is ultimately a desire to eat or ultimately a desire for the pleasure of eating. And, even if the point were conceded, it would not really matter. Psychological hedonism could easily be modified accordingly. The basic claim of psychological hedonism is that there is no way for a person to develop new ultimate ends; one is stuck with the ends that one is born with. As one gets older, the hedonist argues, one does not learn new ultimate ends; one learns new ways of satisfying the intrinsic desires that one was born with. If these original intrinsic desires include not only desires for pleasure but also desires for food, water, etc., then the hedonistic thesis should be restated to say that one's motivation is always ultimately to satisfy one's desires for pleasure, for the absence of pain, for food, for water, etc. This is still to say that motivation is basically selfish, and it is not very different from the original claim that one is motivated always to get pleasure and avoid pain.

Two further modifications in the thesis of psychological hedonism are needed in order to accommodate the indirect connection between motivation and desire discussed above. First, there is the fact that intentions have an inertia that allows them to survive the desires on which they were originally based. The desire for food leads Sam to form the intention of eating a steak. Halfway through, the desire is satisfied; he finishes the rest of his steak out of the inertia of his original intention. While he is eating the rest of his steak, his motivation does not derive from a current desire of his for pleasure or for food, although such a desire originally motivated that intention.

A second point is that, as previously indicated, one may form the intention of doing something, not because of the benefits of doing it, but because of the benefits of forming the intention. This happens, for example, when one forms an intention simply in order to settle an issue, so that one can go on to other things.

But neither of these modifications seriously undermines psychological hedonism, which sees the ultimate source of motivation in intrinsic desires for pleasure, for the absence of pain, and possibly for food, water, etc. As argued earlier in this essay, the connection between desire and motivation is an indirect one, depending on the role that intrinsic desires play in practical reasoning. Psychological hedonism is, at bottom, the claim that the intrinsic desires that play that role in the adult are essentially the same as the intrinsic desires of the infant. If psychological hedonism is to be seriously challenged, therefore, some account must be given of how new kinds of intrinsic desires might arise.

Actually, the answer is simple. One can often simply adopt at will a new intrinsic desire. And, if one regularly adopts the same intrinsic desire under certain conditions, one will develop a habit of doing so—a disposition to have that desire under those conditions. One adopts a new desire in this way because adopting a new intrinsic desire can often promote one's antecedent ends.

In watching a game, for example, one may temporarily adopt a desire for a particular team to win—not because of any benefits one expects from that team's winning, but because it is more fun to watch a game when one wants a particular team to win. Or, at a party, one may take an interest in a topic of conversation, not because one supposes that further information about that subject is of any use, given one's prior interests, but because the conversation will be found enjoyable only if one is interested in the topic of conversation.

It has often been observed that pure hedonism is self-defeating because a person whose ultimate desires are desires for pleasure will not in any usual case get as much out of life as someone with a variety of interests who genuinely cares for other people. The present point is that a variety of interests and a concern for others can be derived from an initial desire for pleasure—not because these concerns and interests have pleasure as their ultimate object (in the sense that they are ultimately concerns for and interests in one's own pleasure, which they are not), but because having those interests and that concern can be a means to one's own pleasure. This is the sort of thing that the child learns as it grows from a selfish hedonistic infant to a loving adult with a concern for society and interests in the arts. Psychological hedonism may be right in seeing the ultimate source of adult desires in the primitive desires of the infant but is wrong in taking this to show that adult intrinsic desires are ultimately desires for the same sorts of things that an infant intrinsically desires.

One can have a selfish reason to develop a genuinely unselfish concern for others. For if one has an unselfish concern for others, it is likely that the others will reciprocate. Furthermore, and more importantly, one's life will be richer and more interesting. But, given such a concern, one may also acquire, for example, an unselfish desire about the distribution of one's property at one's death, which can lead one to write a will in order to bring about that distribution even though one will not be around at that point to be affected by that distribution.

Similarly, it is often useful for reasons of efficiency to develop an intrinsic interest in something in which one already has an instrumental interest, for example money or physical fitness. When such intrinsic interests have developed they may lead to actions that go beyond what would have been needed to satisfy one's original purposes. One may come to want to amass a large fortune, more than anyone would 'need', or one may wish to retain the sort of physical fitness only a professional athlete ordinarily has. An analogous point helps to explain why one may hope to be remembered after death. It is often in one's interest that others should think of one and not forget one; fame has its uses. It is, therefore, useful to acquire an intrinsic interest in being remembered and thought well of. Having acquired that interest, however, one may well want to be remembered after one has died, even though being remembered at that point will not be useful in terms of one's original purposes.

All this is based on the assumption that it is within one's power to adopt new intrinsic desires at will. Let us now consider some reasons for thinking that this assumption is true.

Observe, first, that we sometimes hold a person responsible for the attitude that he takes toward what he is doing. In such a case, we must be supposing that his attitude is to some extent within his control. Now, in particular, we sometimes blame the person playing Monopoly with us for not being interested in winning, and that is to hold him responsible for the attitude with which he is playing. We therefore must be supposing that he could change his attitude at least temporarily by an act of will.

Furthermore, and more importantly, if we suppose that a person can adopt a temporary desire by an act of will, we can give a better explanation of the acquisition of dispositions to have new intrinsic desires than if we do not make this supposition. Given this supposition, we can account for dispositions to have new intrinsic desires in terms of simple habit formation. Without this supposition, we must either accept psychological hedonism or appeal to some sort of novel ad hoc psychological mechanism in order to account for new intrinsic desires and dispositions.

It is true that we avoid the supposition that there is such an ad hoc mechanism only by making a different supposition. But we do not have to invoke any new ad hoc mechanism. We appeal to a mechanism that is needed in any event. Any theory must allow that there are certain attitudes that one can adopt more or less at will. One can, for example, direct one's thoughts in various ways, one can imagine various things, and one can attend to various aspects of things at will. More to the point, one can temporarily suspend one's disbelief, one can suppress hostility, and one can even decide that one will, for the moment, believe someone or accept a particular hypothesis. To say that one can also adopt a temporary desire for something is, therefore, just to add another item to this list. It is not to invoke a wholly new mechanism.

This is not to say that one can always take a temporary interest in something. Sometimes one cannot—just as sometimes one cannot concentrate on what one is doing.

There is another way in which practical reasoning can lead one to adopt new ends. Sometimes one adopts an end so that things that one has already done or plans to do can gain significance as means toward the end that one now adopts. This is how some people choose careers—so that their earlier training will not be wasted.

The typical teacher of physics, for example, did not originally study the subject with the purpose of becoming a physics teacher. He studied the subject because it interested him or perhaps because it was a required subject. Later he decided to become a teacher of physics; at that point he was able to see his earlier study as part of the means by which he is able to become a physics teacher—and that is part of his reason for becoming a physics teacher: so that his earlier study will not have been wasted. It is true that he enjoys physics (let us suppose), so he is choosing a career that will allow him to do something that he enjoys doing. But that is only one consideration. It is also relevant that in becoming a physics teacher he gives significance to his earlier study and to that extent helps to unify his life. If he had chosen instead to do something else, he might always have felt some unhappiness over his decision even if he fully enjoyed his life. His training in physics might in that case have had no significance—it would have been wasted. It would have lost connection with his later life, a connection that could have helped to give his life unity. In the same way someone who is musical or athletic in his youth will often feel unhappy if he does not continue those activities as he grows older.

People create their lives at least to some extent. They adopt purposes which give their lives meaning. But they do not adopt these purposes ahead of time—only after the fact. To choose a career is for many people to drift into a career. Past acts done for other reasons assume a pattern in the light of ends adopted only now.

We adopt ends that help to rationalize and give significance to what we have been and are doing—not only in large decisions, as in choosing careers, but even in our smallest and most insignificant acts. A dramatic illustration of this occurs when someone who has been hypnotized is told that later after he 'comes out of it' at a given signal he is to open a window. When he does later open the window and is asked why, he will be found to have constructed some appropriate end that will rationalize what he is doing. This is no mere parlour curiosity worthy of interest only as a parlour trick. It represents an important aspect of rationality, an aspect that promotes stability in one's plans and allows one to assume that one's long-range plans will be carried out. For in the midst of them, one will be strongly motivated to continue so as not to waste what has gone before. In the midst of some minor activity one may forget what one intends to be doing, but one will often then reconstruct an end on the basis of what is being done at the moment, and one will finish—simply for the sake of finishing what one is doing. One does something because that was what one was doing. Otherwise, one's earlier activities would be pointless.

The same idea keeps one going in more serious activities. A student continues in graduate school, for example, because he has gone this far already and if he stops now the earlier years would amount to nothing. This is, of course, not always for the best. Some people irrationally continue careers, political or religious activities, or their families because they do not want to have to count what they have been doing so far as a waste of time. The aspect of practical reasoning that we are now discussing is not its only aspect and it should not always prevail. But it is an important aspect, and an account of practical reasoning that ignores it is incomplete.

Practical reasoning is, like theoretical reasoning, holistic. In practical reasoning, one seeks a conception of one's life that is both explanatorily coherent and coherent with one's desires. One can increase coherence by adopting means to already existing ends—but that is not the only way. One can also increase coherence by adopting new ends, either because the adoption of those ends will help get one something previously wanted, or because adopting those ends gives a significance to things one has already done or plans to do.

3

Simplicity as a Pragmatic Criterion for Deciding what Hypotheses to Take Seriously

The most basic form of Goodman's (1965) 'new riddle of induction' arises from the fact that, when scientists take certain data to support a hypothesis, there will almost always be infinitely many other, less simple, hypotheses that fit the data as well. None, or almost none, of these less simple hypotheses are even considered by scientists, nor would they be taken seriously if suggested. Goodman's riddle can be interpreted as asking how to characterize the relevant sort of simplicity.

For example, given two variables P and V, suppose that, for some constant K, the data are generally consistent with the principle $V = K \times P$. Suppose also that there are no data for $P = 16$. Then the data are also consistent with the following complicated principle: If $P \neq 16$, then $V = K \times P$, and if $P = 16$, then $V = K^2 \times P$. No scientist would even consider the more complicated principle and no scientist would take seriously the more complicated principle if his or her attention were called to it, unless there was some special reason to consider the more complicated principle, a reason deriving from other evidence.

A similar point holds for most inductive inferences made by almost anyone, scientist or not. When a person reaches almost any sort of conclusion at all, there are almost always infinitely many complicated alternative hypotheses equally compatible with the evidence. Almost all of these hypotheses will not be considered and would be taken to be absurd if someone were to suggest that they be considered.

For example, if a speaker says 'I went to the bank', a hearer might not be sure whether the speaker means a financial institution or the edge of a body of water. No normal hearer will consider the possibility that the speaker means that he went to the circus because on this occasion the speaker uses the word 'bank' to mean 'ciank', where a ciank at time t is a financial institution unless t is today, in which case a ciank is a circus!

This interpretation of 'bank' is logically possible, since a speaker could use the word with that meaning and because the past practice of this and other speakers is compatible with bank having that meaning. But it is an abstract possibility that it would be absurd to take seriously, so absurd that you may wonder why I bring it up at all.

Why do philosophers think about such absurd possibilities? Because it is interesting that such possibilities are absurd. Why is it interesting? Because the data available to a hearer are as compatible with any of the infinitely many absurd hypotheses as with one of the normal, unabsurd hypotheses (edge of water, financial institution). The absurd hypotheses are not absurd because they conflict with the data. They are absurd because they are too complicated when compared with more normal unabsurd hypotheses.

3.1 DIFFERENT USES OF DIFFERENT KINDS OF SIMPLICITY

In this essay I am concerned with the use that scientists and ordinary people make of simplicity in order to decide what hypotheses to take seriously and what hypotheses to treat as absurd and not worth taking seriously.

This is not the only use that scientists make of simplicity. Sometimes they make an explicit appeal to one or another sort of simplicity or 'parsimony' in order to argue for one out of several hypotheses that are worth being taken seriously. One theory is supposed to be better than another because it appeals to fewer kinds of entities: it is more parsimonious in its ontological assumptions. Or one theory is supposed to be better because it requires fewer accidents or coincidences.

As Sober (1988, 1990) points out, using examples from evolutionary biology, the success of such explicit appeals to simplicity or parsimony can depend on what it is reasonable to believe about the domain in question. Robins and sparrows have wings; iguanas do not. It is in one respect simpler to suppose that wings evolved once in W, a descendant of A and ancestor of robins and sparrows, rather than that twice, in one descendant X of A that was an ancestor of robins and in a separate descendant Y of A that was an ancestor of sparrows. The simpler hypothesis would reduce coincidence. But it is controversial whether this particular kind of appeal to simplicity is reasonable in the context of evolutionary theory. Sober argues persuasively that the success of this particular kind of appeal to simplicity depends on special assumptions about the frequency of certain sorts of evolutionary events. Under certain assumptions about evolution, such coincidences are more likely than the one-time evolution of wings.

Sober goes on to question whether there is any useful domain-independent notion of simplicity that always makes one hypothesis more reasonable than another hypothesis that accounts equally well for the data. And Sober's scepticism may be right when it comes to explicit appeals to simplicity.

But I am not concerned with explicit appeals to simplicity to decide among hypotheses that are already being taken seriously. I am concerned with the sort of relative simplicity that distinguishes those hypotheses that are taken seriously from other hypotheses that account equally well for the data but are not taken seriously.

3.2 BASIC ISSUES

By simplicity, I will mean whatever distinguishes the hypotheses people take seriously from those other hypotheses they (normally) do not take seriously even though the other hypotheses account equally well for the data.

With this understanding, then, one task for the philosophy of science is to specify what makes one hypothesis simpler than another in the relevant sense. A second task is to indicate in what respects simpler hypotheses in this respect are worth taking seriously in a way that sufficiently less simple hypotheses are not.

There are two ways to approach these issues. One can begin by looking at how scientists and others actually distinguish hypotheses worth taking seriously from others. If one determines what criterion scientists use, one can next consider what is desirable about limiting consideration to simpler hypotheses as picked out by that criterion. Alternatively, one can think more abstractly about why it might be desirable to limit consideration to hypotheses with certain features, and one might then ask how to determine what theories have the desirable features.

The two tasks are related, of course. For example, if simpler theories are to be preferred because they are easier to use for certain scientific purposes, then it would seem that ease of use ought to be the relevant criterion for distinguishing those hypotheses to be taken seriously from others that account equally well for the data.

One important issue about simplicity is whether the fact that one theory is simpler than another is ever a reason to think that the first theory is more likely to be true than the second. If simplicity has to do with ease of use, the question becomes whether a theory's being easier to use than another can make the first theory more likely to be true than the second theory.

The philosophical outlook called 'instrumentalism' holds that the goal of science is not to come up with true theories but rather to come up with theories that are observationally adequate. For example, van Fraassen (1980, 1989) argues that scientists do not, qua scientists, believe that the theories they accept are true; as scientists, they believe at most that the theories they accept are observationally adequate (or more observationally adequate than their current competitors). Scientists may actually believe that (some of) their theories are true, but they do it on their own time, so to speak, just as they may have various (other) religious and philosophical beliefs that are not implicated in their science, qua science. The fact that one theory may be simpler than another may permit that theory to give a better explanation of the evidence but, according to van Fraassen, that cannot make the theory any more likely to be true. Indeed, van Fraassen (1989) argues that to allow simplicity or any other pragmatic advantage of a theory to affect one's view of its probability would leave one open to a 'Temporal Dutch Book' argument.

I propose to develop a pragmatic theory of simplicity that rejects this sort of instrumentalism. I believe that instrumentalism is itself an example of a parasitical theory of a sort that is less simple than the theory on which it is parasitical. If I am right, there are pragmatic reasons not to be an instrumentalist. I will also defend the use of simplicity as one indicator of the relative likelihood of truth against objections by van Fraassen and others.

The main goal of my project, then, is to indicate what makes one theory simpler than another and to say why simplicity is a desirable feature in a hypothesis, where simplicity is identified with whatever it is that leads us to distinguish the hypotheses to take seriously from other hypotheses that account equally well for the data.

3.3 LESSONS OF CURVE FITTING

Simplicity plays an important role in fitting curves to data points (Glymour, 1980). Suppose, for example, that we measure the relation between two variables, P and C, and obtain the following limited data, rounded to the nearest whole number (and, for the moment, ignoring what the units of measurement are).

P = 1, C = 2
P = 3, C = 6
P = 4, C = 8
P = 8, C = 16

Various hypotheses fit these data equally well. Consider, in particular,

HYPOTHESIS 1:
$C = 2 \times P$

HYPOTHESIS 2:
$C = (2 \times P) + (P{-}1) \times (P{-}3) \times (P{-}4) \times (P{-}8)$

Given this evidence a scientist would normally on grounds of simplicity take HYPOTHESIS 1 seriously and would not take HYPOTHESIS 2 seriously.

Notice that the two hypotheses make quite different predictions for other values of P. To take one example, for P = 6, HYPOTHESIS 1 predicts C = 12 and HYPOTHESIS 2 predicts C = −48. Do data of this sort make one of these predictions more likely than the other? A scientist would normally suppose that the answer is 'Yes' and would suppose that the first prediction is much more likely to be true than the second.

Notice, furthermore, that there are many other hypotheses equally compatible with the data that make different predictions about the value of C when P = 6. Indeed, for any value N there are hypotheses compatible with the data that entail that C = N when P = 6, for example,

$$C = 2 \times P - \frac{(N{-}12) \times (P{-}1) \times (P{-}3) \times (P{-}4) \times (P{-}8)}{60}$$

A scientist will on grounds of simplicity prefer to make further predictions using HYPOTHESIS 1 rather than HYPOTHESIS 2 or any of the other hypotheses just considered. Our questions, then, are (a) 'What makes HYPOTHESIS 1 simpler than these other hypotheses?' and (b) 'Is this difference between the hypotheses a reason for a scientist to prefer using HYPOTHESIS 1 to make predictions?'

3.4 SIMPLICITY AS SIMPLICITY OF REPRESENTATION

Consider the suggestion that the relevant type of simplicity of a hypothesis consists in the simplicity of its representation. One version of this suggestion would measure the complexity of a hypothesis by the number of symbols used to express the hypothesis. HYPOTHESIS 1 uses five symbols: C = 2 × P. HYPOTHESIS 2 uses thirty-one symbols: C = (2 × P) + (P−1) × (P−3) × (P−4) × (P−8). By this criterion, HYPOTHESIS 1 is simpler and more inferable.

Another version of the same suggestion applies to hypotheses that can be graphed. In such a case the simpler hypothesis is the one that has the simpler graph. Now, the graph of HYPOTHESIS 1 is a straight line whereas the graph of HYPOTHESIS 2 is a complex curve that swoops down and up and down and up. So, by this criterion also, HYPOTHESIS 1 is simpler than HYPOTHESIS 2.

But there is a problem. Simplicity of representation is obviously dependent on the system of representation. One hypothesis can have a simpler representation than a second given one way of representing the hypotheses and a more complex representation given a second system.

Putting the point in another way: any hypothesis can be given an arbitrarily simple representation, because any hypothesis can be represented by a single symbol, e.g. 'H'.

Similarly, the simplicity of the shape of a graph depends on the coordinate scales used. In comparing the graph of HYPOTHESIS 1 with the graph of HYPOTHESIS 2, we might use coordinate scales uniform in standard units for measuring P and C. But we can use other scales also: log, loglog, and more complex scales. A change in coordinate scale can change a straight line into a curve and vice versa. There will always be a scale that gives a selected function a simple graph, at the cost of giving other functions more complex graphs. For example, if the X axis is a measure of standard units of P and the Y axis is a measure of

$$\frac{C}{(2 \times P) + (P−1) \times (P−3) \times (P−4) \times (P−8)},$$

then HYPOTHESIS 2 will be graphed by a horizontal straight line, and HYPOTHESIS 1 will be represented by a very complicated curve.

The same point applies to various computational approaches to induction and simplicity (Angluin and Smith, 1983; Blum and Blum, 1975; Blum, 1967; Gold, 1967; Kugel, 1977; Solomonoff, 1964; Turney, 1988; and Valiant, 1979). I explain below how a different computational theory might handle it.

So, if simplicity is to be measured by representational simplicity, restrictions must be placed on allowable kinds of representation. But it is unclear what restrictions would do the trick and also unclear whether it would be desirable all things considered to restrict representations in this way.

For example, it might be suggested that abbreviations are not allowed, so that we cannot use an arbitrary symbol like 'H' to stand for a longer hypothesis. At least, we cannot do this when we are assessing the simplicity of the hypothesis. For that purpose, we must consider the hypothesis as stated in 'primitive notation'. Similarly, it might be suggested that in graphs we must use 'natural scales' and not, e.g.

$$\frac{C}{(2 \times P) + (P-1) \times (P-3) \times (P-4) \times (P-8)}.$$

But it is doubtful that there is any way to restrict the relevant representations in a reasonable way. Any reasonable restrictions would allow new scientific concepts to be introduced, and there is no real difference between introducing an abbreviation and introducing a new concept and then using this concept to state an equivalence as a new theoretical postulate (Quine, 1936; Goodman, 1965; Harman, 1973).

3.5 A SEMANTIC THEORY OF SIMPLICITY

The theory that identifies the simplicity of a hypothesis with the simplicity of its representation might be thought of as a syntactic theory of simplicity, if syntax is concerned with the symbols used to represent something. A semantic theory of simplicity is concerned with the meaning or information contained in a hypothesis, apart from how that information is represented. For example, in Sober's early (1975) theory, one hypothesis is simpler than another if less information is needed in conjunction with the first hypothesis in order to answer certain questions.

As I mentioned earlier, Sober (1990) repudiates his earlier theory and now doubts that scientists ever appeal to a domain-independent kind of simplicity. But I am not now concerned with explicit appeals to simplicity to decide among hypotheses under active consideration. I am instead concerned with the sort of relative simplicity that distinguishes those hypotheses that will be taken seriously from those that are automatically ruled out. So I want for a moment to see whether Sober's earlier (1975) theory provides an account of this sort of simplicity.

In this view, the hypothesis that a particular function $F(x)$ is constant, e.g. $F(x) = 7$, is simpler than the hypothesis that the function is linear, e.g.

$F(x) = 7x$, because the first hypothesis allows one to determine the value of the function for a given value of x without any information at all about the given value of x, whereas the second hypothesis allows one to determine the value of the function only when one is given as information what the numerical value of x is.

'All emeralds are green' is simpler by this measure than 'All emeralds are either green, if first observed before AD 2000, or are blue, if not first observed before AD 2000'. (This example is from Goodman, 1965.) With the first hypothesis, the information that a given stone is an emerald is sufficient to determine that the emerald is green. With the second hypothesis, it is also necessary to have information as to whether the emerald has been observed before AD 2000.

The semantic theory has something to say about why simplicity is scientifically desirable. It is desirable because scientists want to use hypotheses to answer certain questions. Scientists prefer hypotheses that make it easier to answer these questions. Simpler hypotheses make it easier to answer these questions in the sense that they require less information in order to answer the questions.

The semantic theory is not sensitive to the syntactic form of a hypothesis, so it is not affected by changes in the system of representation, e.g. abbreviations, or changes in the scales of graphs. However, the measure is intended to be sensitive to the questions in which one might be interested. 'All emeralds are green' counts as simpler if one tends to be interested in whether emeralds are green. 'All emeralds are green if first observed before AD 2000 and are blue if not first observed before AD 2000' counts as simpler if one tends instead to be interested in whether particular emeralds are grue, in other words, if one is interested in whether particular emeralds are green if first observed before AD 2000 and are blue if not first observed before AD 2000.

According to Sober (1975), people normally take the first hypothesis to be simpler than the second because people are normally interested in colour, not in the sort of complex property represented by 'green if first observed before AD 2000 and blue if not first observed before AD 2000'.

But now consider HYPOTHESES 1 and 2 concerning the relation between C and P. If science had only an interest in answering questions about the value of C for various values of P, the hypotheses would have to count as equally simple by Sober's measure. In both cases, to answer this sort of question information is needed about the relevant value of P, and that is all the information needed.

Sober (1975) suggests somewhat surprisingly that the relative simplicity of the first hypothesis as compared with the second in a case like this arises because of an interest a scientist would have in answering questions about the derivative of C with respect to P, i.e. the slope of the curve for various values of P. Since this slope is constant for HYPOTHESIS 1 and not constant for HYPOTHESIS 2, HYPOTHESIS 1 allows one to answer this question without any further information about P, unlike HYPOTHESIS 2. So HYPOTHESIS 1 is simpler than HYPOTHESIS 2 with respect to answering such a question.

One reason that this is a surprising suggestion is that there would seem to be a clear difference in simplicity between HYPOTHESIS 1 and HYPOTHESIS 2 quite apart from any interest one would have in the derivatives of these functions. I will come back to this point in a moment.

A second reason that this is a surprising answer is that it makes simplicity indirectly relative to how hypotheses are represented after all. The slope of a line in a graph depends on the coordinate scale used. As I have already observed, there is a coordinate scale that graphs HYPOTHESIS 2 as a straight line with zero slope and graphs HYPOTHESIS 1 as a complex curve with a slope that changes in a complex way. To be interested in the derivative of a function is in part to be interested in a particular way in which that function is represented.

3.6 A COMPUTATIONAL OR PRAGMATIC THEORY OF SIMPLICITY

I now want to consider a third theory of simplicity. This theory, like the semantic theory, takes simpler theories to be those that are easier to use to answer questions. But this third theory measures ease of use computationally rather than semantically, and does not require an interest in derivatives in order to account for the difference between HYPOTHESES 1 and 2.

Suppose there is a reason to know what the value of C is when $P = 6$, and consider how this value might be deduced from HYPOTHESIS 1 and HYPOTHESIS 2 respectively.

HYPOTHESIS 1:
$C = 2 \times P$
$C = 2 \times 6$
$C = 12$.

HYPOTHESIS 2:
$$C = (2 \times P) + (P-1) \times (P-3) \times (P-4) \times (P-8)$$
$$C = (2 \times 6) + (6-1) \times (6-3) \times (6-4) \times (6-8)$$
$$C = 12 + 5 \times 3 \times 2 \times (-2)$$
$$C = 12 + 30 \times (-2) = 12-60 = -48.$$

In an obvious sense it is easier to use HYPOTHESIS 1 to get the answer in this case, because the calculation involved is less complex. So it is this that makes HYPOTHESIS 1 simpler, according to the third theory of simplicity, which is a computational, pragmatic theory of simplicity.

The computational theory, like the semantic theory takes it to be relevant what questions scientists are interested in: simpler theories are easier to use in getting results in which scientists are interested even though more complex theories might be easier to use in getting other results.

Consider the calculations involved using HYPOTHESES 1 and 2 to obtain the value of

$$R = \frac{C}{(2 \times P) + (P-1) \times (P-3) \times (P-4) \times (P-8)},$$

when $P = 6$.

HYPOTHESIS 1:
$$R = 2 \times P/(2 \times P) + (P-1) \times (P-3) \times (P-4) \times (P-8)$$
$$R = 2 \times 6/(2 \times 6) + (6-1) \times (6-3) \times (6-4) \times (6-8)$$
$$R = 12/(12) + 5 \times 3 \times 2 \times (-2)$$
$$R = 12/(12) + 15 \times 2 \times (-2) = 12/-48 = 1/4.$$

HYPOTHESIS 2:
$$R = 1.$$

Of course, the two hypotheses disagree about the answer here. And HYPOTHESIS 2 is much easier to use in getting an answer to this question for this or any other value of P. Whether a hypothesis is easier or harder to use depends on what it is to be used for. Relative to an interest in the value of C rather than the value of R, HYPOTHESIS 1 is easier to use and so simpler.

One advantage of the computational theory over Sober's semantic theory is that HYPOTHESIS 1 counts as simpler than HYPOTHESIS 2 in relation to an interest in the value of C for given values of P. There is no need for a further interest in what the derivative of the function is relating C and P.

The computational theory shares with the semantic theory the advantage that the measure of simplicity cannot normally be trivialized by introducing abbreviations. Adding abbreviations will not automatically make derivations easier. For suppose a complex hypothesis is abbreviated as 'H'. That makes the hypothesis very simple according to the syntactic theory of simplicity, but it does not normally make the hypothesis any simpler according to the computational theory. If, in order to use that hypothesis to derive data from it, a scientist must first expand it to its complex formulation, nothing is gained. In fact, derivations from the abbreviated hypothesis will be more complex than derivations from the original unabbreviated hypothesis, because of the need for the expansion step.

3.7 OBJECTIONS

Now we must consider certain objections to a computational theory of simplicity of this sort. First, why should this sort of ease of use matter to scientists who have calculators and computers? The function of HYPOTHESIS 2 can easily be programmed into a calculator in such a way that entering a given value of P will result in the immediate calculation of the corresponding value of C. So why is it relevant that, if a scientist had to do the calculation 'by hand', it might be more difficult to get answers using HYPOTHESIS 1 than using HYPOTHESIS 2? Since a scientist does not have to do the calculation by hand, and since no more effort is involved in the one case than the other if a calculator with the relevant function programmed in is used, what is the relevance of the difference in difficulty in doing the calculation by hand?

Second, suppose that we use a table of values or graph to represent a hypothesis like HYPOTHESIS 2. Then we can get the value of C when P = 6 from HYPOTHESIS 2 in a single step simply by looking it up. So it would seem that, as in the case of the initial syntactic theory of simplicity, the computational theory is heavily dependent on the system of representation used. It would seem that the computational theory cannot allow hypotheses to be represented with tables or graphs. But that is absurd. We cannot rule out using graphs and tables, since scientists need to use them all the time.

3.7.1 *Using Tables and Graphs as Hypotheses*

A possible reply to the second objection is that the use of a table or graph as the hypothesis itself will make the derivation very big even though there is only one step to the derivation. The derivation will be very big because the hypothesis from which the step is made is very big. Consider how this would work for HYPOTHESIS 2.

> H = (if P = 1, C = 2) & (if P = 2, C = −8) & (if P = 3, C = 6) & . . .
> & (if P = 6, C = −48) & . . . [very big conjunction]; so, in one step,
> if P = 6, C = −48.

So we can meet the objection if we consider the complexity or size of entire derivations, including the size of initial assumptions (and intermediate conclusions), not just the number of steps. A derivation including a table is huge and therefore complex in at least one respect. By this measure, replacing the table with the formula in our initial statement of HYPOTHE-SIS 2 is a simplification of the derivation in this case even though more steps are involved in the derivation.

Instead of including a table or graph as part of a derivation, a scientist includes the results of looking things up. Contrast

> x = sin 45 deg
> [Huge table of sines]
> sin 45 deg = 0.70710678
> x = 0.70710678

with

> x = sin 45 deg
> The sine table says: sin 45 deg = 0.70710678
> sin 45 deg = 0.70710678
> x = 0.70710678.

A hypothesis or intermediate assumption that literally included a table or complex graph would be impossible to grasp, impossible to understand, impossible to remember. So a computational account of simplicity might suppose that a scientist's interest in simplicity is an interest in having answers that are relatively easy to grasp to certain scientific questions.

Why? Perhaps because when a scientist accepts a hypothesis, he or she accepts it as an explanation of the certain data. So the scientist is really accepting a collection of explanations, not just a single proposition. What is at issue, then, is the complexity of that collection of explanations. Complexity can arise either because of the number of steps involved in the explanations or because of the complexity of one of the statements from which (or to which) a step is made. Either kind of complexity can make explanations harder to use, especially explanations involved in explaining new data.

The usefulness in question is usefulness in obtaining scientific under-standing, not just usefulness in predicting new data, although that is a good thing too!

3.7.2 *Using Calculators or Tables*

This suggests that, if a scientist uses a calculator or table to help with a cal-culation, then the resulting explanation or derivation should be taken to be something like this:

$P = 6$
$C = 2 \times P + (P-1) \times (P-3) \times (P-4) \times (P-8)$
$C = 2 \times 6 + (6-1) \times (6-3) \times (6-4) \times (P-8)$
According to the calculator, that $= -48$.
So, $C = -48$.

If the calculator is preprogrammed with the relevant function H for HYPOTHESIS 2, we might have this:

$P = 6$
$C = H(P)$
$C = H(6)$
According to the calculator, that $= -48$.
So, $C = -48$.

Clearly, this is not going to be sensitive to the complexity of hypothesis H. At the same time, it provides little understanding of why the result is what it is. To get more understanding, it is necessary to have a better idea of why the calculation comes out as it does. In the computational view, the rele-vant complexity of various hypotheses only emerges from what is needed for this further understanding.

3.8 THE COMPUTATIONAL THEORY VERSUS THE SEMANTIC THEORY

Recall that Sober's semantic theory of simplicity can treat a linear function as simpler than a quadratic function only by considering answers to such questions as 'What is the derivative of $F(x)$?' (We do not need to know the value of x to answer that question if $F(x)$ is a linear function, but we do have to know the value of x if $F(x)$ is a quadratic function.) A computational theory takes the linear function to be simpler without having to consider questions about derivatives, since it is less difficult to calculate the value of $F(x)$ if it is a linear function than if it is a quadratic function.

Perhaps there is a testable difference between a semantic and a computational account. The semantic account may predict that a linear function will seem simpler than a quadratic equation only to someone who knows about derivatives, whereas the computational account predicts that the linear function will seem simpler even to someone who does not know about derivatives. An informal survey among eighth-grade students (who had not had calculus) supports the prediction of the computational theory on this point. The eighth-graders all considered the linear function simpler, despite not knowing anything about derivatives.

3.9 SIMPLICITY AS AN INDICATOR OF VERISIMILITUDE

Newton-Smith (1981: 230–1) expresses a widespread view when he says:

Many scientists and philosophers of science would include simplicity as a good-making feature of a theory. This is, however, problematic for a number of reasons. . . . The case for simplicity is pragmatic: it simply is easier to calculate with simpler theories. But there is no reason to see greater relative simplicity of this sort as an indicator of greater verisimilitude.

Is simplicity 'an indicator of greater verisimilitude' according to the computational theory of simplicity? We must distinguish two senses of the word 'indicator'.

> (1) X is an indicator of Y if the presence of X is in fact correlated with the presence of Y
> (2) X is an indicator of Y if the presence of X gives a reason to believe Y.

According to the computational theory of simplicity, simplicity is an 'indicator' of verisimilitude in the second sense. Simplicity provides a reason to believe something, a practical reason.

But can a practical reason to believe something be an 'indicator' in any relevant sense? Some philosophers (e.g. Foley, 1983) distinguish such pragmatic reasons from what they take to be more properly 'epistemic' reasons to believe something.

Pragmatic reasons include such things as believing something because people will despise you for not believing it and believing in a friend's innocence because that is what loyalty requires.

Here it may seem natural to object, 'Is your friendship any reason to think it is true that your friend is innocent?' But there is no difference between believing that your friend is innocent and believing that it is true your friend is innocent. So a reason to believe your friend is innocent is automatically a reason to believe it is true that your friend is innocent. There is no difference between a reason to believe something and a reason to believe that something is true.

There has always been a controversy as to whether pragmatic reasons to believe something are somehow to be distinguished from more properly epistemic reasons to believe something. Philosophical pragmatism denies that there is any such distinction. Other views take it to be obvious that there is such a distinction.

The issue comes up, for example, between Rudolf Carnap and W. V. Quine. Carnap (1950) famously distinguishes 'internal' from 'external' questions. 'Are there numbers?' is an external question, which asks whether we should adopt a linguistic framework in which we refer to numbers. 'Is there a prime number between 11 and 17?' is an internal question which makes sense only after we have selected such a framework. Carnap argues that external questions call for practical pragmatic decisions: which system of representation will serve our purposes better? Internal questions are then answered in ways that are determined by the system of representation that has been chosen.

In this instance, pragmatism is defended by W. V. Quine (1960a):

I grant that one's hypothesis as to what there is, e.g., as to there being universals, is at bottom just as arbitrary or pragmatic a matter as one's adoption of a new brand of set theory or even a new system of bookkeeping. . . . But what impresses me more than it does Carnap is how well this whole attitude is suited also to the theoretical hypotheses of natural science itself, and how little basis there is for a distinction.

In Essay 4, I show how pragmatism can allow for a distinction between epistemic and nonepistemic reasons that captures our ordinary views but also allows pragmatic considerations to be relevant to epistemic reasons.

3.10 OBJECTIONS TO EXPLANATORY INFERENCE

Replies can be given to a couple of objections that may be raised against a principle of explanatory inference that would make use of simplicity as a principle of theory choice in certain cases.

First, it may be argued that no intuitively appealing rule of inference to the best explanation has ever been given an explicit statement of the sort that can be given for deductive rules.

In reply, it can be said that it is important to distinguish rules of implication from rules of inference. Plausible rules of implication have been given explicit statement in deductive logic, but they are not rules of inference. It might be said that no intuitively appealing rules of inference of any sort have ever been given an explicit statement of the sort that can be given for deductive rules. If this is an objection to inference to the best explanation, it is an objection to inference in general.

Second, Bas van Fraassen (1989) argues that allowing considerations of best explanation to modify probabilities leads to a kind of irrationality over time that permits Dutch book arguments against someone who does this.

This is a complex issue. But if considerations of best explanation affect probabilities in a Bayesian framework, the effect is in the initial a priori probability distribution. So, the Dutch book will not arise, as explained further in Essay 4.

3.11 PARASITICAL THEORIES

A theory is parasitical on a second theory if the first theory says that the phenomena are 'as if' the second theory were true. For example, in one version of 'creation science', God is supposed to have created the fossil record as if there had been an age of dinosaurs. Similarly, Descartes worried about the possibility that his experiences were created by an evil demon who made things appear as if there were a world of objects that in fact does not really exist. Closer to real science, there are linguistic theories that do not themselves lead to interesting new discoveries about language and that instead merely offer reanalyses of discoveries made within other approaches. (For example, I suspect that Harman (1963) exemplifies the parasitical approach in linguistics in defending phrase structure grammar. Compare Gazdar *et al.* (1985) who offer a similar theory that is somewhat less parasitical. These and other parasitical theories are discussed briefly in Harman, 1978.)

Parasitical theories normally count as less simple than the theories on which they are parasites, according to the computational theory of simplicity. A derivation of data within the parasitical theory will go like this:

It is as if theory T were true. Theory T provides the following derivation of data D. (This is spelled out.) So, D would be true if T were true. So D is true.

The parasitical derivation will contain as a part the derivation that is provided by the nonderivative theory. So, the parasitical derivation will necessarily be longer and more complex than the nonparasitical derivation. The nonparasitical theory will therefore provide simpler derivations of the data than will the parasitical theory.

A particular instance of this result is that instrumentalist versions of theories often provide less simple derivations of the data than their non-instrumentalist counterparts.

3.12 IDEALIZATIONS AND ARCANE DATA

If we suppose that simplicity is one of the guides to truth, can we account for the natural view that certain idealizations are useful in arriving at good predictions even though the truth is more complex (Cartwright, 1983)? A natural reply is that we accept the more complex theory as true in this case because there are data that the more complex theory can account for better than the idealization.

But this raises a problem for pragmatic and instrumental approaches which say that we accept theories because they help us answer questions in which we are interested. It would seem that the data that we are interested in are the data that can be handled by the idealization, not the more complex theory. So should a pragmatic or instrumentalist approach not tell us to accept the idealization rather than the more complex theory?

But then what about arcane data? If we are not really interested in such data, does the pragmatic account not imply that we should not use the data to decide among theories? My answer is that we *are* interested in the data. However, we are interested in the data because they help us decide between theories in which we are interested!

This is where (one form of) instrumentalism goes wrong. Our interest in theory is not completely derivative from our interest in the predictions of the theory. We acquire an interest in whether the theory itself is true. That is how we can be interested in certain arcane data.

An adequate pragmatism has to avoid foundationalism in two different respects. There are no absolutely privileged evidential statements and no absolutely privileged interests. At any point, one has certain beliefs and intentions, and one has certain interests and desires. These all get modified as time goes on. One can acquire new intrinsic desires, including desires to know whether certain theories are true.

3.13 CONCLUSION

More needs to be said about all of these issues, but this essay has become too long. What I have tried to do is to formulate an issue about simplicity, suggest a pragmatic account of simplicity, discuss possible objections, and indicate how the resulting theory might have something to say about parasitic theories and idealizations.

4

Pragmatism and Reasons
for Belief

4.1 REALISM, ANTIREALISM, PRAGMATISM

Realism and antirealism with respect to a given question are competing claims about what makes an answer to the question correct. Realism says that what makes an answer correct is that it represents things as they really are. Antirealism denies this.

Consider the question whether numbers exist. According to realism, the answer to this question depends on whether in reality numbers exist. If they do, the correct answer is yes; otherwise the correct answer is no.

One form of antirealism about this question denies that it makes sense to suppose that numbers do or do not exist in reality and interprets the question as a practical question about whether things work out better if one allows quantification over numbers in a theory one is developing.

Pragmatism supposes that all or almost all questions are at least in part practical questions. Since one answers many of these questions by adopting certain beliefs, pragmatism tends to emphasize practical reasons for belief. Pragmatism might be considered a form of antirealism, but it is probably better seen as a rejection of the distinction between realism and antirealism on the grounds that there is no sharp distinction between theoretical and practical questions. (Here I am indebted to Richard Rorty.)

From an intuitive realist point of view, there is a clear distinction between reasons to believe something that are relevant to the truth of what is to be believed and other reasons that indicate something to be gained through belief without making the belief any more likely to be true. One intuitively distinguishes *purely epistemic reasons* to believe something from other more pragmatic *nonepistemic reasons*.

My concern in this essay is with what pragmatism can say about this intuitive distinction.

4.2 EPISTEMIC AND NONEPISTEMIC REASONS
FOR BELIEF

Consider possible reasons for believing that cigarette smoking does not cause cancer. One reason might involve a statistical study of identical twins who differ in their smoking habits. If the life expectancy of the smokers were on average the same as the life expectancy of the nonsmokers, that would provide an epistemic reason to believe that cigarette smoking does not cause cancer. Another reason might be a practical one. An advertiser who wants to obtain the RST Tobacco Company advertising account, knowing that RST will only use advertisers who believe that cigarettes do not cause cancer, has a practical reason to believe that cigarettes do not cause cancer. Having that belief is a necessary condition of obtaining the RST advertising account. Clearly this is not an epistemic reason to believe that cigarettes do not cause cancer. It is a purely practical reason. The fact that having such a belief is needed to obtain the account is not evidence for the belief and does not make the belief more likely to be true.

Similarly, statistical evidence about crime rates in states with and without capital punishment might provide an epistemic reason for a belief about this subject. The consideration that one's friends will think badly of one unless one agrees with their position might very well constitute only a practical reason for a certain belief. If a friend has been charged with theft from a local store, the testimony of the store detective provides an epistemic reason to believe one's friend is guilty, whereas loyalty toward one's friend provides a nonepistemic moral or pragmatic reason to believe one's friend is innocent.

Suppose one is trying to persuade people to join the army to fight against the evil Rudu. One needs to convince people that the war will be short, something one does not oneself believe. One will be more persuasive if one can get oneself to believe that the war will be a short one. This gives one a reason to believe that the war will be short, but it is a purely pragmatic, nonepistemic reason. The fact that one will be more persuasive if one believes the war will be short does not make it more likely that the war will be short. In contrast, learning that Rudu is low on supplies would provide an epistemic reason for one to believe that the war will be short, since it would make it more likely that the war will be short.

4.3 PRACTICAL REASONS FOR A BELIEF

It might be objected that one can have only practical reasons for an action and that believing something is not an action. In this view, one can have practical reasons to do something that may lead one to have a belief, but one's practical reasons cannot be one's reasons for believing it. If one is asked one's reason for believing that cigarettes do not cause cancer, it makes sense to appeal to a statistical study of smokers and nonsmokers. It does not make sense to appeal to the fact that such a belief is needed if one is to obtain an advertising account. That might be one's reason for pretending to have the relevant belief or for undertaking activities that will bring about that belief, but it cannot be the reason for one's belief. In this view, belief is passive and practical reasons are always reasons for something active (Pojman, 1985).

Opposed to this is the observation that there are various situations in which one can decide to believe something. A friend gives her version of what happened; one decides to believe her; one decides to believe that she is telling the truth (Meiland, 1980).

It is true that one can find oneself almost passively accepting certain beliefs. Sometimes a speaker is so persuasive that one cannot help believing him. But one can find oneself doing all sorts of things—stroking one's beard, brushing one's teeth when one intended merely to get a drink of water, and so forth. Finding oneself doing something does not distinguish coming to believe something from other actions. And coming to believe something is not always a matter of finding oneself believing something.

What is it to believe something? At least two things are involved, both of which are things one can decide to do. Beliefs serve as the basis for other acts one may undertake, and beliefs end one's inquiry into an issue. One can certainly decide to accept a given proposition as a basis for action; that is, one can decide to act as if one believed it. Furthermore, one can decide to end one's inquiry into an issue and hold to a certain conclusion.

Jonathan Bennett (1990) observes in effect that there is a difference between increasing one's strength of belief (subjective probability) and doing other things that may be involved in belief, such as ending inquiry. These are separable matters, since, for example, whether or not to end inquiry is not always completely determined by the subjective probabilities. Like Bennett, I am here concerned with reasons for increasing the strength of one's belief. So, it is important to note that one can decide to increase one's strength of belief, inasmuch as one can decide that in further decisions one will treat a certain proposition as being highly probable.

To do this is like deciding to adopt a particular working hypothesis to try out over the long haul, in depth. Such a decision is hard to distinguish from deciding to believe something.

4.4 INTERNAL VERSUS EXTERNAL QUESTIONS

Something like the distinction between epistemic and nonepistemic practical reasons plays an important role in Rudolf Carnap's distinction between internal and external questions. Carnap (1950) argues that certain philosophical puzzles arise through not distinguishing issues to which epistemic reasons apply from issues to which practical reasons apply. A question like 'Do numbers exist?' is confused with a question like 'Do prime numbers greater than 1,000 exist?' The first sort of question seems very 'philosophical', pitting Platonists against conceptualists. The second sort of question seems to raise no serious philosophical issues, requiring only the briefest of calculations to answer it. Yet if there are prime numbers greater than 1,000, then there are numbers, so a positive answer to the non-philosophical second question seems to imply a positive answer to the philosophical first question.

To take another example, philosophers agonize over whether it is possible to know that there are any external objects, where, for example, a human hand would be an instance of an external object. Yet it seems easy enough to determine whether a given individual has hands. G. E. Moore took this to imply that of course one knows that there are external objects. Holding up his hands, he would say, 'Here's one and here's another.' But many philosophers feel that Moore's approach is not relevant to answering the philosophical question.

Carnap's response is to distinguish 'internal questions' from 'external questions'. An external question concerns how philosophers are to talk about or otherwise represent a given subject matter. It is a question concerning choice of language. Carnap takes this to be a practical question. What system of representation enables one best to fulfil one's purposes? What allows the most efficient representation of what one wants to say? What most facilitates the sorts of calculations one needs to perform?

Choice of language in this sense determines the methods to be used to settle issues within a given framework. In choosing a language of arithmetic in which one refers to numbers, one chooses a system of calculation that allows one to answer such questions as whether there are prime numbers greater than 1,000. When one chooses a language in which one refers to external objects like tables, chairs, and hands, one chooses a system that enables one to find evidence for and against such propositions as that a certain person has two hands.

The internal question presupposes an answer to the external question. It presupposes that one has already chosen a system of representation with rules for answering such internal questions. One has to answer the external question before one can intelligibly ask the internal question. Moore's way of answering external questions simply begs the point at issue.

In Carnap's view, a system of representation determines what is to count as evidence, as an epistemic reason, but one cannot in the same way appeal to evidence to decide on a system of representation. Such a decision can be based only on practical or pragmatic reasons.

Carnap is therefore an antirealist about external, philosophical questions and a kind of realist about internal questions. He is an external antirealist and an internal realist.

4.5 PRAGMATISM

Pragmatists deny that there is the sort of distinction between internal and external questions that Carnap describes and therefore deny the distinction between internal and external realism and antirealism.

W. V. Quine famously responded to Carnap in the following way:

I grant that one's hypothesis as to what there is, e.g., as to there being universals, is at bottom just as arbitrary or pragmatic a matter as one's adoption of a new brand of set theory or even a new system of bookkeeping. . . . But what impresses me more than it does Carnap is how well this whole attitude is suited also to the theoretical hypotheses of natural science itself, and how little basis there is for a distinction. (Quine, 1960*a*)

In Quine's view there is no principled distinction between choice of system of representation and choice of theory, and there is no principled distinction between changing the system of representation and changing the views expressed in that system. There is no principled difference between keeping the same system of representation and changing one's view as expressed in that system, and changing the system of representation by changing the meanings of representations. Choice of principles of theory is often dictated by how useful these principles will be in getting interesting results, simplifying calculation, and so forth. If the relevance of such considerations makes the choice a choice of system of representation rather than a choice of theory to be expressed in that system, then one is always choosing and changing the system of representation, just as one is always choosing and changing the view expressed in that system (see Essays 5–6, below).

Quine is a pragmatist. In general, pragmatists deny that there is any sharp distinction between purely epistemic reasons to believe something and more practical reasons. Reasons to believe one thing rather than another are strongly connected with goals and interests. For one thing, goals and interests determine those questions there is a reason to be interested in answering. In addition, practical considerations lie behind a certain conservatism or momentum in reasoning. Initial beliefs provide the starting point for reasoning and one tries to minimize the change in one's beliefs subject to other demands. It would be impractical to follow Descartes and abandon every belief for which one cannot provide an indubitable justification from premises one cannot doubt (see Essay 1, above).

Furthermore, and this is important, when faced with inferring some explanation of the evidence, one finds oneself with infinitely many possible explanations, all of which account for the evidence. Without thinking much about it, one often immediately chooses the simplest of these hypotheses and ignores the others, where the simplest hypothesis is generally the hypothesis that would be easiest to use in order to answer questions of the sort in which one is interested. The reasons for selecting the simplest hypothesis are entirely pragmatic (Essay 3, above).

4.6 PRAGMATISM AND PURELY EVIDENTIAL REASONS

This leaves a problem. On the one hand, there is a clear intuitive basis for distinguishing purely epistemic reasons for believing something from other merely pragmatic reasons, such as obtaining the RST advertising account. There seems to be an intuitively clear distinction between reasons for belief that make the belief more likely to be true and reasons for belief that merely promise some practical benefit of belief without making the belief more likely to be true. On the other hand, pragmatism is surely correct in emphasizing the practical side to ordinary standards of evidence, the goal-directed character of reasoning, conservatism, the role of simplicity, and so forth. How can the intuitively realist distinction between epistemic and nonepistemic reasons be accommodated while allowing for the insights of pragmatism?

Clearly, there is an accommodation only if the distinction between epistemic and nonepistemic reasons is not just a distinction between epistemic and practical considerations. Some practical considerations must be allowed to fall on the purely epistemic side of the distinction. But then what could distinguish epistemic from nonepistemic reasons?

4.7 ARE EPISTEMIC REASONS CONNECTED WITH TRUTH?

Here's a suggestion:

> A reason is an epistemic reason for believing a particular proposition P if and only if one is justified in believing that there is an explanatory connection between the reason and the truth of P. (The phrase 'explanatory connection' is to be understood in a wide sense that includes causal and logical connections: Goldman, 1967; Harman, 1973).

In this view, one can suppose that a statistical study is evidence that cigarette smoking does not cause cancer because one can conclude that smoking's not causing cancer is part of an explanation of the results of the study. One cannot reasonably take the opportunity to obtain the RST advertising account to be evidence that cigarette smoking does not cause cancer because (I am supposing) one cannot reasonably conclude that smoking's not causing cancer is any part of the explanation of the company's policy with respect to advertisers.

How might this apply to simplicity as an epistemic factor? In any particular instance, many different hypotheses might explain the evidence. Now, it may seem that one can take simplicity to be a relevant epistemic consideration without having to suppose that the simplicity of a hypothesis is what explains why that hypothesis rather than some other hypothesis is what accounts for the data. For example, one can take simplicity to be a relevant epistemic consideration without supposing that statistics show that simpler hypotheses are more likely to be what account for the data than other less simple hypotheses that are equally compatible with the same data.

But people do think that the simplicity of a hypothesis has *something* to do with an explanation of the data, since people do suppose that, other things being equal, simpler hypotheses provide better explanations than complicated hypotheses do (as discussed in the previous essay). So the suggested criterion *could* allow people to count the simplicity of a hypothesis to be an epistemic reason for accepting the hypothesis, since anyone can suppose that the simplicity of the hypothesis is part of what makes the truth of the hypothesis a good explanation of the evidence. The suggested criterion would not allow one to count the opportunity to obtain the RST account as an epistemic reason for believing that cigarette smoking does not cause cancer, because one cannot see this opportunity as part of an explanatory connection between the truth of that belief and one's evidence.

So the suggested criterion would give an intuitively acceptable account of many cases. But, alas, it would also give incorrect results for certain cases. Suppose, for example, that the company requires advertisers to believe in the relevant explanatory connection. That is, suppose that the company requires advertisers to believe that cigarettes' not causing cancer is part of the explanation of the company's policy of hiring only advertisers who believe cigarette smoking does not cause cancer. Then the suggested criterion seems to imply that the offer provides an epistemic reason to believe that cigarettes do not cause cancer, which is the wrong result. In this case, there are practical reasons to conclude that, because cigarette smoking does not cause cancer, the company has the policy, which gives one the practical reason. One is justified in believing that the required connection between truth and reasons holds, but the reasons are still merely practical, not epistemic. So this criterion seems to fail. (However, I return to something like this idea at the end of this essay.)

4.8 ARE THERE PRACTICAL SOURCES OF EPISTEMIC REASONS?

It is interesting that one common realist approach to explaining the distinction between epistemic and nonepistemic practical reasons for belief identifies an epistemic reason with a certain sort of practical reason! In this view, an epistemic reason to believe something is a practical reason to believe it deriving solely from an interest in believing what is true and not believing what is false (e.g. Foley, 1987).

Of course, people do not actually have this general desire. Curiosity is more specialized. One wants to know whether P, who did D, what things are F, and so forth. With respect to some limited range of options one wants to arrive at an answer P if and only if it is true that P. Typically, one wants to know whether P because finding out whether P will help one achieve some further goal, although one's goal may be simply to find out more about a certain subject.

So we might put the suggestion as follows. An epistemic reason to believe P is any practical reason to believe P that derives solely from the desire to know whether P is true, ignoring all other desires.

Epistemic reasons are not just reasons that derive from a desire to believe what is true and avoid believing what is false. Perhaps one will be given a copy of the RST encyclopaedia only if one believes that cigarettes do not cause cancer. There are a lot of truths in that encyclopaedia, so believing that cigarettes do not cause cancer would definitely promote one's desire to believe what is true and avoid believing what is false. But that will not count by the present criterion as an epistemic reason to believe that cigarettes do not cause cancer, because the reason in question here does not derive solely from a desire to know whether cigarettes cause cancer.

What if one wants to read the encyclopaedia to find out whether cigarettes cause cancer? One may have reason to believe that the correct answer is in the encyclopaedia. However, one can obtain the encyclopaedia only if one already believes that cigarettes do not cause cancer! Here one's desire to have a true belief about whether cigarettes cause cancer provides one with a nonepistemic practical reason to believe that cigarettes do not cause cancer. So the criterion needs to be understood in a way that does not count this sort of reason as an epistemic reason (Conee, 1992).

One idea is to require that the desire motivating the belief be a desire to have a true belief on this subject *now* (Foley, 1987: 7–8). But what if the encyclopaedia is right here, opened to the right page, and all that is needed is to glance down and read what it says, something one will be permitted to do only if one first has the belief that cigarettes do not cause cancer. Does one second make the difference between now and the future? Then how does one allow for the time it takes to form a belief? Might there be a case in which forming a certain belief would be a necessary condition for simultaneously learning the truth?

Perhaps the criterion should be this: a reason is an epistemic reason to believe P if and only if it depends only on the desire that one's belief in this instance be true (or the desire that one's belief in this instance should constitute knowledge). The fact that the encyclopaedia can be consulted only by someone with the appropriate belief does not give one an epistemic reason to form that belief. That is so even if this fact gives one a reason that derives from one's desire to know the truth about this subject, because one's reason for forming that belief does not derive from the desire that it, that very belief, be true (or be knowledge).

The criterion is still not obviously adequate. It may turn out to be impossible to separate the factors leading to belief into those that do and those that do not depend only on the relevant desire for truth (or knowledge) in this case. It may turn out that everything is tainted by other desires or interests, so that no reasons count as epistemic by this criterion. Or there may turn out to be very few instances of epistemic reasons by this criterion. This may lead to a conflict with the original intuitions about the distinction. And other sorts of conflict are possible.

For example, one natural way to develop this proposal assigns +1 units of epistemic value to believing any proposition P if P is true, −1 units of epistemic value to believing P if P is not true, and 0 units to failing to believe P whether P is true or false. Then the expected epistemic value of believing P = prob(P) − prob(not-P). This is greater than zero if, and only if, P is more probable than not. So, this approach entails that one should believe all and only those propositions that are more likely to be true than false (Hempel, 1965*b*).

However, this consequence is bizarre. We might try a more complicated measure of epistemic value (Levi, 1967), but it is unclear how to do this in a way that retains the intuitive appeal of the principles that lead to the bizarre consequence.

Instead, I suggest that we simply stay with the idea we started with. An epistemic reason for believing something is a consideration that makes that belief more likely to be true. A nonepistemic reason for believing something is a consideration that provides a reason for belief without making the belief more likely to be true. But what is meant by 'likely to be true'?

4.9 WHEN IS A CONCLUSION 'LIKELY TO BE TRUE'?

It is often supposed that there are at least two kinds of likelihood or probability, probability as objective chance, which may or may not be known, and probability as rational degree of belief. These can diverge, and it is degree of rational belief that is relevant here. Suppose one has a six-sided die of unknown constitution. It may be true in fact that the die is weighted to favour side six in the sense that if the die is rolled over and over again, six tends to come up about seventy-five per cent of the time. Before one first rolls the die, one may know nothing about this. One's evidence about the die may not indicate one side's being favoured rather than another. So one's rational degree of belief in the proposition that the die will come up six when one rolls it for the first time may equal 1/6, even though the objective chance of the die's coming up six when one rolls it for the first time may equal 3/4.

Epistemic reasons have to do with rational degree of belief, not directly with objective chance. One's evidence consists in what one learns by studying the die. By hypothesis, the evidence does not favour one side of the die over another. In the relevant sense, the evidence does not make six more likely than any of the other five outcomes. The evidence does not increase the epistemic likelihood of getting a six even though the objective chance is higher than with some other die.

So, if an epistemic reason is a consideration that makes a certain proposition more likely to be true, it is a consideration that raises the rational degree of belief one should attach to that proposition, not just a consideration that increases the objective chance of the proposition's being true. In other words, an epistemic reason is a consideration whose acceptance should rationally increase one's degree of belief in a proposition.

Alas, this way of understanding an epistemic reason does not distinguish epistemic reasons from nonepistemic reasons. Any reason at all that makes it rational to increase one's degree of belief in a proposition is a reason that raises the degree of belief one ought rationally to place in that proposition. Any reason, including the most blatant practical reason, will do. The fact that RST will accept only advertisers who believe that cigarettes do not cause cancer may increase the degree to which it is rational for one to believe that cigarettes do not cause lung cancer. It is rational for one to increase one's degree of belief in that proposition inasmuch as doing so may enable one to acquire the RST advertising account.

But something must have gone wrong here. This consideration (that RST will give its advertising only to someone who believes cigarettes do not cause lung cancer) is surely not a consideration that makes it more likely that cigarettes do not cause lung cancer. Increase in rational belief is not always increase in likelihood. How then is the relevant sort of likelihood to be understood? It is certainly not objective chance.

In order to begin to answer this question, I turn to basic issues of subjective probability theory.

4.10 COHERENCE AND INCOHERENCE

Contemporary accounts of subjective probability do not provide necessary and sufficient conditions for determining the degree of rational belief one should place in a proposition. These accounts are instead concerned with the consistency or coherence of one's degrees of belief. For example, such accounts require that logically equivalent propositions be assigned the same degree of belief even though it is obvious that logically equivalent propositions often admit of different rational degrees of belief. It is inconsistent to assign different degrees of belief to logically equivalent propositions even though one may have every reason to do so.

As I have already mentioned, contemporary accounts relate subjective probability or degree of belief to certain practical considerations. Inconsistency in degrees of belief is represented by a certain sort of practical incoherence, or at least an incoherence in one's views about what it would be good for one to do or what transactions are fair.

The relevant sort of incoherence holds, for example, if a person's preferences are intransitive. In this case, probabilities do not enter the picture; only preferences are relevant. Suppose Jack has the following preferences with respect to a painting by Alice Abbott, a novel by Barbara Baker, and a recording by Connie Cooper:

(1) He would rather have Abbott's painting than Cooper's recording.
(2) He would rather have Baker's novel than Abbott's painting.
(3) He would rather have Cooper's recording than Baker's novel.

Suppose Jack has the painting by Abbott and suppose he also attaches value to money. He prefers having the Baker novel to having the Abbott painting. So he should be willing to pay some amount of money, say a dollar, for the opportunity of trading the Abbott painting for the Baker novel. But he also prefers having the Cooper recording to having the Baker novel, so he should be willing to pay some amount of money, say another dollar, for the opportunity to trade the Baker novel for the Cooper recording, if he should be in possession of the Baker novel. Finally, he also prefers having the Abbott painting to having the Cooper recording. So he should be willing to pay some amount of money, perhaps yet another dollar, for the opportunity to trade the Cooper recording for the Abbott painting, if he should ever be in possession of the Cooper recording.

But this means he should now be willing to pay first one dollar, then a second, and then a third, simply to be able to return to his original situation in possession of the Abbott painting. This willingness to be a 'money pump' illustrates the incoherence involved in having intransitive preferences of this sort (Davidson *et al.*, 1955).

But it is important to understand that the relevant incoherence does not consist in Jack's actually serving as a money pump in this case. Nor does there have to be any real threat that he will lose money in this way. His attitudes are incoherent in that they commit him to thinking that each of several transactions would be good for him to do and also thinking that it would not be good for him to undertake all of them (Skyrms, 1980, 1987).

4.11 DUTCH BOOKS

Similar considerations apply to subjective probability or degree of belief if, as is normally supposed, one's degree of belief in a proposition commits one to a view about what a fair bet would be concerning the truth of that proposition. If one's degree of belief in the proposition A is 0.6, then one is committed to taking it to be fair to offer odds of 0.6 to 0.4 (or 3 to 2) that A is true. Supposing that one values money (and that diminishing marginal utility of money is not a factor), one is committed to thinking the following bet is fair: if A is true, one gets four dollars; if A is not true, one loses six dollars. One's 'expectation' with respect to this bet is determined by multiplying the gain or loss of each possible outcome by the probability of that outcome. So one's expectation is $0.06 \times \$4 - 0.04 \times \$6 = \$0$. One is committed to supposing that the expectation is zero, which is to say one is committed to supposing that this is a fair bet.

A *book* is a collection of bets of this sort. A *Dutch Book* from P's point of view is a collection of bets that P is committed to thinking would guarantee a loss for him or herself. To take a trivial example, consider the following two bets:

(1) If A is true, one receives four dollars; if A is not true, one loses six dollars.
(2) If not-A is true, one receives four dollars; if not-A is not true, one loses six dollars.

If one takes both bets, one is guaranteed to lose two dollars. Either one wins four dollars from the first bet and loses six dollars from the second or one loses six dollars from the first bet and wins four dollars from the second. Since (by hypothesis) one values money, one is committed to thinking that this is not a fair set of bets. More generally, since a Dutch Book is a set of bets that one is committed to thinking guarantees that one ends up in a worse situation than one is now in, one is committed to thinking that no Dutch Book is a fair set of bets.

Now, suppose that one's subjective probabilities or degrees of belief commit one to thinking that each bet in a book of bets would be a fair bet, and suppose that this book of bets is a Dutch Book from one's point of view. Then one's probabilities are incoherent; they commit one to thinking both that each individual bet in the book is fair and that the book of bets as a whole is not fair.

If one's probabilities are not incoherent in this way, that is, if they are coherent, then one's probabilities must satisfy the usual axioms of probability theory (van Fraassen, 1989: 159–60). In the example just considered, the Dutch Book is made possible because the probabilities assigned to A and not-A violate the axiom that says that the probability of A and the probability of not-A should sum to exactly 1.0. The argument for the basic principles of probability is that if one's probabilities do not satisfy these axioms, they are incoherent.

4.12 CONDITIONALIZATION AND TEMPORAL DUTCH BOOKS

A similar argument can be given for the rule of Conditionalization (Teller, 1973, reporting an observation by David Lewis). This is a rule about updating probabilities over time. This rule says that if one's evidence between now and time t can be expressed in the proposition E, where priorprob(E) > 0 then one's subjective probabilities at time t should be in accord with the following principle:

$$\text{Conditionalization: newprob}(p) = \frac{\text{priorprob}(p \,\&\, e)}{\text{priorprob}(p)}.$$

The quotient on the right-hand side of this equation is called one's prior conditional probability of P given evidence E, and might be represented as condprob(P, E).

The argument for Conditionalization involves consideration of sets or books of bets that may be offered at various times. A *temporal book* of bets might include some bets to be made now and other bets to be made in the future if certain events should occur. A *Temporal Dutch Book* from one's point of view is a temporal book of bets with the property that one is committed to thinking that if one accepts all the bets if and when they are offered, one is guaranteed to lose.

One's current commitments subject one to a Temporal Dutch Book if one is committed to supposing that each bet in the Temporal Dutch Book is or would be fair. If one's current commitments subject one to a Temporal

Dutch Book, those commitments are incoherent, since they commit one to thinking that each of the bets is fair and also commit one to thinking that the book as a whole is not fair.

For example, suppose one now takes the probability of a coin's coming up heads on the next toss to be 0.5 and one takes the probability of its coming up heads on both of the next two tosses to be 0.25. Suppose one also accepts a principle for changing one's probabilities that has the following consequence: if the coin comes up heads on the first toss, then change one's probability of its coming up heads on the second toss to 0.75 (perhaps because one takes the first head to be evidence that this is a two headed coin). Given these commitments, one is subject to thinking that all the bets in the following Temporal Dutch Book will be fair bets at the time they are made:

(A) A bet made now: if the coin comes up heads on the first toss, one receives $45; otherwise one loses $45.
(B) A bet made now: if the coin comes up heads on both the first toss and second toss, one loses $90; otherwise one wins $30.
(C) A bet made after the first toss yields a heads (should that happen): if on the second toss, the coin comes up tails, one loses $90; otherwise one wins $30.

If one accepts this book of bets, one is guaranteed to lose $15, as should be clear from the following table:

Outcome	(A)	(B)	(C)	Total
Heads–Heads	+$45	−$90	+$30	−$15
Heads–Tails	+$45	+$30	−$90	−$15
Tails–Heads	−$45	+$30		−$15
Tails–Tails	−$45	+$30		−$15

These commitments are incoherent. One is committed to thinking that it would be rational for one to be prepared to accept all these bets (since one is committed to thinking that they are or will be fair when they are made). One is also committed to thinking that it would be irrational to be prepared to accept all these bets because one would be guaranteed to lose at least $10 if one did so. (One is now committed to thinking that bet (C) will be fair when it is made because one is now committed to assigning a probability of 0.75 to getting a second heads, if the first toss comes up heads. So one is committed to thinking that odds of 3 to 1 would be fair at that point.)

If one is committed to updating one's subjective probabilities in a way that diverges from Conditionalization, then one is subject to a Temporal Dutch Book and one's commitments are incoherent in this way. In the example just given, the conditional probability of coming up heads on the second toss given that it comes up heads on the first toss equals the probability of getting heads on both tosses (0.25) divided by the probability of getting heads on the first toss (0.50), which equals 0.5. This is not the same as the probability that one is committed to assigning to getting heads on the second toss if heads comes up on the first toss, namely 0.75. This discrepancy makes one subject to the Temporal Dutch Book.

This is not to agree with Christensen (1991) that it is always incoherent to *expect* to have degrees of belief that, together with one's present degrees of belief, would (if one acted on them) subject one to a Temporal Dutch Book. Christensen argues against the principle of Reflection in van Fraassen (1984) and to cast doubt on Temporal Dutch Book arguments in general. Christensen bases his objection to Reflection on van Fraassen's rough statement: 'To satisfy the principle, the agent's present subjective probability for proposition A, on the supposition that his subjective probability for this proposition will equal r at some later time, must equal this same number r' (van Fraassen, 1984: 244). A better statement of Reflection begins with the supposition that the agent is committed to a certain principle P for changing the probability distribution to use for determining what bets would be fair, in the light of new evidence E. The agent further supposes that at a later time t the subjective probability for A determined by P given the evidence up to that time will equal r. Reflection says that the agent's present subjective probability for A, conditional on this supposition, must also equal r. Christensen's observation is no objection to the Temporal Dutch Book argument for Reflection, if the principle is understood in this way.

I make a similar point about the correct formulation of Conditionalization in section 4.18, below.

4.13 THE ALLEGED INCOHERENCE OF INFERENCE TO THE BEST EXPLANATION

Van Fraassen (1989: 160–76) argues that any substantive commitment to using inference to the best explanation is incoherent. Given evidence E, inference to the best explanation considers possible explanations of E and either directly infers, or at least assigns higher probability to, the best of these explanations, where the criteria for best explanation might include the extent to which an explanation accommodates the data, conservatism, simplicity, and other factors. If one is committed to allowing such explanatory considerations to influence the way one updates one's probabilities beyond what is entailed by Conditionalization, then one is subject to a Temporal Dutch Book and one's overall commitments are incoherent. Van Fraassen concludes that it is necessary to reject any use of inference to the best explanation that goes beyond Conditionalization. Inference to the best explanation is therefore either superfluous or incoherent, in his view.

As he observes, the same argument applies to any ampliative rule, any rule that goes beyond Conditionalization. For example, Goodman's (1965) theory of entrenchment assigns greater predictability to hypotheses using predicates that have appeared in previous projections than to hypotheses that do not use such predicates. If one is committed to allowing considerations of predictability to influence the way one updates probabilities, given new evidence, in a way that goes beyond what Conditionalization allows, then one is subject to a Temporal Dutch Book and one's commitments are incoherent.

4.14 WHERE PRIOR PROBABILITIES COME FROM

Now, Goodman (1965) can accept van Fraassen's (1989) argument yet respond that there is still a role for entrenchment in determining prior probabilities. Considerations of entrenchment might affect a person's conditional probabilities, condprob(h,e). That is to say, considerations of entrenchment might affect the ratio between priorprob(h & e) and priorprob(e), for hypotheses with entrenched predicates. The effect on this ratio might itself be taken to be the result of Conditionalization on evidence about entrenchment of predicates, call that evidence f. Then

$$\text{condprob}(h,e \,\&\, f) > \text{condprob}(h,e).$$

Here, for example, h might be 'All emeralds are green', e might be evidence indicating that all emeralds examined for colour have been found to be green (i.e. grue), and f might be evidence that 'green' rather than 'grue' has been used in past projections. (See Essay 3 for more discussion of this example.)

This can seem strange, as if one were supposing that one would have made it more likely that all emeralds are grue if one had made predictions using 'grue' rather than 'green'. But the issue is degree of rational belief, not objective chance. There is no suggestion that the way one uses language to make predictions will have an effect on the objective frequencies with which nonlinguistic properties are correlated with each other.

It might be suggested that, as one finds out what projections one is inclined to make, one finds out which hypotheses are more likely to be true, given certain evidence. But that is not quite right. Even at the beginning, one is inclined to project 'green' rather than 'grue'. It is true even at the beginning that the probability that all emeralds are green, given that some have been observed to be green, is greater than the probability that all emeralds are grue, given that some have been observed to be grue.

What one learns from patterns of past projection is what one's inductive principles are. Not what principles one explicitly accepts, but what principles one implicitly follows. Initially, one just made inferences, without having a theory about how one did it. As one sees what predicates one projects, one acquires information about one's prior probabilities, one's inductive principles.

4.15 EXPLANATION AND PRIOR PROBABILITIES

In the same way, explanatory considerations, like simplicity, play a role in determining prior probabilities. Suppose one has two hypotheses, h and h', both of which accommodate the evidence e, but one takes h to be the better explanation, because it is simpler. Suppose that this difference inclines one to infer h rather than h' or any of the infinitely many other competing hypotheses that could account for e. This does not mean that such explanatory considerations play a role in addition to Conditionalization. Rather, the fact that one is inclined to infer h rather than h' shows that

$$\text{condprob}(h,e) \gg 0.5 \gg \text{condprob}(h',e).$$

This implies that

$$\text{prob}(h \ \& \ e) \gg \text{prob}(h' \ \& \ e)$$

in one's prior probability distribution.

Here it may be useful to observe that the requirements of probabilistic coherence are *consistency* requirements, not directly requirements about inference. To take another example, if one believes both P and Q, and sees that these propositions together imply R, that is not necessarily a reason to believe R. One may, for example, also believe not-R. So maybe one has a reason to stop believing P or stop believing Q.

Nothing in logic or probability theory says that one has to stick with previous commitments (van Fraassen, 1984; see also Essay 1, above). When one realizes what those commitments entail, one is free to revise them, as far as anything that logic says goes. At best one sees that something has to be done, but what is done may be to change some of one's initial assumptions.

It may also be useful to notice an ambiguity in the notion of 'prior probability'. The relevant meaning is not: *a probability arrived at ahead of time*. Rather, what is meant is something mathematical: a probability distribution *priorprob* that is related to one's current probability distribution *prob* via the formula of Conditionalization:

$$\text{prob}(p) = \frac{\text{priorprob}(p \ \& \ e)}{\text{priorprob}(p)} \ .$$

The distribution *priorprob* can be a prior probability in the relevant sense without being a probability distribution one had ahead of time.

4.16 BELIEF AND DEGREE OF BELIEF

To think of matters in terms of subjective probabilities is not to suppose that people have explicit degrees of belief that they use in deciding what to do and how to change their views in the light of new evidence. Nor is it even to suppose that degrees of belief are precisely determined. Degrees of belief are vaguely determined by a person's overall psychological or neurophysiological state, or perhaps by one or another part of that overall state. Something like a behaviouristic account of degrees of belief may be right. Degrees of belief may be determined by a person's dispositions to make choices.

Perhaps people have all-or-nothing beliefs and goals that are responsible for these behavioural dispositions. Degrees of belief can be determined by these dispositions without being functional aspects of a person's psychology (Harman, 1986*a*: ch. 3).

4.17 NONEPISTEMIC REASONS AND TEMPORAL DUTCH BOOKS

One believes H, that smoking cigarettes greatly increases a person's chances of getting cancer and dying early. One assigns a high probability to this conclusion. One thinks this probability would be unaffected by O, receiving an offer from a tobacco company of a large amount of money if one would come to believe that smoking does not increase a person's risk of getting cancer. Let us suppose that prob(H) = 0.9 and condprob(H,O) = 0.9, according to one's current probability distribution. Suppose one also thinks that if the tobacco company were to make one such an offer, one would have a strong reason to form the belief that smoking is not bad for people. In other words, one thinks that if O, the value of one's prob(H) should become very low.

But then one seems to be subject to a Temporal Dutch Book (note: 'seems to be'). One seems to be committed to thinking that each bet in a Temporal Dutch Book should be accepted when offered even though one is also committed to thinking one is guaranteed to lose.

The point is tricky in the present case, because it is hard to bet on something like H. What counts as winning or losing the bet? So let us change the example slightly. Suppose a governmental study is being made and the question concerns how that study will come out. Suppose H is the proposition that the study will conclude that cigarettes cause cancer and that not-H is the proposition that the study will not reach that conclusion. This study will come out a year from now and O is that the cigarette company offers one $100,000 to believe not-H.

Part of the relevant Temporal Dutch Book would be a bet on not-O. Part would be a bet on O&H. Part would occur only if O. At that point one would be offered to bet on not-H. Consider this last bet: at that point one would have shifted one's degree of belief in H to 0.1. So one would at that point be prepared to bet heavily against H, giving 9 to 1 odds!

Now, when one is considering the offer of the tobacco company, should one conclude that one should change one's opinion of what a fair bet would be in this way? Should one really be prepared to give 9 to 1 odds against H? If one thought that someone would actually bet a large amount with one if one were to offer them such odds, then one now (before changing one's degree of belief) must conclude this offer from the tobacco company is not a good deal after all. One will get the $100,000 but almost certainly lose even more betting against H.

In this case, whether one is willing to modify one's degrees of belief will depend on how one thinks one will have to act on one's modified degrees of belief after one makes the change. Here is a distinction between evidence and other sorts of reasons for believing something.

Putting the point in another way, one will not want to view the sort of change of belief resulting from the tobacco company's offer as simple Conditionalization. Envisioning the possibility of the offer ahead of time does not lead one to change one's prior probabilities in the way that envisioning getting certain sorts of evidence can lead one to change or firm up prior probabilities. So, it looks as if epistemic reasons can be distinguished from other sorts of reasons by the following criterion. Suppose one would consider R to be a reason to believe H. If one's subjective probabilities are such that

$$\frac{\text{prob(H \& R)}}{\text{prob(R)}} > \text{prob(H)},$$

then one is treating R as an evidential or epistemic reason. Otherwise one is treating R as a different sort of reason, possibly a purely pragmatic reason.

It remains possible that some pragmatic reasons are also epistemic reasons. In particular, considerations of simplicity do seem to affect prior probabilities in the way that is characteristic of evidential reasons and not characteristic of the tobacco company's offer by the current test. This is so even if the only justification for this use of simplicity is a pragmatic justification to the effect that simpler hypotheses are easier to use.

4.18 WHY AREN'T NONEPISTEMIC REASONS INCOHERENT?

This still leaves a problem. On the one hand, there is the Temporal Dutch Book argument that it is incoherent, and so irrational, to be committed to a policy of updating degrees of belief in a way that does not coincide with Conditionalization. On the other hand, there is the rationality of the policy of updating degrees of belief for the sorts of practical reasons that are involved in the RST example. Since it can be rational to be ready to increase one's degree of belief in a proposition simply in order to obtain the RST advertising account, something has to be wrong with the Temporal Dutch Book argument applied to this case.

To see what is wrong, we need to distinguish two ways in which one might be committed to a policy P for updating one's degrees of belief given certain considerations e:

(1) one is committed to thinking *now* that, given e, the probability assignment according to P determines what bets would fair;

(2) one is committed to adopting a new probability assignment according to P given e for determining what bets one *then* thinks would be fair.

These commitments are different. With respect to the RST account, one may have commitment (2) without having commitment (1). The Temporal Dutch Book argument is a good argument only with respect to commitment (1), not with respect to commitment (2). (This is the same point I made in section 4.12 about the principle of Reflection.)

A Temporal Dutch Book argument with respect to commitment (2) would overlook how the rationality of committing oneself to what one will do in hypothetical situations can depend on how likely such situations are and, more generally, on what is to be gained from undertaking such a commitment. To attach a high degree of belief to 'Cigarettes don't cause cancer' is to commit oneself to accepting a bet that one antecedently expects would be ruinous. It can be rational to make such a commitment if one thinks it sufficiently unlikely that one will be called upon to keep the commitment. It can be rational to allow oneself to have commitments that subject one to a hypothetical Temporal Dutch Book if the chances are sufficiently low that one will have to accept the relevant bets. It can even be rational to be committed to an actual Dutch Book, temporal or otherwise, if one's expected losses from the Dutch Book are not as great as the expected gains from the commitment.

A similar point arises in discussions of deterrence: it can be rational to commit oneself to an act of retaliation that would be very costly by one's present lights, if the expected gains from so committing oneself outweigh the expected loss from retaliation, discounted by the probability that retaliation will be required (Schelling, 1960, 1966).

4.19 EXPLANATION, REASONS, AND TRUTH AGAIN

If, as I suppose, degrees of belief and probabilities are not themselves basic but are derivative from considerations of inference to the best explanation, then there ought to be a way of accounting for the distinction between epistemic and nonepistemic reasons that does not make such a heavy appeal to considerations about degrees of belief. I would like to be able to offer a nonprobabilistic account, but I have not found a fully satisfactory one.

The best I can do is to return to the suggestion considered earlier, that epistemic reasons involve an explanatory connection to the truth of what they are reasons for. A problem case is that in which RST requires of its advertisers that they do not just believe P, that cigarette smoking does not cause cancer, but also believe that the truth of P is part of the explanation of their policy with respect to advertisers. The trouble is that this reason now does involve accepting a connection between the truth of P and the nonepistemic practical reasons that one has to believe that P.

Here two possibilities need to be considered: (a) part of the reason for the policy is in fact that cigarettes don't cause cancer; (b) their making the offer is explained entirely in some other way. The question is whether (a) is a better account than (b). Suppose that one's reason for concluding that (a) is a better explanation than (b) is that one will gain financially from so concluding. This makes (a) a better explanation in the sense of being more inferable, but it does not make (a) better as an explanation. It does not make (a) explain any better.

On the other hand, the simplicity of a hypothesis may make an explanation better in the sense that the explanation explains better. Perhaps simpler explanations provide a better explanation in the sense that they provide a better understanding.

It may still be true that this is entirely a pragmatic matter. Simpler explanations may be easier to grasp in some way. Nevertheless, simplicity may play the relevant sort of role in connecting a belief to the truth of what is believed, a role not played by expected monetary gain when RST is looking for an advertiser.

So, maybe there is a way to salvage the idea that an epistemic reason for P must involve a relevant sort of explanatory connection between the truth of P and the reason. But this idea needs further development.

4.20 CONCLUDING SUMMARY

There is an intuitive realist distinction between epistemic and nonepistemic practical reasons for belief. This poses a problem for pragmatism, which holds that what are normally considered epistemic reasons often depend on practical considerations. Foundational considerations in the theory of subjective probability point to a solution to the problem. A commitment to inference to the best explanation does not lead to the incoherence of supposing that Temporal Dutch Books can be fair, because the commitment to inference to the best explanation helps to determine one's prior probability distribution (in the relevant sense of 'prior probability'). Acceptance of nonepistemic reasons differs in not helping to determine one's prior probability distribution, and that allows a pragmatist to make the relevant distinction.

I conclude that pragmatists can allow for a distinction between epistemic and nonepistemic reasons without supposing that all practical reasons for belief are nonepistemic reasons.

PART II

Analyticity

5

The Death of Meaning

5.1 AGAINST THE ANALYTIC–SYNTHETIC DISTINCTION

What I shall call a 'full-blooded theory of analytic truth' takes the analytic truths to be those that hold solely by virtue of meaning or that are knowable solely by virtue of meaning (Bennett, 1966: 6; Carnap, 1966: 260, 267; Pap, 1958: 423). By virtue of the phrase 'by virtue', a full-blooded theory of analytic truth commits its defenders to an explanatory claim about meaning. The main problem for the theory is to make clear what sort of explanation this could be.

The idea behind the full-blooded theory seems to be this: meaning is always part of the reason why a statement expresses a truth, since the statement could be made to express a falsehood by assigning different meaning to the words that make up the statement. Some statements express a truth by virtue of their meanings plus the way the world is. The statement 'Copper conducts electricity' expresses a truth because it means what it does and because of the way the world is. If its meaning were suitably different, or if the laws of nature in the world were suitably different, the statement would not express a truth. According to the full-blooded theory of analytic truth, there are other statements that express truths solely by virtue of their meanings and independently of the way the world is. The statements 'Copper is a metal' and 'Copper is copper' would be said to express truths solely by virtue of their meanings. That they express truths would be said to have nothing to do with the way the world is, apart from the fact that these statements have the meaning they have.

There is an obvious problem in understanding how the truth of a statement can be independent of the way the world is and depend entirely on the meaning of the statement. Why is it not a fact about the world that copper is a metal such that, if this were not a fact, the statement 'Copper is a metal' would not express a truth? And why doesn't the truth expressed by 'Copper is copper' depend in part on the general fact that everything is self-identical (Quine, 1960a)?

A similar problem arises if analyticity is identified with knowability by virtue of knowledge of meaning. Why is it not to know something about the world to know that copper is a metal or that copper is copper? It is not sufficient to reply that if someone sincerely denies these statements, she must fail to understand what she is saying or must be using at least some of her words in a new sense. This does not by itself show how something can be true or knowable solely by virtue of meaning. Perhaps a psychological compulsion prevents one from denying these claims. Or perhaps they are claims that everyone finds obviously true, so that if any of them were to be denied we would have the best possible evidence for thinking the speaker either misunderstands what she says or uses her words in new senses (Quine, 1960a). The problem for a defender of analyticity is to show how in certain cases such compulsion or obviousness can be a sign of truth or knowability in virtue of meaning alone.

The only serious attempt to do this invokes the notion of convention. The argument begins by noting that it is, in some sense, a matter of convention that a given word means what it does. Our conventions might have been different and we can change them now if we want to. We might decide to use the word 'wood' as we now use the word 'copper' and vice versa. Such a change in our conventions would affect the truth and falsity of statements like 'Copper conducts electricity' and 'Wood conducts electricity'. A conventionalist argues further that meaning depends on conventions for the use of an expression, and that in the present instance the relevant conventions specify which statements are to be counted true and which false. The claim is that we have adopted certain rules or conventions that assign truth or falsity to statements like 'Copper is a metal', 'Wood is not a metal', the truths and falsehoods of logic and perhaps mathematics, etc. These conventions determine the meanings of the words 'copper', 'metal', 'wood', and of logical words like 'if', 'not', 'every', etc. As a result, certain principles ('Copper is a metal' or the truths of logic) are true by virtue of meaning, that is, by virtue of convention, in the sense that we have given meaning to the words used to state these principles by conventionally counting these and other principles true. If we were to change our conventional assignments of truth and falsity, we would thereby change the meaning of at least some of those words (Hahn, 1959; Black, 1958b; Quinton, 1963; Scriven, 1966).

Quine (1936, 1960a) points out that conventionalism faces a major technical difficulty if it is supposed to account for all logical truth and falsity. An infinite number of statements of logic require conventional assignments of truth or falsity. Presumably the conventionalist holds that we make certain general conventions that together assign truth or falsity to this infinite set. But the statement of these general conventions must use logical words like 'if', 'whenever', 'every', etc., and by hypothesis these words are given meaning by the conventions. To understand and apply the conventions that give meaning to logical words one would already have to understand some logical words. Conventionalism in logic thus either proves circular or leads to an infinite regress.

But there is a more basic problem with conventionalism. Even if conventional assignments of truth or falsity determine meaning, it does not follow that a statement assigned truth is true by virtue of convention. It does not even follow that the statement is true. For the relevant notion of convention cannot be distinguished from the notion of postulation. If one can assign truth and falsity to statements in logic, set theory, or mathematics by general conventions, that is, postulates that determine the meaning of one's words, the same is true in geometry, physics, or chemistry. The meanings of 'molecule', 'electron', 'quantum', etc. are determined by the postulates of one's physics in the same way as the meaning of 'is a member of' is determined by the postulates of one's set theory.

But not every physical theory is true; for example, Newton's theory is not true, the theory of the ether is not true, etc. Since 'truth by convention' is 'truth according to one's conventions', i.e. postulates, truth by convention does not guarantee truth and therefore cannot account for truth. For similar reasons conventionalism must fail to account for knowledge of truth by virtue of knowledge of meaning, since knowledge that something is true according to one's conventions, that is, knowledge that it follows from one's postulates, is not sufficient for knowledge that it is true (Quine, 1936, 1960*a*).

The ultimate defence of the full-blooded theory of analytic truth rests on the claim that some truths are either necessarily true or knowable a priori, where the notions of necessary truth and a priori knowledge are given special meaning. The argument is that all necessary or a priori truth must be analytic truth, true by virtue of meaning and knowable by virtue of knowledge of meaning. For it is said that a statement expresses a necessary truth if, given the meaning of the statement, it must be true no matter what; and a statement expresses an a priori truth if knowledge of its meaning can suffice for knowledge of its truth. The meaning of such a statement guarantees its truth; knowledge of meaning is enough for knowledge of truth; and either the a priori or the necessary (or both) can be identified with the analytic. The statements 'Copper is a metal' and 'Copper is copper', various principles of logic and mathematics, etc., are said to express necessary truths and are said to be knowable a priori; so they are also said to be analytic truths.

Unfortunately the relevant notions of necessity and a prioricity are not very clear. In a particular inquiry certain premises may be taken for granted and not questioned. We could say such premises are known a priori, i.e. at the beginning of the inquiry, while other things, discovered in the course of the inquiry, come to be known only a posteriori. But this would not mean that we have a priori knowledge of the premises of the inquiry in any sense usable by a philosophical defender of analyticity. For these premises need not be known solely by virtue of knowledge of their meaning. They may well be known as the result of prior empirical inquiry. They may not be known at all, but only assumed to be known. The defender of analyticity needs more than such relatively a priori knowledge. He needs absolutely a priori knowledge, whatever that would be. Similarly, certain truths may be necessary in that they are laws of nature, for example, as discovered by science (Quine, 1966*a*). But such natural necessity cannot guarantee analyticity, since a contrast between laws of nature and necessary truths is intended, the former synthetic, the latter analytic. Laws of nature do not hold solely by virtue of the meaning of words used to express those laws. The point, if you like, is that laws of nature are not absolutely necessary (again: whatever that would be); they need not have been true. There are conceivable worlds in which they do not hold. The notions of relatively a priori knowledge and of truths necessary by virtue of laws of nature are (relatively) clear notions. The notions of absolutely a priori knowledge and of truths absolutely necessary (no matter what the laws of nature) are obscure.

One test of the a priori or necessary character of a view has been whether it is possible to conceive of its failing to hold, or whether it is possible to imagine circumstances in which we would give it up. It would seem that any simple basic assertion that can be conceived not to hold cannot be necessary, knowable a priori, or analytic (in the full-blooded sense). If, given its meaning, a statement could conceivably fail to hold, its meaning does not guarantee its truth, nor can knowledge of its meaning suffice for knowledge of truth. Now, Quine (1953*c*) claims that we can conceive of any statement failing to hold and that for any view we can imagine circumstances in which we would give it up. He concludes that no truths are a priori or necessary and therefore that no truths are analytic in the full-blooded sense.

We have granted that a person who denies our basic logical principles thereby indicates that she misunderstands what she says or means something different by her words from what we would mean. This does not imply that we cannot conceive of someone giving up our basic logical principles, nor does it imply that we cannot conceive of these principles failing to hold. At best it implies that these principles cannot be false, that they cannot be given up by simply denying them. However, someone can refuse to accept our principles and instead adopt principles that cannot be translated into ours; and we can conceive of his principles being correct. Perhaps the law of the excluded middle (P or not-P) fails to hold, even though it is not false. A person who accepts a logic without this law may mean something different by 'not' from what we mean; but his language may contain no principle we can identify with our law. According to such a person, our law of the excluded middle fails to have a truth-value: he rejects our notion of 'not' (Quine, 1960*a*).

Similarly, even the principle of noncontradiction (not both P and not-P) can be conceived to fail to hold. We may not be able to conceive of its falsity, that is, we may not be able to envisage a counterexample; but we can conceive of its failing to have a truth-value. We can easily imagine someone giving up the principle and refusing to accept any equivalent principle. For one thing, it is sometimes said that any logic that fails to accept the law of the excluded middle shifts the meaning of the word 'not'. If so, this shift will affect the meaning of the principle of noncontradiction. Furthermore, in a logic like Strawson's (1952) in which failure of reference deprives a statement of a truth-value, the principle of noncontradiction does not hold, since if P contains a referring term that does not refer, so will both P and not-P. Nor must every logic contain the principle that both a statement and its denial cannot both be true, for again one's logic may have nothing that qualifies as such a principle. A similar point can be made about any putatively necessary truth. One may give up even 'Copper is copper' by refusing to have any expression corresponding to 'copper' or by refusing to countenance the 'is' of identity (Wittgenstein, 1961).

It is a familiar point in ethics that, to reject certain principles sometimes requires us to reject certain terminology, for example, the principles that give meaning to words like 'nigger' or 'queer', at least as these words have been used by some people. Perhaps the same is true of the principles that give meaning to the words 'phlogiston', 'ether', 'God', and 'witch'. Again, perhaps it makes no sense to deny the conjunction of the nonlogical postulates of a weak set theory, since these postulates give meaning to 'is a member of'. But one may reject the theory without denying it.

I have described Quine's arguments against the full-blooded theory of analyticity. He argues that it has not been shown how meaning can account for truth, or how knowledge of meaning can account for knowledge of truth. In particular, he denies that this can be shown by appeal to conventional postulation or to necessary or a priori truth, even backed by reference to what can be conceived. The same arguments are also effective against a weaker theory that identifies the analytic truths as those that are either explicitly or implicitly truths of logic. The statement 'A male sibling is male' represents an explicit logical truth. The statement 'A brother is a male' is supposed to represent an implicit logical truth in this sense, since it is supposed to be equivalent (on 'analysis') to an explicit logical truth, where the equivalence is equivalence by virtue of meaning. Both statements count as analytic truths according to the weaker theory.

Putting aside issues about how to characterize explicit logical truth, the claim that two statements can be equivalent by virtue of meaning requires further discussion. It may seem that there is no problem here. 'If two statements are meaningful, each has a meaning; if they have the same meaning the statements are equivalent by virtue of meaning'. Such an argument assumes that there are such things as meanings which a statement may or may not 'have', that the meaning one statement has may be the same as another, and that the possession of the same meaning can account for equivalence in truth-value.

Notice that the postulation of meaning can be related to the notion of equivalence by virtue of meaning in two different ways, depending on which is taken to explain the other. Meaning equivalence is used to explain meanings if, for example, we identify the meaning of a given statement with the class of statements equivalent to it by virtue of meaning. Alternatively, postulation of meanings would account for meaning equivalence if by virtue of such postulation we could show how two statements can be equivalent in truth-value because they have the same meaning. But we cannot have it both ways. We cannot simply identify meanings with equivalence classes of statements if the only account we give of the relevant type of equivalence is to say that statements are equivalent that have the same meaning.

I shall argue, first, that there is a difficulty here that cannot be avoided by appeal to ordinary talk about meaning, synonymy, definition, etc. I shall then argue that taking meaning equivalence as basic leads immediately to the sort of problem that faces the full-blooded theory of analyticity. Finally, I shall present Quine's arguments against any theory of meaning that postulates intensional objects, meanings, propositions, etc.

From the beginning it is important to recognize the following point. When philosophers say that analytic truths are those truths that are synonymous with or mean the same as truths of logic, they use 'synonymous' and 'mean the same' as technical expressions. They do not use these expressions in their ordinary senses. One has only to examine a dictionary of synonyms in order to appreciate this point with respect to 'synonym'. A synonym is another expression that can in certain contexts replace the first expression and serve our purposes in speaking at least as well, often better. And ordinarily when we say that one thing means another, we indicate that the second follows from the first, given also certain background information we share. We say that one statement means the same as, comes to the same thing as, or is synonymous with another if the two statements are relatively obviously equivalent in truth-value, given shared background information. Philosophical talk about sameness of meaning differs from this ordinary talk, since philosophers take synonymy to hold by virtue of meaning alone and not by virtue of shared information. The same point tells against those philosophers who would distinguish meaning equivalence from synthetic equivalence by appeal to dictionary definitions. These philosophers assume a type of distinction between dictionaries and encyclopaedias that does not exist. This is obvious to anyone who has examined a few random entries in any large dictionary (Scriven, 1958), and it will be supported by the discussion of definition below. So the important question is whether or not philosophers can give sense to their particular technical notion of synonymy or meaning equivalence.

The claim that two statements are equivalent by virtue of meaning is an explanatory claim, which raises the issue of how meaning can be any more useful in explaining equivalence than it is in explaining truth. To stop accepting a previously accepted equivalence may change the meaning of one's words; but that can be the result of giving up any equivalence one takes to be obvious or accepts as a basic part of some view or theory. That a rejection of an equivalence would lead to change in meaning fails to show how there can be equivalence by virtue of meaning; and appeal to convention or necessity would seem to give no better an account of equivalence by virtue of meaning than of truth by virtue of meaning.

Some philosophers believe a weaker theory of analyticity can be set forth without any explanatory claim; it is not easy to see how. I shall discuss the possibility of such nonexplanatory theories of analytic truth for a moment and then return to the stronger explanatory theories.

Quine (1953c) and White (1950) have pointed out that, as technical terms, 'analytic', 'synonymous', 'necessary', etc., form a small circle definable in terms of each other but not usually otherwise explained. Philosophers who accept the analytic–synthetic distinction have not always appreciated the difficulty this raises, since they have not always appreciated the technical character of the terms used to state the distinction. It is irrelevant that definitions, if followed back, eventually always become circular (Grice and Strawson, 1956). Ordinarily the circle will contain terms antecedently understood; but this is not the case with technical terms used by philosophers who accept the analytic–synthetic distinction. Perhaps the point has been obscured by a fallacious identification of these technical terms with their more ordinary counterparts.

There are restrictions on what can count as an explanation of this technical distinction. One cannot claim that a particular distinction is the analytic–synthetic distinction if there is no relationship between the specified distinction and what philosophers have wanted to say about analytic and synthetic truth. It would be pointless to call a true statement 'analytic' if and only if it is more than ten words long; and this would not provide an account of the analytic–synthetic distinction. The major constraint on such a distinction is that it must be explanatory. A notion of 'analytic truth' or 'meaning equivalence' that had no explanatory use would fail sufficiently to resemble anything philosophers have in the past meant by those expressions.

Several philosophers deny this (Grice and Strawson, 1956; Bennett, 1959; Putnam, 1962a). They argue that philosophers tend to agree in classifying new cases as either analytic or synthetic and they claim that 'where there is agreement on the use of the expressions involved with respect to an open class, there must necessarily be some kind of distinction present' (Putnam, 1962a: 360). They identify the distinction concerning which there is such agreement with the analytic–synthetic distinction, taking it to be a further question whether philosophical claims about the distinction, e.g. about its explanatory power, can be supported. The only restriction these philosophers place on an account of the technical distinction is that on any adequate account truths generally called 'analytic' should turn out to be analytic and truths generally called 'synthetic' should turn out to be synthetic. For these philosophers, the ascription of analyticity does not commit one to an explanatory claim.

This amounts to a paradigm case argument for the existence of analytic truths; and it is no more convincing than any other such argument. An analogous argument might show that there are or were witches, although it turns out that witches fail to have supernatural powers. It is true that there is a distinction between truths that seem analytic and truths that seem synthetic (to those who accept the analytic–synthetic distinction), and that permits general agreement (within that group) on the use of 'analytic' and 'synthetic' with respect to an open class. But to call this distinction the analytic–synthetic distinction is like identifying the witch–non-witch distinction with the distinction between people who seem and people who do not seem to be witches (to those who believe in witches).

Quine (1960*a*: 56–7, 66–7) agrees that there are apparently analytic truths and he speculates on the mechanism of analyticity 'intuitions'. But he refuses to identify the notion of analyticity with that of apparent analyticity. 'The intuitions are blameless in their way, but it would be a mistake to look to them for a sweeping epistemological dichotomy between analytic truths as by-products of language and synthetic truths as reports on the world' (67). Compare: 'Even if logical truth were specifiable in syntactical terms, this would not show it was grounded in language' (Quine, 1960*a*: 110; see also Quine, 1967: 52–4).

One has only to reflect on why philosophers introduced talk about analyticity to see that they have generally taken ascription of analyticity to possess explanatory power. The analytic–synthetic distinction has always reflected an epistemological or metaphysical distinction, 'How do we know this is true?' or 'Why is this true?' One has only to mention those views associated with the introduction of talk about analyticity or meaning equivalence to see the purported epistemological or metaphysical point of such talk. Phenomenalism was supposed to account for our knowledge of the external world. Behaviourism was supposed by some to account for the relation between mind and body; and it (or talk about 'logically adequate criteria') was supposed by others to account for our knowledge of other minds. Ethical naturalism was intended by some to account for how we can know the truth of ethical principles. And so on.

Consider, furthermore, how the usage of philosophers who distinguish analytic and synthetic truths is affected by changes in their beliefs about the limits of what can be conceived or imagined. As they come to see that more can be imagined than they had thought, they retract certain ascriptions of analyticity. At first, most philosophers would take the following to be analytic: 'All cats are animals', 'All bachelors are unmarried', 'Red is a colour'. After having certain imaginary or (in some cases) real situations described to them, some (but not all) of these philosophers no longer take these to be analytic. After imagining what it would be like if those things we call 'cats' should turn out to be radio-controlled robots, some philosophers refuse to ascribe analyticity to 'All cats are animals' (Putnam, 1962*b*). After imagining what it would be like if a flaw in the divorce courts had made almost all recent divorces invalid, some philosophers no longer attribute analyticity to 'All bachelors are unmarried' (Moravscik, 1965).

After imagining what it would be like to discover that things look red partly as the result of an extremely high-pitched sound emitted by red objects such that, if we were to go deaf, the objects would look grey, some philosophers no longer ascribe analyticity to 'Red is a colour'. Given these and other examples, some philosophers give up all ascription of analyticity.

Consideration of such examples tends to destroy one's ability to identify statements as analytic, just as careful study of certain women can destroy one's ability to identify people as witches. Therefore one cannot vindicate a theory of analytic truth by simple appeal to ordinary or philosophical talk about meaning, synonymy, definition, and analyticity. Instead one must explicitly justify the explanatory claim involved in 'equivalent by virtue of meaning'. In a moment I shall discuss a defence of this claim that postulates intensional objects (meanings and/or propositions). But first I want to say something about explicit conventional definition.

Such definition is supposed to be more than mere explication, that is, more than the provision of necessary and sufficient conditions, since explicit conventional definition is supposed to provide analytically necessary and sufficient conditions. The claim is that when we introduce a new expression by explicitly defining it to be equivalent with an old expression, the two expressions are thereby made equivalent by virtue of meaning.

But now the same old worry returns. Conventional definition is a kind of postulation, the postulation of an equivalence. Equivalence by virtue of conventional definition is equivalence according to certain of one's postulates. The difficulty lies in seeing how equivalence by virtue of conventional definitions can ensure equivalence, just as the corresponding difficulty with the full-blooded theory lies in seeing how truth according to one's postulates can guarantee truth.

People who believe that definition holds the key to analyticity may be misled by what happens in the formalization of some body of information or theory. Often this is done by specifying certain primitive terms, giving postulates that use only those terms, then introducing other terms by 'definition'. It may appear that the desired analytic truths of the interpreted theory are those equivalent by such definition to logical truths. But this is an illusion. A body of doctrine can be formalized in various ways for various purposes: one way will take certain predicates as primitive and others as defined, another way will make a different distinction between primitive and defined predicates. Different sets of statements will count as definitionally equivalent to logical truths depending on how one has decided to formalize. Definitional equivalence to a logical truth varies depending on formalization, even though the meanings of one's terms do not. Therefore, definitional equivalence to a logical truth is not the same as equivalence in meaning with a logical truth.

Postulation often provides a way of partially specifying the meaning of one's terms when one introduces a new theory or wants to describe an old theory, even though such postulation does not by itself guarantee truth. In particular, the postulation of an equivalence in a definition can help to specify the meaning of a certain person's terms even though such postulation cannot guarantee equivalence. Furthermore, two people may introduce the same theory in different ways such that 'synthetic' statements according to the one presentation are true by definition plus logic according to the other, although the corresponding terms in the two presentations of the theory will not for that reason differ in meaning. Therefore definition does not hold the key to analyticity (Quine, 1953*c*, 1960*a*).

To sum, the ascription of analyticity commits one to an explanatory claim: the claim that something can be true or knowable by virtue of meaning, or at least that two statements can be equivalent by virtue of meaning. But so far we have seen no way in which meaning might provide such explanation. We must now consider theories of meaning that postulate the existence of intensional objects, e.g. meanings or propositions. When we have seen what is wrong with such theories and have understood Quine's alternative, we will be able to appreciate more fully what is wrong with the analytic–synthetic distinction.

5.2 AGAINST INTENSIONAL OBJECTS

Language is often used to express a speaker's psychological attitudes. To some philosophers this fact is incompatible with the rejection of the notion of meaning equivalence. They hold that two statements are equivalent by virtue of meaning if they express the same psychological attitude, for example, if they express the same belief.

If the same belief can be expressed by several different statements, then a belief cannot be construed simply as the acceptance of a statement. Therefore some philosophers hold that psychological states involve something else, language-independent *propositions*, so that, for example, belief is the acceptance of a language-independent proposition. Quine (1960*b*: 220–1; 1953*a*: 47–8) responds that the postulation of such language-independent propositional attitudes purports to offer an explanation without really doing so. In particular, Quine denies that a person accepts a statement because he accepts a language-independent proposition expressed by the statement.

Philosophers have noticed that people often identify beliefs that have been expressed by different statements. They infer that belief must be the acceptance of something more basic than a statement. They have also noticed that when two different statements are ordinarily said to express the same belief, these statements are also said to have the same meaning. So they have identified the underlying belief as the acceptance of a proposition or meaning.

The fallacy in the argument lies in a switch between the ordinary and philosophical use of 'means the same'. People ordinarily say that two statements mean the same if they are relatively obviously equivalent in truth-value by virtue of generally accepted principles. For example, in 1966 the statement 'Lyndon Johnson has travelled to Vietnam' would have been taken to mean the same (in the ordinary sense of 'means the same') as the statement 'The President of the United States has travelled to Vietnam', although a linguistic philosopher would not want to say the statements are equivalent by virtue of meaning. Therefore the theory of propositional attitudes not only fails to account for ordinary talk about beliefs, desires, etc., but, taken as an account of ordinary talk about sameness of meaning, even implies things that are false, since it would predict that the two cited statements would not ordinarily be said to mean the same. Quine's theory has no such problem. To account for ordinary views he need not assume that an attitude toward a language-independent proposition underlies a psychological attitude. He can observe that different attitudes are often 'identified' in ordinary speech but note such identification is a shifting thing that depends on context and does not presuppose postulation of some language-independent thing behind the statement.

Translation provides another reason for postulating language-independent propositions or meanings, since translation is supposed by some philosophers to consist in finding a statement in one language that 'has' the same meaning or expresses the same proposition as a given statement in the other. Quine (1960*b*) argues that this is not a correct account of translation, because it makes no sense to speak of the translation of a single statement of one language into a statement of another language apart from other translations one would make. That is, Quine says that translation must always proceed against the background of a general scheme of translation from the one language to the other. Ordinarily, in talking of translation from English to French or German, etc., such a scheme is generally accepted. Without some presupposed general scheme, the notion of translation (i.e. the notion of 'radical' translation) is indeterminate; hence Quine's (1960*a*) thesis of the indeterminacy of radical translation.

Here is an analogy. There are various ways to translate number theory into set theory. Following von Neumann, one may identify each (natural) number with the set of all smaller numbers. Following Zermelo, one may identify each number with the unit set of its predecessor. Either series of identifications permits translation of all statements of number theory; and apart from some such general scheme of translation, it makes no sense to ask what is the correct translation of an isolated statement of number theory or what is the correct way to identify number with sets (Benacerraf, 1965; Goodman, 1966; C. Parsons, 1965). Without reference to a general scheme of translation, the notion of the translation of an isolated statement of number theory is indeterminate. Quine (1960*b*) claims that this kind of indeterminacy holds for radical translation in general.

When all reasonable conditions have been placed on possible general schemes of translation from number theory into set theory, several schemes still satisfy all the conditions. Both schemes mentioned above preserve truth. Both are relatively simple. Nothing can decide between them except the purposes of the moment. Either scheme provides a set of acceptable translations. Yet they do not provide equivalent translations. There are even statements for which they provide translations that differ in truthvalue. These latter statements are counted neither true nor false before translation. (Consider, for example, the statement 'The number 2 has exactly one member'. This statement receives no truth-value in number theory before translation into set theory. It is translated into a true statement by von Neumann's scheme of translation; it comes out false on Zermelo's scheme.) Quine (1960*b*) claims that these points can be generalized to all interesting cases of radical translation. In general there will be several possible schemes of translation that satisfy all reasonable conditions on such a scheme, yet provide nonequivalent translations. Therefore we cannot speak of translation apart from a scheme of translation; radical translation is always indeterminate; and consequently the postulation of meanings or propositions is not vindicated by the possibilities of translation from one language into another.

In order to see this more clearly we must examine the intimate connection between translation and psychology. A general theory of language must ultimately attempt to explain linguistic and other behaviour, and this requires the postulation of certain psychological states, e.g. desires and beliefs. Some explanation requires postulation only of sentences, for example, one can explain why a person has uttered a particular sentence by assuming he is freely expressing his thoughts and accepts the sentence he has uttered.

So far, this is not controversial. Disagreement arises over the explanatory value of knowing the radical translation of the sentence involved. The more one must know about such a translation in order to provide good psychological explanations, the more justified one is in postulating propositional attitudes that underlie sentential attitudes.

The behavioural evidence relevant to a particular hypothesis about translation may be construed as the behavioural evidence relevant to a particular hypothesis about the psychological explanation of that behaviour. The issue then is whether this evidence warrants postulation of propositional attitudes. Quine argues that we do not need to know a very complete scheme of translation in order to provide the required explanations; in other words, that beyond a certain point, various schemes of translation serve equally well. In order to explain behaviour we may need to assume nonradical translatability, that is, we may need to assume that there is some possible way to translate from his language to ours; but, according to Quine, we do not need to assume that the speaker's statement has a particular meaning, i.e. in this context a particular translation, apart from some general scheme of translation, where several nonequivalent schemes are equally possible.

Whether or not Quine is right depends largely on what sort of conditions must be satisfied by schemes of translation. Indeterminacy is clearly inevitable unless there are fairly strong constraints. For example, we must assume that beliefs, desires, etc., of people speaking the language to be translated are similar to our own beliefs and desires and that these beliefs and desires arise in similar ways through observation, deprivation, etc. If we did not make such an assumption, there would be strong indeterminacy. In a particular case, one scheme of translation might represent certain statements of the language to be about cats. On this scheme the relevant beliefs and desires would be similar to ours. An alternative scheme might represent these statements as being about dogs, where on this scheme the relevant beliefs and desires come out quite different from ours such that these people are taken to believe that something looking like what we call a 'cat' is really a dog, such that they want dogs when there are mice to be caught, such that they believe that dogs miaow rather than bark, etc. If someone speaking English expressed the cited beliefs and desires, we would say that he meant by 'dog' what we mean by 'cat'. A good scheme of translation ascribes to the people whose language is translated beliefs, desires, etc. that are similar to our own and arise in ways similar to the ways in which our beliefs, desires, etc. arise.

Someone who believes that propositional attitudes underlie one's sentential attitudes should be bothered by the problem of ruling out the possibility of such strange beliefs. Compare the philosophical problem of the inverted spectrum: for certain philosophers there is the problem that I might mean by 'green' what you mean by 'red', etc., although there is no way of discovering this (Quine, 1960b: 78–9; also Essay 14, below).

More generally, some translations are partially determined by the psychological explanations we want to give; for example, we may be able to discover that certain statements are denials of others since we may have to postulate this in order to explain why a person says some things but not others. We may have to assume that a particular construction represents 'P, if Q' so that we can explain how a person comes to accept P, given that he accepts that construction and also accepts Q. The same translation of the construction may enable us to explain how a person comes to desire true Q, given that he desires true the construction and also desires true P (Quine, 1960b: 57–61).

Even at this level some indeterminacy arises. Instead of translating the construction as 'P, if Q' we might just as well use 'not both Q and not-P' or 'P or not-Q'. Some comfort may be taken from the fact that these translations are always equivalent in truth-value. Similarly, indeterminacy in the translation of fairly simple talk about rabbits seems to be indeterminacy among translations equivalent in truth-value. A particular statement may receive as possible translations statements like 'Here is a rabbit', 'Here is an instance of rabbithood', 'Here is an undetached rabbit part', etc. These are equivalent in that one is true if and only if the others are true (Quine, 1960b: 40–6, 68–72). But where translation of truth-functional connectives is indeterminate among truth-functional equivalents, indeterminacy of translation of this talk about rabbits is indeterminate among statements equivalent by virtue of more complicated principles. This leads one to expect that, in general, translation will be indeterminate among statements equivalent by virtue of the basic principles of the area translated. One would expect that the translation of statements of chemistry is indeterminate among statements equivalent by virtue of chemical theory, etc.

Such indeterminacy is incompatible with the view that translation must equate statements that express the same proposition, and is enough to refute the view that propositional attitudes underlie one's sentential attitudes; but even more can be said. There will be indeterminacy among 'utterly disparate translations. Two such translations might even be patently contrary in truth-value, provided there is no stimulation that would encourage assent to either' (Quine, 1960*b*: 73–4).

Suppose on one scheme of translation the people whose language is being translated are assigned beliefs about numbers, and suppose we have reduced our number theory to set theory. Then there will be alternative schemes of translation from their number theory into our set theory, where some of these alternatives produce nonequivalent translations of single statements; and there is no reason to prefer one of these schemes to the other. This example provides an instance of the strong indeterminacy of radical translation that Quine describes in the passage cited above. The statement corresponding to 'The number 2 has exactly one member' is a statement such that the speakers of the given language assign it no truth-value (no stimulation would encourage assent to either it or its denial); and it is assigned contrary truth-values by the von Neumann and Zermelo translations.

Therefore, the possibility of translation from one language to another does not support the postulation of intentional objects, meanings, or propositions. Translation does not require antecedently existing meaning relations between statements in different languages apart from some pre-supposed scheme of translation from the one language to the other. A person's acceptance of a statement in another language does not represent an underlying propositional attitude such that, apart from a presupposed scheme of translation, the same attitude could be said to underlie our acceptance of a statement in our language.

5.3 QUINE'S THEORY OF MEANING

Quine believes that the basic psychological reality consists in attitudes involving statements in one's language along with connections among these attitudes and between these attitudes and their causes and effects (e.g. observation and speech). His opponents must agree that there are such attitudes, connections, causes, and effects; but they also postulate underlying meanings, propositions, intensional objects, etc. We have seen that Quine argues that this postulation is wrong because it is incompatible with the indeterminacy of radical translation. In order to make his case more plausible, I shall now say a few things about Quine's theory of meaning.

His account of translation provides the basis of an account of verbal dis-agreement. Ordinarily a person interprets the words spoken by other speakers of the 'same language' in the same way that he interprets his own words, that is, he takes the obvious translation scheme to apply—call it the 'identity scheme'. He can do this because the identity scheme ascribes to others roughly the same beliefs he has and roughly the same methods of belief formation (and similarly for desires and other psychological attitudes), because there is no obvious alternative that does as well, and also because of an epistemological conservatism that favours assumptions one has been making all along. Occasionally there are reasons for overriding this conservatism. Sometimes a relatively obvious modification of the identity translation will translate beliefs, etc. that appear to diverge from one's own beliefs, etc. into beliefs, etc. that are similar to one's own. If so, one will accept the modified translation scheme and take the apparent disagreement in belief to be 'merely verbal'. In general there is no real (underlying) distinction between a difference in view and a difference in meaning. But if the disagreement is systematic to a degree sufficient to override our conservative commitment to the identity scheme, then we call it a difference in meaning; otherwise we call it a difference in belief.

To understand this is to begin to see the mistake involved in the analytic–synthetic distinction. Proponents of this distinction claim that one cannot give up basic analytic principles without changing the meaning of one's words. This presupposes a real distinction between changing one's view and only appearing to change one's view by changing the meaning of words used to state it. The trouble with this is that any change from one view to another tends to involve a change in meaning; it will tend to make the identity translation less good, since one defect in a scheme of translation may be that it ascribes to others beliefs diverging too radically from ours. We can say that any change in view represents some change in meaning, since a sufficient number of small changes in view will lead to the sort of change we describe as a clear change in meaning. (To see this, imagine small successive changes in one's beliefs about cats and dogs so that one eventually comes to believe about cats what one believes about dogs and vice versa.)

Given a small change in view, the change in meaning (or the tendency to change in meaning) is slight. Should we say that our terms no longer mean what they used to mean? This resembles the question whether something is still the same colour if its colour has changed slightly. Sameness of meaning can represent a strict equivalence relation or a similarity relation. Ordinarily it represents the latter.

The theory that there is an analytic–synthetic distinction may well be the result of confusing similarity in meaning with exact sameness in meaning. When one gives up certain principles the meaning of one's words may remain sufficiently similar to permit us to say they still mean the same thing; and this may fail to be true if one gives up certain other principles. But that does not support the analytic–synthetic distinction. Meaning has changed somewhat in either case, that is, the identity translation between persons with different theories is not as good a translation as it is between two people who both hold the same theory. Whether we actually say there is a change in meaning depends on whether we can find a simple translation that preserves beliefs, etc. better than the identity translation.

To see where proponents of the analytic–synthetic distinction may go wrong, suppose that a theory changes twice and let A, B, and C represent successive states of the theory. The change between A and B and also that between B and C can both be slight enough so that we say our theoretical terms have not changed meaning in the move from A to B or again in the move from B to C. That is, in translating between A and B or between B and C, the identity translation, although not perfect, is best. It does not follow that in the overall move from A to C our theoretical terms have not changed meaning, since in translating between A and C some other translation may be better than the identity translation. Thus when same meaning is similar meaning, sameness of meaning is not transitive (similarly for same colour when this is similar colour). But proponents of the analytic–synthetic distinction need transitivity. They want to say that because there has been no change in meaning, the move from A to B has not changed the analytic statements or 'meaning postulates' of the theory, and similarly for the move from B to C. Therefore there ought to be no such change in the move from A to C; and this means there ought to be no change in meaning in the move from A to C. The mistake lies in confusing similarity of meaning, which holds between A and B and also between B and C but not between A and C, with exact sameness of meaning, which holds between none of those (although if it did hold between A and B and also between B and C it would also hold between A and C). No doubt other confusions are also responsible for the analytic–synthetic distinction; but confusing similarity with exact sameness probably plays a major role.

Finally, a word about ambiguity. Quine takes ambiguity to be a special case of the effect of context on acceptance and rejection of statements. Roughly speaking, a statement is ambiguous if its truth-value changes with context (Quine, 1960*b*: 129). Here one may feel that something has been left out of Quine's theory: the difference in interpretation one can place on an ambiguous statement. A statement may come out true on all such interpretations yet still be ambiguous. Can Quine account for these differences without assuming one associates varying meanings or propositions with ambiguous statements? Yes, he can. According to him, a person associates varying paraphrases with ambiguous statements (Quine, 1960*b*: 129, 191–5). Paraphrases will be statements in the speaker's language, not statements or statement substitutes in some universal language of propositional attitudes. The varying paraphrases represent what the speaker takes to be equivalent to the ambiguous statement given a particular context. The notion of equivalence here is not that of 'meaning equivalence', but rather the notion of an equivalence taken to follow fairly obviously from what the relevant group of people (possibly only the speaker or hearer) accepts.

In this essay I have tried to explain Quine's arguments that the analytic–synthetic distinction, and the postulation of intensional objects—meanings and propositions—cannot be justified by appeal either to ordinary or to philosophical talk about meaning, or by the view that meaning can explain truth or knowledge, or by a correct account of translation that also accounts for verbal disagreement and ambiguity. According to this argument, such theories of meaning are no better off than other bad scientific theories such as the theories of phlogiston and of the ether. To continue to accept such a theory of meaning in the light of Quine's arguments, without offering some reply, is to make the theory meaningless. It is to render it into a religious theory. This suggests that such theories of meaning will prove difficult to dislodge by mere argument. Quine's greatest achievement lies in having shown that they ought to be dislodged.

6

Doubts about Conceptual Analysis

In these brief remarks, I want to indicate why conceptual analyses by philosophers are unlikely to deliver the sorts of a priori connections that Jackson (1994) argues are needed for armchair metaphysics.

Paradigm cases of the a priori include basic principles of logic, definitions, and other 'axioms' into the truth of which we seem (I say 'seem' because I recognize that this may be an illusion) to have intuitive insight. In such cases we seem to be able to tell that something is true just by considering the matter clearly. In addition, we seem to be able to tell a priori that when certain things are true, certain other things are also true. There are patterns of implication that we seem to be able to recognize a priori: modus ponens, for example. So paradigm cases of the a priori include axioms that can be immediately recognized as obviously true and anything that follows from these axioms via one or more steps of obvious implication.

My first point is that philosophical analysis does not often yield a priori results of this paradigmatic sort.

6.1 PHILOSOPHICAL ANALYSIS: WHAT'S GOING ON?

It is true that philosophical analyses of 'know', 'good', 'refers', etc. are often presented as accounts of meaning. They are confirmed not by empirical testing but, as Jackson points out, by thought experiments. An analysis is accepted because it cannot be imagined false. So it may seem that successful analyses aim to provide analytic a priori truths.

But there is an obvious immediate difference between these cases and paradigm cases of the a priori. We do not normally have the sort of direct intuitive insight into the truth of philosophical analyses that we may seem to have into basic principles of logic. Nor can philosophical analyses ordinarily be demonstrated as following by obvious principles from obvious axioms.

Typically, attempts at philosophical analysis proceed by the formulation of one or more tentative analyses and then the consideration of test cases. If exactly one of the proposed analyses does not conflict with 'intuitions' about any test cases, it is taken to be at least tentatively confirmed. Further research then uncovers new test cases in which intuitions conflict with the analysis. The analysis is then modified or replaced by a completely different one, which is in turn tested against imagined cases, and so on.

There is an inductive component to the acceptance of any philosophical analysis that is defended in this way. From the fact that an analysis conflicts with none of the test cases considered so far, one concludes that the analysis gives the right results for all possible test cases. Compare this with inductive reasoning that might be offered in support of a mathematical hypothesis, such as Goldbach's conjecture: from the fact that no counterexamples have been found so far, one concludes that the conjecture holds for all natural numbers.

Even in the judgement that an analysis fits a particular case there is an inductive element. When we speak of 'intuitions about cases', we refer to the fact that, given a description of a possible situation, we find that we are more or less strongly inclined to make a particular judgement about the situation on the basis of that description. Notoriously, such a judgement can depend on exactly what description of the case is given, other assumptions we may be making, etc. It happens more often that some philosophers like to admit that we change our mind about what our intuitions are about a given case, especially if we discover that others have different intuitions.

We have some data, namely, that people P have actually made judgements J about cases C as described by D. Given the data, we infer that P and others would make the same judgements J about the same cases C on other occasions. This is clearly an inductive and fallible inference, because it is a type of inference that is very often mistaken. An analysis is defended in the way one defends any inductive hypothesis, namely, as offering the simplest most plausible explanation of certain data.

6.2 ANALYTIC–SYNTHETIC

Philosophical analyses must be understood as involving hypotheses about how we, the people in question, use certain terms. But that is not to say that to engage in philosophical analysis one must accept a distinction between substantive theoretical assumptions and conceptual truths.

When Jackson speaks of 'extremists' who reject 'conceptual analysis', I take it that he is referring to those who reject the analytic–synthetic distinction. In my view, the distinction was conclusively undermined at least thirty years ago. I am surprised that this fact has not been universally appreciated.

Why do people reject 'conceptual analysis'? Jackson says they 'are forgetting about biased samples. True, the well known and much discussed examples of putative analyses in the philosophy journals are highly controversial but that is why they are much discussed in the philosophy journals.'

But this simply misrepresents the opposition. When Quine, Putnam, Winograd, and a host of others raised objections to the analytic–synthetic distinction, they did not mention controversial philosophical analyses. When problems were raised about particular conceptual claims, they were problems about the examples that had been offered as seemingly clear cases of a priori truth—the principles of Euclidean geometry, the law of excluded middle, 'Cats are animals', 'Unmarried adult male humans are bachelors', 'Women are female', and 'Red is a colour'. Physics leads to the rejection of Euclidean geometry and at least considers rejecting the law of excluded middle (Quine, 1936, 1953c). We can imagine discovering that cats are not animals but are radio controlled robots from Mars (Putnam, 1962b). Speakers do not consider the Pope a bachelor (Winograd and Flores, 1986). People will not apply the term 'bachelor' to a man who lives with the same woman over a long enough period of time even if they are not married. Society pages in newspapers will identify as eligible 'bachelors' men who are in the process of being divorced but are still married. The Olympic Committee may have rejected certain women as sufficiently female on the basis of their chromosomes. (Robert Schwartz pointed this out to me many years ago.) Just as a certain flavour is really detected by smell rather than taste, we can imagine that the colour red might be detected aurally rather than by sight.

Furthermore, the heart of the objection to analyticity was not simply that there are problems with all the usual paradigms of analytic truth, but that, whatever we are to say about these paradigms, the analytic–synthetic distinction rests on substantive assumptions that turn out to be false.

The basic idea behind the analytic–synthetic distinction was that certain propositions could be true solely by virtue of what is meant by the words used to express them and could be known to be true simply by knowing the meaning of these words. These propositions were the analytic truths; all other truths were synthetic. The analytic truths were supposed to be a subset, proper or improper, of the truths knowable a priori. A priori knowledge was supposed to be knowledge that was justified without appeal to experiential evidence. The relevant notion of justification required a 'foundations' account: knowledge of P might depend on knowledge of Q, and so forth, eventually culminating in foundations that were either known a priori or deliverences of immediate conscious experience.

When foundationalism was discredited, so was a priori knowledge (and vice versa).

6.3 THE ALTERNATIVE TO A FOUNDATIONS APPROACH

Foundationalism went away once it was realized that one's beliefs are not structured via justification relations. Beliefs do not need justification unless there is a specific challenge to them. Some beliefs may be more 'central' than others—more theoretical, more taken for granted (in a way that needs more explication than I can provide). These more central beliefs will seem obvious, because it is hard to take seriously revising them, but they are not therefore guaranteed to be true and there will normally be circumstances in which such previously obvious beliefs will be revised.

There is no sharp, principled distinction between changing what one means and changing what one believes. We can, to be sure, consider how to translate between someone's language before and after a given change in view. If the best translation is the homophonic translation, we say there has been a change in doctrine; if some other (nonhomophonic) translation is better, we say there has been a change in meaning. What we say about this depends on context and our purposes of the moment.

6.3.1 *Definitions*

There are various kinds of definitions. Definitions in dictionaries try to capture ordinary meaning. Sometimes definitions are offered in the course of discussion in order to fix meanings. Sometimes this is a matter of making definite a term that is already in use, for example defining a metre in a certain way. Sometimes this is a matter of setting out a subject in a rigorous way, where there might be several different ways to proceed, for example defining numbers in terms of sets. Sometimes a new term is introduced for certain purposes.

No matter what sort of definition is in question, no long-term epistemological status for the definition is guaranteed. As time goes by, we may as easily modify a definition as change our belief in something else. And whether we will speak of change in meaning is not determined by whether we changed what was called a 'definition'.

What about the short term? Here definitions do have a privileged status, but it is a status that is shared by anything being assumed. If we agree that we are going to make certain assumptions, then for the time being we do not challenge those assumptions.

6.3.2 *A Rough, Serviceable, Commonsense Distinction?*

Grice and Strawson (1956) suggested that the analytic–synthetic distinction was an ordinary one, or at least that ordinary people could easily be brought to make it and understand it; whether or not we had an acceptable theoretical account of the distinction was another matter, they said. That was clearly wrong. Ordinary people do not make the distinction and it turns out to be hard to teach it to students, as they confuse it with all sorts of other distinctions. It turns out that someone could be taught to make the analytic–synthetic distinction only by being taught a rather substantial theory, a theory including such principles as that meaning can make something true and that knowledge of meaning can give knowledge of truth.

In Essay 5, I compare the analytic–synthetic distinction with the rough ordinary distinction made in historic Salem, Massachusetts, between witches and other women. The fact that people in Salem distinguished witches from other women did not show there was a real distinction. They were able to make the distinction they made only because they accepted a false theory along with some purported examples of witches. Similarly, people can make the analytic–synthetic distinction only if they accept the false analytic–synthetic theory along with purported examples of analytic truth.

This is the point at which it is relevant that many of the supposed analytic truths mentioned by philosophers are either false or easily imagined false—'Bachelors are always unmarried', 'Cats are animals', etc.

6.4 FINAL REMARK

The fact that once-paradigmatic analytic truths are false or easily imagined false shows that we do not have a priori insight into even what seem to be the clearest cases. This reinforces my main objections to armchair meta-physics of the sort defended by Jackson. The analyses that philosophers come up with do not appear to provide a priori connections of the required sort. Prospects for armchair metaphysics are therefore dim.

7

Analyticity Regained?

We can distinguish two issues about analyticity. First, is there a useful philosophical distinction between analytic and synthetic truths? Second, does analyticity help to explain a priori knowledge? Quine's 'Truth by Convention' (1936) provides a negative answer to the second question. His 'Two Dogmas of Empiricism' (1953c) offers a negative answer to the first.

Boghossian (1996) challenges both of Quine's answers. In the first part (7.1) of these comments, I discuss the issue of analyticity and a priori knowledge, saying what I take to be required for an analytic or semantic explanation of a priori knowledge, and I indicate how difficult it is to provide an adequate account of this sort. Then in the second part (7.2), I make some remarks about Boghossian's response to Quine's 'Two Dogmas of Empiricism'.

7.1 AN ANALYTIC THEORY OF THE A PRIORI?

7.1.1 Explaining Direct A Priori Knowledge

The apparent existence of direct a priori knowledge poses a problem for empiricism or scientific philosophy. A priori knowledge would be knowledge that is not directly knowledge of experience and does not depend for its justification on knowledge of experience. Knowledge of logical mathematical truths appears at least sometimes to be a priori knowledge in this sense, as does various other knowledge, for example, that if Jack is taller than Bob and Bob is taller than Sue, then Jack is taller than Sue; or that all uncles are male.

If there is any a priori knowledge, it is likely that some is derivative from other a priori knowledge. One knows something a priori through recognizing its relation to other things one knows a priori, for example, recognizing that it is implied by other things one knows a priori. But it would seem that some a priori knowledge would have to be direct and not derivative. One problem about a priori knowledge would be how to account for direct a priori knowledge in a way that is acceptable to a scientific philosophy, where brute appeal to direct insight, or intuition, or the memory of a stroll among Platonic Forms, is not acceptable to such a philosophy in the absence of a further explanation.

Might a purely semantic explanation of such knowledge be given? Can we say that direct a priori knowledge derives from one's knowledge of the meanings of words used to express that knowledge? If so, how?

It might be suggested that a priori knowledge that P could be based on something like the following argument:

(1) I know that expression S means that P.
(2) I know that if expression S means that P, expression S is true.
So, (3) I know that S is true.
(4) I know that S is true if and only if P.
So, (5) I know that P.

However, no argument of this or any other sort could account for *direct* a priori knowledge, because direct knowledge does not derive from the acceptance of any sort of argument from other things one knows.

If my direct a priori knowledge that P is to be explained by my knowledge of the meaning of S, then my knowledge of the meaning of S must already include my knowledge that P. How could that be so?

Linguistic conventionalism promises one way of answering this question. I am not aware of any other even remotely plausible proposals.

Here is a possible conventionalist answer. Everything I know is something represented either in language or in some other system of representation that I use for thought. The terms or symbols in a language or system of representation that I use have meaning by virtue of my conventions for the use of terms or symbols, i.e. by my intentions to use these terms or symbols in one or another way, including, for example, an intention to use my terms in such a way that S is true. But an intention to do something is or involves the belief that I will do it, and so in certain cases, including this one, involves the knowledge that I will do it. One does not infer that one will do something from one's intention to do it; rather, the intention includes that belief as an inseparable part, a belief not based on evidence of any sort.

In this view, in intending to use my terms in such a way that S is true, given the way I am using my terms, I know directly that S is true, given the way I am using my terms. Furthermore, my belief that S is true, given the way I am using my terms, is in this case (we need to suppose) constituted by my *using* S as a belief, that is, the belief that P. Given the way I am using my terms, in so using S, what I believe is that P. I have an immediate belief that P, not based on evidence, and in this context such a belief counts as knowledge. So, I know that P, where this knowledge is direct in the same way that in intentionally raising my hand I have direct knowledge that I am raising my hand.

This view relies on two assumptions: (A) that intentions can give one knowledge of what one is doing and (B) that sometimes a belief that S is true can be identified with the belief one has in accepting S and therefore with the belief that P.

It is an important question for this view how to explain a priori knowledge in such a way as not to count the knowledge that I am raising my hand, while counting my direct a priori knowledge that P. Perhaps it is relevant that there are conceivable circumstances in which I intend to be raising my hand but am not actually doing so, even though I may be having the illusion that I am raising my hand. In that case, although my intention may involve the belief that I am raising my hand, it does not involve the knowledge that I am raising my hand. But, in this view of direct a priori knowledge, there are no conceivable circumstances in which (a) I intend to be using my terms in such a way that S is true but (b) S is not true given the way I am using my terms.

In this view, then, my intention to use my terms in a certain way (i) makes S true and so (ii) gives me direct knowledge of the truth of S. Part (i) invokes what Boghossian calls a 'metaphysical' notion of analyticity—truth by virtue of meaning. Part (ii) invokes what he calls the 'epistemological' notion—knowledge of truth by virtue of knowledge of meaning. In this approach, the epistemological notion is not independent of the metaphysical notion, as Boghossian says it must be. Indeed, the epistemological explanation depends on the metaphysical explanation.

Boghossian suggests that we must accept the following equivalence:

S is true if and only if for some P, S means that P and P.

Let us ignore some obvious (and quite serious) problems: (1) it is unclear how to interpret this quantification over sentence position and (2) the suggested equivalence cannot be correct since it leads immediately to the liar paradox.

Boghossian allows that my intention might make it the case that S means that P, but asks how that could 'make it the case that S is true. Doesn't it also have to be the case that P?' The answer, in the view sketched, is that in the first instance my intention makes it the case that S is true and in the second place that fact about my intention (is part of what of what) makes it the case that S means that P, where it is the case that P. This view has no commitment whatsoever as to what makes it the case that P.

7.1.2 *Derivative A Priori Knowledge*

As suggested above, if there is any a priori knowledge, some is derivative from other a priori knowledge. One knows something through directly recognizing its relation to other things one knows a priori, for example, directly recognizing that it is implied by other things one knows a priori, where the direct recognition of this relation must itself be a priori.

If we apply the same strategy to this direct recognition of a particular implication (say), then we must suppose that the conventions that give meanings to one's terms include, for each such implication, the intention that the implication holds. However, it seems that one does not and cannot have separate particular intentions for each such implication one can recognize, since one can recognize indefinitely many. One has to make do with general intentions, for example, the intention that all instances of modus ponens are to be implicative, as one is using the conditional construction 'if . . . then'.

But then Quine's objections apply. The intentions that are assumed to give meaning to one's logical terms, such as 'if . . . then', make use of and so presuppose those or equivalent logical notions. It then becomes obscure how such general intentions can give one the needed *direct* knowledge of their instances.

For example, suppose one recognizes as an implication a complex instance of modus ponens: *P* and *if P, then Q* imply Q. Suppose further that this recognition is not based on a specific intention concerning that very instance but is based on the more general intention that all instances of modus ponens are to be implicative. Then one's recognition of that implication derives from one's acceptance of the following argument:

(1) *P* and *if P, then Q* stand in the modus ponens relation to Q.
(2) For all X, Y, and Z, if X and Y stand in the modus ponens relation to Z, then X and Y imply Z.
(3) If (*P* and *if P, then Q* stand in the modus ponens relation to Q) then (*P* and *if P, then Q* imply Q).
So, (4) *P* and *if P, then Q* imply Q.

Ignore the question of how (1) is recognized. Step (2) is a usable version of the intended result that all instances of modus ponens are to be implicative.

Step (3) is implied by (2), the implication presumably mediated by the intention that generalizations imply their instances.

But how am I supposed to recognize that (4) is implied by the preceding steps? The step from (1) and (3) to (4) is an instance of modus ponens. So the recognition of the one modus ponens implication requires the recognition of a more complex modus ponens implication, which in turn will require the recognition of a still more complex modus ponens implication. And so on in a vicious infinite regress.

How is the regress to be avoided? Clearly, I need to do more than adopt a general intention to use 'if . . . then' in such a way that instances of modus ponens are to be implicative. I must also acquire a disposition directly to accept such instances as implicative. Boghossian favours this move. Quine (1936) explicitly considers it but objects, correctly, that treating such a general disposition as a convention deprives the notion of convention of any explanatory force.

Notice that, if the point is to account for derived a priori knowledge, the central issue is not 'How do we distinguish those dispositions that give meaning to our terms from those that do not?' The issue is how our having such dispositions might account for our having direct knowledge of certain implications in the way, for example, that our having certain intentions might account for our having direct knowledge of what we are doing.

7.2 BOGHOSSIAN ON 'TWO DOGMAS'

7.2.1 *The Rise and Fall of the Analytic–Synthetic Distinction*

Despite the failure of the analytic theory of a priori knowledge, the analytic–synthetic distinction was widely deployed as an important philosophical tool through much of the twentieth century until the middle 1960s. Analytic philosophers tried to show why certain claims were necessarily true and/or knowable a priori without appeal to exotic realms of being or special faculties of intuition, by providing analyses of key terms that would show the claims in question to be tautologies, equivalent by definition or analysis to logical truths.

During this period, philosophers of a speculative bent were sometimes asked, 'Is your claim supposed to be analytic or synthetic?' This was a trick question, because if the speculative claim was supposed to be analytic, then it was shown to be a trivial tautology, whereas if it was supposed to be synthetic, then it was shown to be a substantive matter to be decided by empirical research that is outside the reach of philosophy.

Quine's paper, 'Two Dogmas of Empiricism', questioned whether it was possible to make any useful analytic–synthetic distinction in an acceptably scientific way. Although few philosophers were converted to Quinean scepticism about the distinction at first, there followed an intense exploration of the issue in which numerous attempts to defend the distinction proved ineffective. By the late 1960s, opinions had shifted to the extent that philosophers of an analytic bent came to fear the challenge, 'Aren't you assuming the analytic–synthetic distinction?'

The change in philosophical climate was not an immediate consequence of the publication of 'Two Dogmas of Empiricism'. So it is a mistake to suppose that this change can be understood or assessed simply by analysing that important paper taken just by itself. The ensuing discussion was equally important in showing that a certain philosophical line was not sustainable.

7.2.2 *Indeterminacy of Meaning and Indeterminacy of Translation*

Consider a formulation of a scientific theory that uses a number of theoretical terms in order to present the basic principles of the theory. Perhaps the role of these terms in this statement of the theory determines their meanings. But it is unclear that we objectively distinguish the analytic principles of the theory or 'meaning postulates', which hold by definition, from the synthetic principles. We might on one occasion treat certain principles as definitional and others as substantive. But this is a matter of presentation. On another occasion we might count the latter principles as definitional and the former as substantive without any change in meaning. In this respect, we can say the rejection of the analytic–synthetic distinction involves accepting a kind of indeterminacy of meaning. To reject the analytic–synthetic distinction is to hold that it is objectively indeterminate which principles are true by virtue of meaning and which are substantive.

'Two Dogmas of Empiricism' is largely a critique of proposals by Carnap. Carnap replies in 'Meaning and Synonymy in Natural Language' (Carnap, 1956). Quine responds in turn in chapter 2 of *Word and Object* (Quine, 1960*b*) which introduces Quine's thesis of the indeterminacy of radical translation. The thesis is that, among the objectively best schemes for translating sentences of another language into one's own, we can expect to find a sentence of the other language that is translated into a sentence S of our language by one such scheme and a sentence T of our language by another such scheme, although we suppose that S is true if and only if T is not true.

Whether the thesis of the indeterminacy of radical translation is to be accepted depends on what count as the objective criteria of good translation. Quine's own criteria are sufficiently limited to support his thesis. If additional criteria are allowed—for example, try to translate short expressions in the other language with short expressions in our own language—the thesis is not obviously true (see Essay 10, below).

I do not want to get into a discussion of the thesis of the indeterminacy of radical translation, except to point out that it is distinct from the thesis of the indeterminacy of meaning that is involved in rejecting the analytic–synthetic distinction.

Boghossian's terminology is unfortunate. He says, '[T]here can be no effective Quinean critique of the a priori that does not ultimately depend on Quine's radical thesis of the indeterminacy of meaning, a thesis that, as I've stressed, many philosophers continue to reject'. The phrase 'radical thesis of the indeterminacy of meaning' suggests the thesis of the indeterminacy of radical translation, and a supporting quotation Boghossian gives from Lycan specifically mentions the thesis of the indeterminacy of radical translation. But the conclusion of Boghossian's argument refers instead to the sort of indeterminacy of meaning that is an immediate consequence of the analytic–synthetic distinction,

if there is no fact of the matter as to which of the various inferences involving a constant are meaning constituting, then there is also no fact of the matter as to what the logical constants themselves mean. And that is just the dreaded indeterminacy of meaning on which the critique of analyticity was supposed not to depend.

This last indeterminacy is an obvious consequence of the critique of analyticity. The issue Boghossian begins by raising seems to be whether that critique is independent of the thesis of the indeterminacy of radical translation, but his ultimate answer is a trivial answer to a different question.

7.2.3 *Frege-Analyticity and the Synthetic A Priori*

Explaining that a statement is Frege-analytic if it is 'transformable into a logical truth by the substitution of synonyms for synonyms', Boghossian adds, 'there do appear to be a significant number of a priori statements that are not Frege-analytic'. His examples are:

> Whatever is red all over is not blue.
> Whatever is coloured is extended.

If X is warmer than Y, then Y is not warmer than X.

One more or less familiar response to such examples by opponents of the (Frege)-synthetic a priori is that the examples can be transformed into logical truths by substituting synonyms as follows: 'red all over' is synonymous with 'red all over and not blue', 'coloured' is synonymous with 'coloured and extended', and 'X is warmer than Y' is synonymous with 'X is warmer than Y and Y is not warmer than X'.

As far as I can see, Boghossian ought to accept those synonymies. He says that '"All bachelors are male" does seem to be transformable into a logical truth by the substitution of synonyms for synonyms', and it is unclear what synonyms he might have in mind apart from the thought that 'bachelor' is synonymous with 'male bachelor'. It is well known that 'bachelor' as ordinarily used in English is not easily analysed, for example, as 'unmarried adult male', because ordinary speakers of English are not willing to count as a bachelor the Pope, or a man who has lived with a woman for several years without getting married, etc.

But, of course, if such 'synonymies' count, then it is obvious that all a priori truths are Frege-analytic! And, if they do not count, what is the criterion of synonymy?

7.2.4 *Different Senses of a Word*

The word 'bank' has several senses. A given occurrence of the word may be intended to have one or another of these senses and two occurrences of the word may or may not have the same sense. Boghossian argues that this much understanding of the sameness of sense of word tokens is enough for the sort of synonymy required for Frege-analyticity.

The suggestion is clearly inadequate. A word with different senses is for present purposes indistinguishable from a set of homonyms—different words that sound the same or are written in the same way. Distinguishing words in this way, we can say that tokens have the same sense if they are instances of the same word. That is not enough for the sort of sameness of sense involved in Frege-analyticity, where what is needed is to replace one or more expressions with different expressions.

7.2.5 *Stipulative Definitions as Assumptions*

It seems that we can create some synonymy and so some Frege-analyticity simply by defining some new terminology. Boghossian notes that this appears to refute any total rejection of Frege-analyticity.

However, as Quine observes in several places, stipulative definition cannot really serve to ground Frege-analyticity. The problem is that stipulative definition is a momentary thing, of no significance in the long term. In presenting a theory we can introduce the same terminology in different ways on different occasions, without any apparent effect on the meanings of our terms. Furthermore, as our views change in the face of new evidence, we are as willing to abandon what used to be a definition as any other theoretical principle, with the same sort of effect on meaning in either case.

To put the point somewhat differently, stipulative definitions are assumptions. To give a definition is to say 'Let's assume for the time being that the following equivalence holds'. The epistemological force of a stipulative definition is the same as the epistemological force of an assumption. While an assumption is in force, it is impolite to challenge it; so too, while the stipulative definition is in force, it is impolite to challenge it. But, after a while, we can look at where we have got to and, at that point, we might very well give up any assumption, including stipulative definitions, without any more change in meaning than what is involved in any other change in view.

The key point with respect to analyticity is that, just as assuming something is not a way of coming to know that it is so, defining two expressions to be equivalent is not by itself a way of coming to know that the equivalence holds. 'True by stipulative definition' is like 'true by assumption': just as something that is assumed to be true can turn out not to be true, something that is true by stipulative definition can turn out not to be true either.

Finally, this is what's *really* wrong with the analytic theory of the a priori. Even if the meanings of my words derive from my intentions as to how to use them, these intentions cannot be distinguished from postulates or other substantive assumptions with respect to their ability to make sentences true and so cannot be distinguished from postulates or other substantive assumptions with respect to their ability to provide a priori knowledge.

PART III

Meaning

8

Three Levels of Meaning

Philosophers approach the theory of meaning in at least three different ways. First, Carnap, Ayer, Lewis, Firth, Hempel, Sellars, Quine, etc. take meaning to be connected with evidence and inference, a function of the place an expression has in one's 'conceptual scheme' or of its role in some inferential 'language game'. Second, Morris, Stevenson, Grice, Katz, etc. take meaning to be a matter of the idea, thought, feeling, or emotion that an expression can be used to communicate. Third, Wittgenstein (?), Austin, Hare, Nowell-Smith, Searle, Alston, etc. take meaning to have something to do with the speech acts the expression can be used to perform. (A fourth approach, which emphasizes truth conditions, is discussed in several of the following essays, particularly Essay 11.)

8.1 FAMILIAR OBJECTIONS TO EACH TYPE OF THEORY

8.1.1 *Meaning as Conceptual Role*

Theories of the first sort, which take meaning to be specified by inferential and observational evidential considerations, are sometimes accused of ignoring the social aspect of language. Such theories, it is said, admit the possibility of a private language in which one might express thoughts without being able to communicate them to another; and this possibility is held to be absurd. More generally, it has been argued that even if meaning depends on considerations of evidential connection, the relevant notion of evidence involves intersubjective objectivity, which requires the possibility of communication among several people. Therefore it is argued that one could not account for meaning via the notion of evidence without also discussion of meaning in communication.

Furthermore, there are many uses of language to which the notion of evidence has no application. If one asks a question or gives an order, it is not appropriate to look for the evidence for what has been said. But if there can be no evidence for a question, in the way that there can be evidence for a conclusion, differences in meaning of different questions cannot be explicated by means of differences in what evidence can be relevant to such questions. So theories of the first sort seem vulnerable in several respects.

8.1.2 *Meaning as Communicated Thought*

On the other hand, theories of the second sort are threatened by circularity from at least two directions. According to Katz (1966*b*), one understands the words someone else says by decoding them into the corresponding thought or idea. But a person ordinarily thinks in words, often the same words he communicates with and the same words others use when they communicate with him. Surely the words mean the same thing when used in these different ways? But to apply Katz's account of meaning to the words one thinks with would seem at best to take us in a circle.

Similarly, consider Grice's theory of meaning. According to Grice (1957, 1969), one means that P by one's words (in communication) if and only if one uses them with the intention of getting one's listener to think one thinks that P. But what is it to think that P? On one plausible view it is to think certain words (or some other representations) by which one means that P. If so, Grice's analysis would seem to be circular: one means that P by one's words if and only if one uses them with the intention of getting one's listener to think one has done something by which one means that P.

Circularity and worse also threaten from another side, if the second type of approach is intended to explain what it is to promise to do something or if it is supposed to be adequate to exhibit the difference between asking someone to do something and telling him to do it, etc. The fact that saying something in a particular context constitutes one or another speech act cannot be represented simply as the speaker's communicating certain thoughts. For example, promising to do something is not simply communicating that you intend to do it, nor is asking (or telling) someone to do something simply a matter of communicating your desire that he do it. At the very least, to perform one or another speech act, one must communicate that one is intending to be performing that act; so, at the very least, to treat all speech acts as cases of communication would involve the same sort of circularity already mentioned. Furthermore, communication of one's intention to be performing a given speech act is not in general sufficient for success. The speaker may not be in a position to promise or to tell someone to do something, no matter what his intentions and desires.

8.1.3 *Meaning as Speech-Act Potential*

Finally, theories of the third sort, which treat meaning as speech-act potential, are also subject to familiar objections. For example, Chomsky (1964, 1966), following Humboldt, argues that this third approach (and probably the second as well) ignores the 'creative aspect of language use'. Language exists primarily for the free expression of thought. Communication and other social uses of language are, according to Chomsky, of only secondary importance.

One of the most important characteristics of human language is its unbounded character. Almost anything that one says has never been said by anyone before. Surely this unboundedness reflects the unbounded creative character of thought and is not simply a reflection of the more or less practical uses to which language can be put in a social context.

Furthermore, approaches of the third sort seem to be at least as afflicted with circularity as are approaches of the second sort. For example, Alston (1964) suggests defining sameness of meaning as sameness of illocutionary-act potential, where illocutionary acts are the relevant subclass of speech acts. He claims that two expressions have the same meaning if and only if they can be used to perform the same illocutionary acts. Now, suppose we ask whether the expressions 'water' and 'H_2O' have the same meaning. They do only if, for example, in saying 'Please pass the water' one performs the same illocutionary act as one does in saying 'Please pass the H_2O'. But it can be argued that we are able to decide whether these acts are the same only by first deciding whether the expressions 'water' and 'H_2O' have the same meaning. If so, Alston's proposal is circular.

8.2 THREE LEVELS OF MEANING

Each of the preceding objections is based on the assumption that the three approaches to the theory of meaning are approaches to the same thing. I suggest that this assumption is false. Theories of meaning may attempt to do any of three different things. One theory might attempt to explain what it is for a thought to be a thought of a certain sort with a given content. Another might attempt to explain what it takes to communicate certain information. A third might offer an account of speech acts. As theories of language, the first would offer an account of the use of language (or other representations) in thinking; the second, an account of the use of language in communication; the third, an account of the use of language in certain institutions, rituals, or practices of a group of speakers.

I shall refer to theories of meaning of level 1, of level 2, and of level 3, respectively. I believe that there is a sense in which later levels presuppose earlier ones. Thus a theory of level 2, i.e. a theory of communication (of thoughts), presupposes a theory of level 1 concerning the nature of thoughts. Similarly, a theory of level 3 (e.g. an account of promising) must almost always presuppose a theory of level 2 (since in promising one must communicate what it is one has promised to do).

The objections I have just discussed show only that a theory of one level does not provide a good theory of another level. A theory of the nature and content of thoughts does not provide a good account of communication. A theory of meaning in communication does not provide a good account of speech acts. And so forth. On the other hand, I do not want to deny that proponents of the various theories have occasionally been confused about their objectives. In the third section of this essay I shall argue that such confusion has led to mistakes in all three types of theory.

But first, from the point of view of the suggested distinctions between such levels of meaning, I shall briefly review the three approaches to the theory of meaning sketched at the beginning of this paper.

8.2.1 *Level 1*

A theory of level 1 attempts to explain what it is to think that P, what it is to believe that P, to desire that P, etc. Let us suppose we are concerned only with thinking done in language. Such a supposition will not affect the argument so long as thinking makes use of some system of representation, whether or not the system is properly part of any natural language.

Even if we do not know what the various expressions of a subject's language mean, we can still describe him as having thoughts, beliefs, desires, and other psychological states. It seems reasonable to assume that the subject has the thought that P if and only if he thinks certain words or other representations that have on this occasion the meaning or content that P; he believes that P if and only if his belief involves a sentence or other representation that has the content that P; and similarly for desires and other psychological attitudes. The problem of saying what it is to think, believe, desire, etc. that P can be reduced to the problem of saying what it is for certain words or other representations used in thinking to have the content that P.

Another way to put the same point is this. A theory of the nature of thought, belief, desire, and other psychological attitudes can appear in the guise of the theory of meaning or content. That is the best way to interpret the first sort of theory discussed at the beginning of this paper. Extreme positivists claim that the content of a thought, i.e. what thought it is, is determined by its conditions of verification and refutation. Its meaning or content is determined by the observational conditions under which the subject would acquire the corresponding belief plus those conditions under which he would acquire the corresponding disbelief. Other empiricists argue that what a thought is or means is determined by its position in a whole structure of thoughts and other psychological attitudes, i.e. its place in a subject's conceptual scheme, including not only relations to experience but also relations to other things in that same scheme.

Several philosophers have argued a similar thesis that makes no explicit reference to meaning or content. Fodor (1965), Putnam (1960), and Scriven (1966) have each taken psychological states to be 'functional states' of the human organism. What is important about such states is not how they are realized; for my psychological states may well be realized in a different neurophysiological way from yours. What is important is that there is a certain relationship among the various states a person can be in, between such states and observational 'input', and between such states and action 'output'. In this regard persons are sometimes compared with non-deterministic automata (Miller, Galanter, and Pribram, 1960). Just as a particular program or flow chart may be instantiated by various automata made from quite different materials, so too the 'same' person (a person with the same psychological characteristics and dispositions) might be instantiated by different neurophysiological set-ups and perhaps even by some robot made of semiconductors, printed circuits, etc. For a person to be in a particular psychological state is like the automaton's being at a certain point in its program or flow chart rather than like something's happening at one or another transistor.

If we conceive the automaton's operation to consist largely in the formation, transfer, and 'storage' of certain representations, the analogy is even better. To say that such an automaton is at a certain point in a particular program is to say, first, that the automaton has various possible states related to one another and to input and output in such a way that it instantiates a particular program and, second, that it is in a particular one of the states or collections so indicated. For the automaton in question, the same point can be made by first specifying the role of various representations it uses in its internal operation, its reaction to input, and its influence on output. Second, one may describe the present state of the automaton by indicating what representations are where (Harman, 1967a, 1968).

It is obvious how such an account may offer a functional account of psychological states via a person's use of language. Thus, according to Sellars (1963), the meanings of one's words are determined by the role of the words in an evidence-inference-action game, which includes the influence of observation on thought, the influence of thought on thought in inference, and the influence of thought on action via decision and intention. Sellars offers a functional account of psychological states in the guise of a theory of meaning. (Sellars, 1974, explicitly agrees.)

It is important that the analogy be with nondeterministic rather than deterministic automata. According to Sellars, the meaning of an expression is given by its role in the evidence-inference-action game, where this role is not causal but rather defined in terms of possible (i.e., more or less legitimate) moves that can be made. A similar point would have to be accepted by anyone who would identify psychological states with functional states (Harman, 1973: 51–3).

Quine's thesis of indeterminacy, discussed above in Essay 5, says that, functionally defined, the content of a thought is not uniquely determined. The thesis ought to be expressible directly as the following claim about instantiations of nondeterministic automata: when a set of possible states of some device can be interpreted in a particular way as instantiations of a given nondeterministic automaton, that interpretation will not in general be the only way to interpret those physical states as instantiations of the given automaton.

I hope I have said enough to show how theories of the first sort may be treated as theories about the nature of the contents of thoughts and other psychological ('intentional') states.

8.2.2 *Level 2*

A theory of level 2 attempts to say what communication is and what is involved in a message's having a particular meaning. Communication is communication of thoughts and ideas; and Katz's description of it (1966b) is perfectly acceptable provided that his talk about 'decoding' is not taken too literally. It is true that Katz's description of communication would have us explain meaning in terms of meaning; but the two sorts of meaning are different. Katz would have us explain the meaning of a message in terms of the meaning or content of a thought, which is to explain meaning of level 2 in terms of meaning of level 1. And there is nothing wrong with that. Similarly, Grice's theory of meaning avoids the charge of circularity by explaining the meaning of a message (what the speaker means) in terms of the content of the thought communicated (which the speaker intends the hearer to think the speaker has).

Communication need not involve use of language. When it does, the language used need not be one either speaker or hearer is able to think in. And even when the language used is one both participants think in, it may (for the purposes of certain communications) be used arbitrarily as a code. But ordinary communication makes use of a language which both participants think in and which is not being used arbitrarily as a code. In such a case the hearer typically assigns, as his interpretation of what the speaker says, either (a) a thought that the hearer expresses using the same words the speaker has used (with possible minor modification, e.g. for first- and second-person in pronouns) or (b) a thought that is some simple function of a thought in those words, where the function is determined by context (e.g. irony). Similarly, the speaker standardly uses in communication (almost) the same words he uses in expressing to himself the thought he intends to communicate. This is no accident, and one will fail to understand the nature of linguistic communication unless one grasps this point. It is obscured when linguistic communication is described as if it involved processes of coding and decoding. We would not be able to use language in communication as we do if communication really involved coding and decoding.

Similarly, it would be a mistake to treat learning one's first language as simply a matter of learning how to communicate one's thoughts to others and how to understand others when they attempt to communicate. When a child is exposed to language he acquires two things. First he acquires a new system of representation for use in thinking and in the formation of various psychological attitudes. This is the primary thing he acquires. Second he acquires the ability, alluded to above, to communicate with and understand other speakers of the language. This ability relies heavily on the fact that the language has been acquired as an instrument of thought. No very complicated principles of interpretation need to be learned to support this ability. All the child needs to do, at first, is to assume that other speakers express by their words thoughts the child would think using those same words. More complicated principles of interpretation are learned later to allow for lying, irony, metaphor, etc. But it would surely be a mistake to think of the child as having an ability to perform a certain sort of complicated decoding.

Aside from that point, I hope it is now clear how, for example, Grice's theory may be treated as a promising attempt at a level 2 theory of meaning; and I hope it is clear why it should not be criticized for failing to do what can be done only by a theory of meaning of another level.

8.2.3 *Level 3*

A theory of level 3 would be a theory of social institutions, games, practices, etc. The theory would explain how the existence of such things can make certain acts possible, for example, how the existence of a game of football can make possible scoring a touchdown or how the existence of an institution of banking can make possible writing a cheque. In a sense such a theory is a theory of meaning. The game or institution confers meaning on an act like carrying a ball to a certain place or writing one's name on a piece of paper.

Some institutions, games, practices, etc. involve the use of language and can therefore confer meaning (significance) on such uses of language. But this is a different sort of meaning from that involved in levels 1 and 2. And, typically, use of certain words within an institution, practice, or game presupposes that the words have meaning as a message (which standardly presupposes that they have meaning when used to express one's thoughts). Despite the priority of levels 1 and 2, meaning on those levels can sometimes presuppose meaning on level 3, but only because one can think and communicate about practices, games, and institutions.

8.3 APPLICATIONS

Distinguishing between the three levels of meaning can clarify many issues in philosophy and linguistics. In this final section, I shall briefly give some examples.

8.3.1 *Private Language and Other Verbal Issues*

The distinction of levels tends to dissolve as verbal certain philosophical worries about what has to be true before someone can be said to use a language. One may use a system of representation in thinking, without being able to use it in communication or speech acts. Children and animals presumably do so, and perhaps some computers may also be said to do so. Similarly, one may use a system of representation in thought and communication without being able to engage in more sophisticated speech acts. (Compare computers that 'communicate' with a user or programmer.) Whether communication or more sophisticated speech acts must be possible before one's system of representation counts as a language can only be a purely verbal issue.

A special case of this issue would be the philosophical question whether there can be a private language. For the issue is simply whether there could be a language used to think in but not to communicate with. There can be a system of representation with such properties; whether it should count as a language is a purely verbal issue. On the other hand, Wittgenstein's private language argument may be directed against a conception of language learning and of the use of language in communication similar to that put forward in transformational linguistics by Katz and Fodor, among others. I shall argue below that this conception is based on failure to distinguish levels of meaning.

8.3.2 *Clarifying Philosophical Theories*

The distinction can be used to help clarify various philosophical accounts of meaning. For example, chapter 2 of *Word and Object* (Quine, 1960*b*) presents considerations mainly relevant to level 1 theories of meaning. But by describing language as a set of dispositions to verbal behaviour, Quine suggests wrongly that he is concerned with communication or more sophisticated speech acts. And this occasionally leads him wrong. He describes the thesis of indeterminacy as the view that a speaker's sentences might be mapped onto themselves in various ways without affecting his dispositions to 'verbal behaviour'. So stated the thesis would be obviously wrong. A conversation containing one sentence would be mapped onto one containing another. Dispositions to verbal behaviour would therefore change under the mappings in question. But Quine is actually interested in only one particular sort of verbal behaviour: assent or dissent to a sentence. And his position would be even clearer if he had entirely avoided the behaviouristic formulation and spoken instead about a speaker's accepting as true (or accepting as false) various sentences.

Grice (1957) presents a level 2 theory of meaning. But later (Grice, 1969) he is troubled by two difficulties: (a) difficulties in accounting for the difference between telling someone one wishes him to do something and ordering him to do it, and (b) difficulties in accounting for meaning something by one's words in silent thought. But (a) can be handled only within a level 3 theory and (b) can be handled only within a level 1 theory. The former point is obscured by Grice's formulation of the notion to be analysed: 'U meant X by uttering.' The locution is at least three ways ambiguous. It may mean (i) that X is the message conveyed by U's uttering Y, (ii) that U intended to say X when he said Y, or (iii) that U really meant it when he said X; i.e. he uttered Y with no fingers crossed, not ironically, not in jest, etc. Grice does not make clear exactly which of these interpretations we are to assign to the locution he is analysing. A theory of communication results if the interpretation is (i). If (ii) were the correct interpretation, Grice's analysis of meaning in terms of the speaker's intentions would be trivialized.

Alston (1964) presents a level 3 theory of meaning. But he believes that such a theory must account for sameness of meaning of linguistic expressions. I have argued above that this cannot be done. We cannot define sameness of meaning of expressions as sameness of illocutionary-act potential. Sameness of meaning is to be accounted for, if at all, within a level 1 theory. Given a theory of level 1, we might hope to define sameness of meaning (i.e. significance) of illocutionary acts via sameness of meaning of linguistic expressions. None of this shows that meaning cannot be approached via speech acts, as long as it is understood what sort of theory of meaning a theory of speech acts is.

8.3.3 *Criticizing Katz and Fodor*

The distinction between levels of meaning can be used to criticize an important aspect of Katz and Fodor's (1964) semantic theory. They claim that an adequate semantic theory must show how the meaning of a sentence is determined by its grammatical structure and the meaning of its lexical items. They say that such a theory must specify the form of dictionary entries for lexical items and must say how such entries are combined, on the basis of grammatical structure, in order to give readings of sentences.

I believe that these claims are the direct result of failure to distinguish a theory of the meaning of language as it is used in thinking from a theory of the meaning of a message, plus a failure to recognize that in the standard case one communicates with a language one thinks in. Thus at first Katz and Fodor purport to be describing the structure of a theory of linguistic communication. They are impressed by the fact that a speaker has the ability to produce and understand sentences he has never previously encountered. As a result, they treat communication as involving a complex process of coding and decoding where readings are assigned to sentences on the basis of grammatical structure and dictionary entries. That this is a mistake has already been noted above. In normal linguistic communication a message is interpreted as expressing the thought (or some simple function of that thought) that is expressed by the same words the message is in.

The fact that a speaker can produce and understand novel sentences is a direct consequence of the facts that he can think novel thoughts and that he thinks in the same language he communicates in. One gives an account of the meaning of words as they are used in thinking by giving an account of their use in the evidence-inference-action game. For a speaker to understand certain words, phrases, and sentences of his language is for him to be able to use them in thinking, etc. It is not at all a matter of his assigning readings to the words, for to assign a reading to an expression is simply to correlate words with words. (I am oversimplifying. There is further discussion in Essays 9 and 10, below.)

Katz and Fodor do have some sense of the distinction between levels 1 and 2. Although their theory is put forward as if it were an account of communication, they describe it as a theory of meanings a sentence has when taken in isolation from its possible settings in linguistic discourse. They do this in order to avoid having to take into account special 'readings' due to codes, figurative uses of language, etc. Their theory of meaning is restricted to giving an account of the meaning of a message for that case in which the message communicates the thought that is expressed in the same words as those in which the message is expressed. They recognize that another theory would have to account for the interpretation that is assigned when a sentence occurs in a particular context.

In a way this amounts to distinguishing my levels 1 and 2. And in a sense Katz and Fodor attempt to provide a theory of level 1. More accurately, their theory falls between levels 1 and 2. It cannot provide a level 1 theory, since a speaker does not understand the words he uses in thinking by assigning readings to them. It cannot provide a level 2 theory, since it treats a relatively simple problem of interpretation as if it were much more complicated.

Analogous objections can be raised against Ziff (1960), and against theories like Davidson's (1967*b*) that attempt to account for meaning in terms of truth conditions (see the following essay).

In this essay I have distinguished three levels in the theory of meaning corresponding to the meaning of thoughts, the meaning of messages, and the meaning of speech acts. I have argued that distinguishing these levels helps to clarify three well-known approaches to the theory of meaning and reveals certain deficiencies in Katz and Fodor's semantics.

9

Language, Thought, and Communication

I shall discuss two apparently conflicting views about our use of natural language. The first view, that language is used primarily in thought, has rarely been given explicit formulation but may be associated with the theories of Noam Chomsky, W. V. Quine, and Wilfrid Sellars. The second view, that language is used primarily in communication, has been explicitly put forward by J. A. Fodor and J. J. Katz and may also be associated (I think) with the theories of Paul Ziff and Donald Davidson. I shall describe each view and then try to say where I think the truth lies.

9.1 THE VIEW THAT LANGUAGE IS USED PRIMARILY IN THOUGHT

Chomsky (1964) takes the primary function of language to be its use in the free expression of thought. He speaks approvingly of Humboldt's emphasis on the connection between language and thought, especially the way in which a particular language brings with it a world view that colours perception, thought, and feeling. According to Chomsky's description of Humboldt's view, to have a language is to have a system of concepts,

and it is the place of a concept within this system (which may differ somewhat from speaker to speaker) that in part, determines the way in which the hearer understands a linguistic expression . . . [T]he concepts so formed are systematically interrelated in an 'inner totality', with varying interconnections and structural relations . . . This inner totality, formed by the use of language in thought, conception, and expression of feeling, functions as a conceptual world interposed through the constant activity of the mind between itself and the actual objects, and it is within this system that a word obtains its value . . . Consequently, a language should not be regarded merely, or primarily, as a means of communication . . . and the instrumental use of language (its use for achieving concrete aims) is derivative and subsidiary. It is, for Humboldt, typical only of parasitic systems (e.g. . . . the lingua franca along the Mediterranean coast). (1964: 58–9)

Now this view, that language is used primarily in thought, need not imply that all or even most thinking or theorizing is in some natural language. We may reasonably suppose that animals think, that children can think before they learn a natural language, and that speakers of a natural language can have thoughts they cannot express in language. The view is, rather, that anyone who fully learns a natural language can and does sometimes think in that language. More precisely, it is that some of a speaker's so-called propositional attitudes are to be construed as, at bottom, attitudes involving sentences of her language. A speaker of English may believe that the door is open by using the sentence, 'The door is open'. Another may fear that the door is open by being in a state of fear that involves that sentence. A third may think of the door's being open by adopting an appropriate attitude involving the sentence.

Strictly speaking, sentential attitudes involve sentences with one or another more or less detailed grammatical analysis. I shall return to this point near the end of this essay. For now, I shall speak loosely of sentential attitudes as attitudes involving sentences. (This is not to say that they are attitudes *toward* sentences. They are not attitudes *about* sentences. See Essay 14, below, on this distinction.)

In this view, linguistic communication is the communication of thought. The parties involved typically communicate using the same language they use in thinking. The words used to communicate a thought are the same as those one 'says to oneself' when one has that thought. Linguistic communication does not typically require any complicated system of coding and decoding. Our usual translation scheme for understanding others is the identity relation. Words are used to communicate thoughts that would ordinarily be thought in those very words. It is true that allowance must sometimes be made for irony and other such devices; but in that case the thought communicated is some simple function of what would be normally communicated by a literal use of those words.

More precisely, linguistic communication typically involves communication of what is sometimes called 'propositional content'. A speaker says, 'The door is shut', 'Shut the door', 'Is the door shut?' or some such thing. He does so in part to get his hearer to think of the door's being shut. This first view holds that in such a situation, if communication is successful, the hearer will think of the door's being shut by adopting a state of mind that consists in part in a token of the sentence, 'The door is shut'. There is no claim that a person can think of the door's being shut *only* by using the sentence, 'The door is shut'. There are various ways in which a person might think of the door's being shut. But, normally, when a speaker successfully communicates in English by saying, 'The door is shut', etc., both speaker and hearer think of the door's being shut by using the English sentence, 'The door is shut'.

Even more precisely, sentential attitudes involve sentences with particular grammatical analyses. It is sufficient that the hearer should use the sentence uttered with the appropriate analysis. In this sense, linguistic communication does not typically make use of complex principles of coding and decoding and our usual translation scheme is the identity scheme. The hearer need only hear the sentence uttered as having the appropriate structural description and does not need to go on to translate the sentence, under that analysis, into anything else in order to understand it.

Proponents of the view that language is primarily used in thought can point out that, although one *can* use a natural language as a code, so that one's listeners would have to use complicated principles of decoding in order to understand what has been said, that is not an ordinary case of linguistic communication. They can also point out that, when a person learns a second language, she may at first have to treat the new language as a code; but hopefully the person soon learns to think directly in the second language and to communicate with other speakers of that language in the ordinary way, which does not involve complex coding and decoding or translation.

Furthermore, proponents can say, when a person thinks out loud, it is not always true that she has to find a linguistic way to express something that exists apart from language. Without language many thoughts and other psychological attitudes would not even be possible. In learning her first natural language, a child does not simply learn a code which she can use in communicating her thoughts to others and in decoding what they say. She acquires a system of representation in which she may express thoughts made possible by that very system. This is obvious when one acquires for the first time the language of a science or of mathematics. The claim is that it is no less true when one learns one's first natural language.

We now have a rough sketch of the view that language is used primarily in thought, I shall say more about that view below. Now I want to describe the apparently conflicting theory that communication provides the primary use of language.

9.2 THE VIEW THAT LANGUAGE IS USED PRIMARILY IN COMMUNICATION

A *compositional theory of meaning* holds that a hearer determines what the meaning of an utterance is on the basis of her knowledge of the meaning of its parts and her knowledge of its syntactic structure. Such a view follows naturally from the picture of communication that takes it to involve complex coding and decoding. On that picture, to understand (the meaning of) a sentence is to know what (nonverbal) thought or thoughts the sentence encodes. Meanings are identified with the relevant thoughts. Hence the view is that to know the meaning of an expression is to know what meaning, i.e. thought, the code associates with that sentence. In this view, a general theory of meaning of a language is given by the principles of the code that defines the sound–meaning correspondence for the language. Because of the unbounded nature of language, these principles would have to be compositional or recursive.

The rules of coding and decoding are to be given by a grammar in a wide sense of this term. The grammar has three components, a syntactic component that connects a phonological component with a semantic component. And as Katz describes it, '[W]hereas the phonological component provides a phonetic shape for a sentence, the semantic component provides a representation of that message which actual utterances having this phonetic shape convey to speakers of the language in normal speech situations' (1966*b*: 151). Katz adds that

The hypothesis on which we will base our model of the semantic component is that the process by which a speaker interprets each of the infinitely many sentences is a compositional process in which the meaning of any syntactically compound constituent of a sentence is obtained as a function of the meanings of the parts of the constituent ...

This means that the semantic component will have two subcomponents: a *dictionary* that provides a representation of the meaning of each of the words in the language, and a system of *projection rules* that provide the combinatorial machinery for projecting the semantic representation for all supraword constituents in a sentence from the representations that are given in the dictionary for the meanings of the words in the sentence. (152–3)

Here meanings are to be identified with what Katz calls 'readings'. He continues,

Projection rules operate on underlying phrase markers that are partially interpreted in the sense of having sets of readings assigned only to the lower level elements in them. They combine readings already assigned to constituents to form derived readings for constituents which, as yet, have had no readings assigned to them ... Each constituent of an underlying phrase marker is thus assigned a set of readings, until the highest constituent, the whole sentence, is reached and assigned a set of readings, too. (164–5)

This theory would be appropriate as an account of the meaning of expressions in one language, e.g. Russian, given in another language taken to be antecedently understood, e.g., English. In that case one would want some general principles for translating Russian into English. Such principles would enable one to know the meaning of Russian expressions because one already knows (in the ordinary sense of this phrase) the meaning of the corresponding English expressions. Katz tries to make the same trick work in order to give an account of the meaning of sentences in English. In effect he envisages a theory that gives principles for translating from English into Mentalese. He thinks these principles are sufficient because one already knows Mentalese.

9.3 MEANING IN MENTALESE?

Katz's theory of communication is circular, if Mentalese is simply English used to think in. And, if Mentalese is not simply English used to think in, the theory simply shifts the problem back one step. How are we to give an account of meaning for Mentalese? We cannot continue forever to give as our theory of meaning a way to translate one system of representation into another. At some point a different account is needed. Katz's theory appears only to delay the moment of confrontation.

There are two distinct issues here. The first is the difficult quasi-empirical question whether thought is in the relevant sense verbal. Let us postpone discussion of that issue for a moment. The second issue is the methodological question whether a semantic theory may presuppose a theory of the nature of thought. Proponents of the view that language is primarily used for thought take semantics to be part of such a theory of the nature of thought. They argue, as it were, that semantics must be concerned in the first instance with the content of thoughts.

Katz assumes that no account need be given of the content of thoughts, as if Mentalese were intrinsically intelligible. That is exactly the sort of view Bloomfield (1933, 1955) attacked as 'mentalistic'. In an influential article,

Katz (1966*a*) attempts to answer Bloomfield but only blurs the issue, since he never considers whether Bloomfield's criticisms of mentalism apply against a theory that assumes semantics can be unconcerned with the meaning of thoughts because of their supposed intrinsic intelligibility.

In Essay 8, above, I argue that a theory of the meaning of messages must presuppose a theory of the content of thoughts. The former theory might resemble that proposed by Paul Grice. According to Grice (1957), the thought meant is the one the speaker intends the hearer to think the speaker has, by virtue of his recognition of the speaker's intention. However that may be, in normal linguistic communication speakers and hearers rely on a regular association between messages and thoughts. Those philosophers and linguists who think that language is used primarily in communication suppose that this association is between sentences in, for example, English (conceived under particular structural descriptions) and, as it were, sentences in Mentalese. Those who believe that language is used primarily in thought suppose that the association is a relatively trivial one, since the language used to communicate with is normally the same as that used to think with.

A theory of the content of thought might exploit the Humboldtian idea that the meaning of a linguistic expression is derived from its function in thought as determined by its place in one's total conceptual scheme. We might consider the influence of perception on thought, the role of inference in allowing one to pass from some thoughts to others, and the way thought leads to action. The resulting theory might be like that proposed in Sellars (1963). Sellars identifies the meaning of an expression with its (potential) role in the evidence-inference-action language game of thought. Similar theories have been proposed by various philosophers, e.g. Carnap (1936, 1937, 1956), Ayer (1936, 1940), and Hampshire (1959). And Quine (1960*b*) has argued that meaning at this level admits of a special sort of indeterminacy.

According to proponents of the view that language is used primarily in thought, a compositional theory of meaning of the sort defended in Katz (1966*b*) provides neither an account of the meaning of language as used to think with nor an account of the meaning of language as used to communicate with. They claim that it cannot provide a theory of the meaning of thought, since a speaker does not understand the words he uses in thinking by assigning readings to them, and that it cannot provide a theory of the meaning of a message, since it treats a relatively simple problem of interpretation as if it were more complicated.

9.4 COMPOSITION AND COMMUNICATION

Compositional theories of meaning assume that language is used primarily in communication. Davidson (1965) argues for compositionality as follows. He says, first, '[W]e are entitled to consider in advance of empirical study what we shall count as knowing a language, how we shall describe the skill or ability of a person who has learned to speak a language'. He wants to argue for the condition 'that we must be able to specify, in a way that depends effectively and solely on formal considerations, what every sentence means. With the right psychological trappings, our theory should equip us to say, for an arbitrary sentence, what a speaker of the language means by that sentence (or takes it to mean).' That last reference, to what a speaker takes the sentence to mean, sounds like Katz's view described above, which assumes that to give an account of meaning for some language is to say how a 'speaker–hearer' is able to correlate meanings, qua thoughts, with sentences. This suspicion is confirmed by Davidson's explicit argument for the compositional theory:

These matters appear to be connected in the following informal way with the possibility of learning a language. When we can regard the meaning of each sentence as a function of a finite number of features of the sentence, we have an insight not only into what there is to be learned; we also understand how an infinite aptitude can be encompassed by finite accomplishments. Suppose on the other hand the language lacks this feature; then no matter how many sentences a would-be speaker learns to produce and understand, there will remain others whose meanings are not given by the rules already mastered. It is natural to say such a language is unlearnable This argument depends, of course, on a number of empirical assumptions: for example, that we do not at some point suddenly acquire an ability to intuit the meanings of sentences on no rule at all; that each new item of vocabulary, or new grammatical rule takes some finite time to be learned; that man is mortal. (1965: 387–8)

This argument makes sense only in the presence of an assumption, which Davidson (1967*b*) explicitly acknowledges, that 'speakers of a language can effectively determine the meaning or meanings of an arbitrary expression (if it has a meaning)', where that is understood to mean that a speaker (hearer) understands a sentence by translating it into its Mentalese counterpart (and where Mentalese is not the language used in communication). If speakers of a language can effectively determine the meaning of messages in ordinary linguistic communication by using the identity mapping of verbal message onto verbal thought, the assumption does not support Davidson's argument for a compositional theory of meaning.

In the end Davidson (1967*b*) argues for a version of the theory that meaning is given by truth conditions. That is not very different from Katz's (1966*b*) theory. According to Katz, a speaker knows the meaning of sentences of his language because he has mastered the complicated rules that correlate sentences with thoughts. According to Davidson, a speaker knows the meaning of sentences of his language because he has mastered the complicated rules of a truth definition for his language that correlate sentences with truth conditions. Katz's theory is in trouble if the relevant thoughts are verbal. The same difficulty faces Davidson in a slightly different form, if the relevant knowledge of truth conditions are verbal. Katz would say that the speaker understands the sentence 'Snow is white' by virtue of the fact that he has correlated it with the thought that snow is white. Davidson would (presumably) say that the speaker understands that sentence by virtue of the fact that he knows it is true if and only if snow is white. The difficulty in either case is that the speaker needs some way to represent to himself snow's being white. If the relevant speaker uses the words 'Snow is white' to represent in the relevant way that snow is white, both Katz's and Davidson's theories are circular. And if speakers have available a form of Mentalese in which they can represent that snow is white, so that the two theories avoid circularity, there is still the problem of meaning for Mentalese.

The point is that no reason has been given for a compositional theory of meaning for any system of representation we think in, be it Mentalese or English. This point has obvious implications for linguistics, and for philosophy too if only of a negative sort. For example, Davidson (1965) uses his theory in order to support objections to certain theories about the logical form of belief sentences. Since his argument for a compositional theory of meaning fails for the language one thinks in, those objections have no force against theories about the logical form of belief sentences used in thinking or theorizing.

Similar remarks apply to the compositional theory of meaning in Ziff (1960). Ziff asserts that '[T]he semantic analysis of an utterance consists in associating with it some set of conditions [and] the semantic analysis of a morphological element having meaning in the language consists in associating with it some set of conditions . . . '. Very roughly speaking, the relevant conditions are those that must obtain if something is to be uttered without deviance from relevant nonsyntactic semantic regularities.

Ziff says, 'In formulating the theory presented here I have had but one objective in mind, viz. that of determining a method and a means of evaluating and choosing between competing analyses of words and utterances'.

If 'analysis' here means 'philosophical analysis', Ziff's enterprise must be counted a success, especially in the light of his careful discussion of the analysis of the word 'good' in the final chapter. And since analysis is perhaps a kind of translation or decoding, it may be possible to defend a compositional theory of meaning as a compositional theory of analysis. (One must see that a proposed analysis of a word is adequate for various contexts and is consistent with analyses suggested for other words.)

But Ziff does not give quite that argument for a compositional theory of meaning; and the argument he does give indicates that he wants more from his theory than a way of evaluating philosophical analyses. His own argument seems to assume that a speaker understands sentences by virtue of being able to give analyses or explications of them. In Ziff (1960) the argument goes like this:

In a general form, the principle of composition is absolutely essential to anything that we are prepared to call a natural language, a language that can be spoken and understood in the way any natural language can in fact be spoken or understood.

How is it that one can understand what is said if what is said has not been said before? Any language whatever allows for the utterance of new utterances both by the reiteration of old ones and by the formation of new ones out of combinations of old elements. Hence any natural language whatever allows for the utterance of both novel utterance tokens and novel utterance types. If a new utterance is uttered and if the utterance is not then and there to be given an arbitrary explication, that one is able to understand what is said in or by uttering the utterance must in some way at least be partially owing to one's familiarity with the syntactic structure of the utterance. (61)

Ziff (1966) is more explicit:

[P]art of what is involved in understanding an utterance is understanding what conditions are relevantly associated with the utterance . . .

Someone says 'Hippopotami are graceful' and we understand what is said. In some cases we understand what is said without attending to the discourse the utterance has occurred in or without attending to the context of utterance. How do we do it?

It seems reasonable to suppose that part of what is involved is this: Such an utterance is understood on the basis of its syntactic structure and morphemic constitution.

Assuming that part of what is involved in understanding an utterance is understanding what conditions are relevantly associated with the utterance, this means that we take a certain set of conditions to be associated with such an utterance on the basis of its syntactic structure and morphemic constitution. (104–5)

To this the same remarks apply as to the theories of Katz and of Davidson.

A speaker can *understand* that certain conditions are associated with an utterance and can take certain conditions to be associated with an utterance only if he has some way to represent to himself that the conditions are associated with the utterance. And even if the speaker uses Mentalese to represent utterance-conditions correlations, the problem of meaning is merely pushed back one step to Mentalese. Ziff fares no better than Katz or Davidson in showing that we need a compositional theory of meaning for the system of representation that we think with. If speakers of English think in English and we rely on that fact in communication, Ziff gives us no reason why we need a compositional theory of meaning for English.

9.5 LANGUAGE USED IN THOUGHT

There are levels of meaning. A theory of the first level must account for the meaning of an expression as a function of its role in thought. A theory of the second level must account for the meaning of an expression used to communicate a thought. A theory of the second level must presuppose the first, since linguistic communication typically communicates a thought that can be expressed (roughly speaking) in the same words used for communication.

Katz and Fodor (1964) put forward a level two theory of meaning in communication. The theory is supposed to account for 'the way that speakers understand sentences'. That may suggest it is the sort of theory Grice (1957) tries to develop. But Katz and Fodor describe it as an account of the meaning or meanings a sentence has when taken in isolation from possible settings in actual discourse. In other words, their theory is restricted to giving an account of meaning for those cases in which the message communicates a thought that in an alternative view can be expressed in (roughly) the same words as those in which the message is expressed. Katz and Fodor say that an additional theory is needed to account for the interpretation or interpretations assigned when a sentence occurs in a particular setting. Furthermore, they argue that the latter theory must presuppose the one they present. Thus they come close to the distinction between levels one and two, and in a way they attempt to provide a theory of level one. Or rather, in their approach three theories are needed, although they do not acknowledge this. First, there is a theory of the content of thought, an account of content for whatever system of representation one uses to think with. Katz and Fodor say nothing about this theory, perhaps because they take thoughts to be intrinsically intelligible. On the alternative view, this theory is the most important part of the theory of meaning. Second, there is the theory Katz and Fodor describe that would associate sentences (under various structural descriptions) used in communication with meanings they have (in isolation from setting and discourse). This theory would associate sentences of English (with their structural descriptions) with 'readings' in the system of representation used in thinking. Katz and Fodor take this theory to be the central part of the theory of meaning, which amounts to a theory of how sentences in e.g. English are to be translated into Mentalese. The alternative view takes this part of the theory to be trivial, on the grounds that speakers of English think in English and can use what amounts to the identity scheme of translation. (I shall say more about this in a moment.) Third, there is the theory of the meaning of a message in a particular linguistic and nonlinguistic setting. Both sides agree that this is an important part of a theory of meaning and that it presupposes the other parts.

How are we to decide between a view like Katz and Fodor's, which takes language to be used primarily in communication, and the alternative which takes language to be used in thought? Katz (1967) claims that his and Fodor's semantic theory is needed in order to explain a great number of different things that cannot be explained on the alternative account, namely, 'semantic anomaly and ambiguity', 'synonymy, paraphrase, antonymy, semantic distinctness, semantic similarity, inclusion of senses, inconsistency, analyticity, contradiction, syntheticity, entailment, possible answer to a question, and so forth'. We have no right to reject their semantic theory unless we have some other method to explain or explain away the phenomena in question.

In the remainder of this essay I want to describe and defend one alternative method. I shall be concerned mainly with the level one theory of meaning, that is, the theory of the content of language used to think in. I shall say something about level two, which is concerned with the meaning of messages, only indirectly and in passing.

What is it for an expression to have a content on level one? It is certainly not that the relevant person, the 'thinker', can assign it one or more 'readings'. It is rather that she can use it in thought, i.e. that it has a role in her evidence-inference-action language game. She may be able to use the expression in direct perceptual reports. She must certainly be able to use it in (theoretical and practical) reasoning. She must be able to recognize implications involving the expression.

Sometimes an implication is formal. It depends only on the logical or grammatical form of relevant expressions and is not a function of nonlogical or nongrammatical vocabulary. In order to account for a person's ability to recognize such a formal implication, it is plausible to suppose that the sentences she uses in thought are grammatically structured. I shall return to this point in a moment. But first I note that it is not sufficient for full understanding of an expression that one be able to recognize formal implications involving that expression; at best this shows merely that one understands the expression as having a particular grammatical form. One must also be able to give paraphrases and notice implications that involve changes in nonlogical and nongrammatical vocabulary. One must be able to see what sentences containing the relevant expression imply, what they are equivalent to, etc.

It is here that Katz and others have thought that appeal must be made to meaning, to entailment by virtue of meaning, to equivalence by virtue of meaning, etc. Not so. The relevant notions of equivalence and of implication are ordinary ones: equivalence or implication with respect to one's background assumptions, where no distinctions need be made between analytic or synthetic background assumptions. One has an understanding of an expression to the extent that one can paraphrase sentences containing it, can make inferences involving such sentences, etc. It adds nothing to one's understanding if one can distinguish 'analytic' equivalence and implications from 'synthetic' ones. In fact, most people cannot do so. Only those who have been 'indoctrinated' can; and they are not the only ones who understand the language they think in. (See Essay 5, above.)

It might be objected that sentences used in thinking are often ambiguous. How can we account for that—and for a person's ability to understand or interpret a sentence one way at one time and another way at another time? Can we account for it without assuming that she assigns an interpretation or 'reading' to the sentence in the way in which Katz suggests? Well, we can and we can't. An expression is ambiguous if a person can sometimes treat it as having one sort of role and at other times treat it as having a different role. Treated one way it admits of paraphrases it does not admit when treated the other way. This difference in paraphrasability represents the difference in interpretation; but recall that paraphrasability is relative to background knowledge and need not permit any analytic–synthetic distinction.

To account for the difference in the ways a person can use an ambiguous expression we must suppose that she does not simply view it as a sequence of words. She views it, or hears it, as having a particular syntactic structure and as containing words in one or another of their possible senses. Let us consider each of these things in turn.

Syntactically ambiguous sentences may be heard as having either of two (or more) different syntactic structures. They are like lines on paper which may be seen as a staircase viewed from the back or from the front. Or they are like a group of dots that may be seen as two groups in one way or as two other groups in another way. Or they are like a figure that can be seen either as a duck or as a rabbit. The sentence, 'They are visiting philosophers', may be understood in two different ways, depending on whether we take 'are visiting' together or 'visiting philosophers' together. We hear the sentence as admitting either of two groups of paraphrases, either 'They are philosophers who are visiting', etc. or 'They are visiting some philosophers', etc. Similarly, the sentence, 'Visiting philosophers can be unpleasant', differs in interpretation depending on its grammatical structure, although the difference is not simply a matter of grouping on the surface. It is rather a matter of the source of 'visiting philosophers'. Roughly speaking, it may come from 'someone visits philosophers' or from 'philosophers visit someone'. It is true that the average person is quite ignorant of the relevant linguistic principles. But that does not mean he fails to hear that sentence as having one or another of the indicated structures. A person can see lines on a page as forming one or another three-dimensional structure without knowing any geometry. In order to account for the way in which a person can deal with ambiguous sentences, we must assume that in some sense she uses a sentence in thought with one or another syntactic structure. The same conclusion is needed in order to account for the formal inferences a person can make, quite apart from considerations of ambiguity.

Similarly, in order to account for the way in which a person deals with ambiguous words, we must assume that she distinguishes a word used in one sense from the same word used in another sense. But we can do that without assuming that she makes the distinction by assigning different readings to the word. She may mark the distinction in sentences by an arbitrary device as simple as a subscript. The inferences and paraphrases that are then permissible depend in general on the subscript selected (Harman, 1966). One reason why no more is needed than a subscript is that the relevant sorts of inference and paraphrase are those possible by virtue of background information. Such background information itself must be 'stored' as sentences under certain structural descriptions including subscripted words. But a person can understand the expressions she uses without having divided her background information into a part that is true by 'definition' (the dictionary) and another part that is not true by definition (the encyclopaedia).

We think with sentences that have particular structural descriptions, where the subscripts that distinguish word senses are part of their structural descriptions. So-called propositional attitudes are structured sentential attitudes, where the relevant sentences have particular structural descriptions. In understanding what someone else says to us, we must determine the content of her utterance taken literally. It is sufficient that we should hear her words as having a particular syntactic structure. That is not to say that we come (even unconsciously) to know that it has a particular structure; and it is certainly not to say that we have knowledge of the principles that relate phonetic representations to structural descriptions. The situation is strictly analogous to other cases of perceiving something as something. We perceive a series of lines as making up a particular three-dimensional structure without explicitly thinking about that structure, indeed without knowing anything about geometrical structure. We can certainly do so without knowing rules that relate two-dimensional figures and three-dimensional structures.

Sounds reach a person's ears and, after physiological processes we know little about, she perceives or conceives a sentence with a particular structural description. Her understanding of that sentence is represented not by her having assigned it a 'reading' in Mentalese but rather by her being able to use the sentence with that structural description in her thought. If we like, we may still speak of 'decoding' here. One decodes certain sounds into a sentence plus structural description. But this is not enough for the sort of decoding that Katz refers to, namely, decoding into intrinsically intelligible Mentalese 'readings'.

I conclude from that it is possible to give an account of how people understand sentences without postulating that a speaker understands sentences by assigning such readings to them.

9.6 ANOMALY AND SYNONYMY

Katz and Fodor have one more argument. They claim that their semantic theory can account for a couple of things that it would be difficult to handle in any other way. First, Katz and Fodor (1964) argue that their theory can show how certain interpretations of a sentence that are grammatically possible are semantically ruled out, so that they can account for a certain amount of disambiguation with their theory. Second, Katz (1964, 1966*b*, 1967) argues that the theory shows how certain sentences are analytic, others contradictory, and still others synthetic, so that the theory can account for native speakers' intuitive judgements about analyticity, etc.

In reply, I say that there is no such thing as semantic anomaly and no such distinction as the analytic–synthetic distinction. To believe otherwise is to suffer from a lack of imagination.

For example, Katz and Fodor argue as follows:

Now let S be the sentence *The paint is silent.* English speakers will at once recognize that this sentence is anomalous in some way. For example, they will distinguish it from such sentences as *The paint is wet* and *The paint is yellow* by applying to it such epithets as 'odd,' 'peculiar,' and 'bizarre.' . . . Hence, another facet of the semantic ability of the speaker is that of detecting semantic anomalies. (1964: 402–3)

But I say that whatever anomaly there is in the phrase 'silent paint' arises from the fact that paints do not emit noise. If some paints did and some did not, 'silent paint' would not be anomalous. And that is to say that there is nothing peculiarly semantic about the anomaly. Its anomaly is a result of our general nonlinguistic knowledge of the world.

Again, Katz and Fodor (1964) argue that a theory that incorporates only the sort of considerations I have sketched above

will not be able to distinguish the correct sense of seal in 'One of the oil seals in my car is leaking' from such incorrect senses as 'a device bearing a design so made that it can impart an impression' or 'an impression made by such a device' or 'the material upon which the impression is made' or 'an ornamental or commemorative stamp' and so forth, since all of these senses can apply to nominal occurrences of *seal.* (409)

But, surely, it requires only a little imagination to see that 'seal' may have any of these senses, although in ordinary discourse it would be more likely to have the sense the authors have in mind (Bolinger, 1965).

McCawley (1970) makes a similar point with respect to purported syntactic anomalies of a certain type

Moreover, it appears incorrect to regard many so-called 'selectional violations' as not corresponding to possible messages, since many of them can turn up in reports of dreams:

(2) I dreamed that my toothbrush was pregnant.
(3) I dreamed that I poured my mother into an inkwell.
(4) I dreamed that I was a proton and fell in love with a shapely green-and-orange-striped electron.

or in reports of the beliefs of other persons:

(5) John thinks that electrons are green with orange stripes.
(6) John thinks that his toothbrush is trying to kill him.

(7) John thinks that ideas are physical objects and are green with orange stripes.

or in the speech of psychotics. While one might suggest that a paranoid who says things like

(8) My toothbrush is alive and is trying to kill me.

has different selectional restrictions from a normal person, it is pointless to do so, since the difference in 'selectional restriction' will correspond exactly to a difference in beliefs as to one's relationship with inanimate objects; a person who utters sentences such as (8) should be referred to a psychiatric clinic, not to a remedial English course.

McCawley's argument supports the conclusion that there is no real distinction between semantic anomaly and anomaly due to 'extralinguistic factors'.

Similar points apply to Katz's claims about analyticity, etc. First, the fact that people have 'intuitions' about analyticity shows at best that there is a distinction between 'seems analytic to certain people' and 'seems synthetic to them'. It does not show that there are sentences that are really analytic as opposed to others that are synthetic. The fact that people once had intuitions that some women were witches and others not, certainly fails to show that there were women that really were witches as opposed to others that were not (see Essay 5, above).

Second, the intuitive distinction Katz and others make between analytic and synthetic truths is easily explained away without appeal to their semantic theory. People who have such intuitions suffer from a lack of imagination. The intuitions come from their inability to imagine that certain sentences are false. But as Putnam (1962*b*), Moravcsik (1965), and others have pointed out, after a little practice such things can be imagined.

9.7 FINAL REMARKS

Consider the two views. On the first view, a person who speaks a natural language can think in that language and does not need to translate sentences conceived into some other system of representation, Mentalese. On this view, Mentalese incorporates one's natural language. On the second view, a person cannot think in language and must translate sentences of her language into Mentalese. The incorporation view has the advantage over the translation view that it provides a natural explanation of the way in which learning one's first language makes possible thoughts and other propositional attitudes one would not otherwise have. The translation view must add some special principle to account for this. Furthermore, the translation view suggests things that are false about anomaly, synonymy, etc.

It is difficult to see how, say, neurophysiological evidence could support one of the views against the other (except by pointing to further relatively behavioural phenomena to be explained). For, as descriptions of the mechanism of the brain, the two views must be taken to be descriptions of a fairly abstract sort. And it is not easy to see how any neurological mechanism that might account for the relevant behaviour and that could be interpreted as an instantiation of one of the descriptions could not also be interpreted as an instantiation of the other. So far then, I see no reason not to accept the incorporation view. However, I discuss the issue further in Essay 10, immediately following.

10

Language Learning

Let us suppose that there is an inner language of thought that may or may not be distinct from the outer language one speaks. I wish to contrast two views of what it is to learn a natural language. A *code-breaking conception* might be provisionally formulated like this:

> (CB) One's inner language, which one thinks in, is distinct from one's outer language, which one speaks. Communication involves coding or translation between inner and outer languages. Learning language is a matter of learning an outer language and involves acquiring the ability to do such coding or translation.

An *incorporation view* might be stated as follows:

> (IV) Knowledge of a language is the ability to use that language; and the primary use of language is in thought. Knowing a language is being able to think in it. Learning an outer language involves the incorporation of that language into one's inner language.

In this essay I try to say what the issue between CB and IV amounts to in the last analysis.

I assume a psychological model of a person as a nondeterministic automaton, whose input is the result of interaction with the environment and whose output consists in actions and reactions, including speech. The assumed model uses a system of representation for framing beliefs, desires, etc. In a very simple version of this sort of model, there might be two places in which representations are stored. Representations of things believed would be stored in one place; representations of things desired in the other. Interaction with the environment would produce new representations that would be stored as beliefs. Needs for food, love, etc. would produce representations to be stored as desires. Reasoning could lead to changes in both the set of beliefs and the set of desires.

I will use the term 'thoughts' broadly to stand for attitudes and occurrences including occurrent thoughts, beliefs, desires, etc. Then CB and IV can be understood as the following proposals about psychological models:

(CBPM) A psychological model of a speaker of a language should use a system of representation for thoughts that is distinct from the language spoken by the person modelled. In a model of communication, the model of the speaker converts an element of this inner system of representation into a sentence of the language; and the model of the hearer converts this sentence back into the proper element of the inner system of representation. A model of a language learner must come to acquire the ability to thus convert elements of the inner system to sentences of the outer language; and vice versa.

(IVPM) A psychological model of a speaker of a language should use a system of representation for thoughts that includes the language spoken by the person modelled. A model of communication need not involve the sort of conversion mentioned in CBPM. A model of a language learner does not acquire the ability to do such conversion; instead it comes to incorporate the outer language into its inner system of representation.

It is plausible that relevant models should make use of a system of representation, given that people have beliefs and desires, that beliefs and desires influence action, that interaction with the environment can give rise to new beliefs, and that needs and drives can give rise to desires. Adequate psychological theories must reflect these facts and add to them. So adequate psychological models must have states that correspond to beliefs, desires, and thoughts such that these states function in the model as psychological states function in the person modelled, and such that they are representational in the way that psychological states are representational. Where there is such representation, there is a system of representation; and that system may be identified with the inner language in which a person thinks.

This reduces the claim that there is an inner language of thought to the trivial assertion that psychological states have a representational character. But it leaves obscure CBPM and IVPM, which respectively deny and assert that one's inner language contains one's outer language. What could it mean to assert or deny that psychological states involve, or even are, instances (i.e. tokens) of sentences of one's language? How can it be serious whether or not to include sentences of a person's language among the representations used in the way suggested above as part of a psychological model of that person?

Of course, one reason it is not clear what it is for a person's psychological states to be or include tokens of his language is that it is unclear what it is for anything to be such a token. Compare uttered and written tokens,

tokens in different dialects, different handwriting, and different styles of type, tokens uttered aloud and said to oneself. What do all the various instances of a sentence have in common?

It is not easy to say; but the following conditions seem necessary. First, any two tokens of the same sentence must have similar (potential) representational properties. Second, the tokens must each be analysable as an ordered sequence of the same words in the same order.

A generalization of the second condition allows us to distinguish tokens of the same old sentences appearing in a new form (e.g. the new written tokens as opposed to the old spoken tokens) from tokens of sentences in another language which are only translations of sentences in the original language. In a language that can be both spoken and written, for every possible spoken word, there is a corresponding written word. Every spoken sentence is a temporal sequence of spoken words; and the corresponding written sentence is a spatial sequence of corresponding written words in the same order, where corresponding written and spoken sentences have the same potential representational properties. This sort of general correspondence does not hold between distinct languages. One cannot, for example, correlate English and Russian words so that whenever a sequence of English words forms a sentence, the corresponding sequence of Russian words forms a sentence that translates the English sentence.

This suggests that we formulate the two conceptions of language learning as follows (recall that we are using 'thoughts' to include beliefs, desires, etc.).

(IVT) The relationship between one's thoughts and the sentences of one's language is relevantly more like the relationship between spoken and written English than it is like the relationship between English and Russian. Thoughts may be analysed as sequences of elements; and some of the elements may be correlated with words in one's language so that corresponding sequences of elements and sequences of words have similar representational characteristics. To learn a language is to acquire thoughts that are (at least in part) tokens of sentences of that language.

(CBT) The relationship between one's thoughts and the sentences of one's language is relevantly more like the relationship between English and Russian than it is like the relationship between spoken and written English. The sort of analysis envisaged in IVT is not possible. To learn a language is not to acquire thoughts that are tokens of sentences of the language but is in part to acquire the ability to encode one's thoughts in such tokens.

Notice, by the way, that so formulated IVT does not commit one to the view that thoughts that are 'in words' have such words occurring in temporal sequence. One can think in words without those words passing through one's head in the proper temporal order. An uttered sentence is a temporal sequence; but a written sentence is a spatial sequence; and a thought sentence need not be a spatiotemporal sequence at all.

However, a moment's reflection suffices to show that, when formulated in this way, IVT is false and CBT is true, because of ambiguity in natural language. Thoughts are not ambiguous in the way that sentences in English are. So there can be no analysis like that suggested in IVT which correlates sentences and thoughts that have similar representational characteristics. IVT is trivially false; and CBT, the relevant denial of IVT, is trivially true.

Now, the ambiguity of a sentence may derive from the ambiguity of certain words in the sentence, from the ambiguity of the grammatical structure of the sentence, or from some combination of factors. Let us make the controversial assumption that the relevant grammatical structure includes what linguists sometimes call the level of LF (loosely: 'logical form'). Assume further that this structure reveals relations such as underlying first argument of a predicate, scope of quantifiers and negation, etc. Let us also assume that the LF structure of a sentence represents in some form or other the words (or morphemes) relevant to the meaning of the sentence. Finally, let us assume that different senses of words are distinguished by subscripts on those words in LF but that LF contains no other purely semantic information. Then, by a sentence under analysis, I shall mean a sentence viewed (or 'heard') as having a particular LF in the sense just described.

We may now state the incorporation view and the code-breaking conception of language learning in such a way that there is a real nontrivial issue between them.

> (IVA) To acquire a language is to acquire thoughts that are, at least in part, instances of sentences of that language under analysis. Spontaneous speech is thinking out loud: one utters a sentence under analysis. Two such sentences sound the same if they contain the same words in the same order, even if their LF structures are different. For someone to understand what is said is for him to hear it as a sentence under analysis.

> (CBA) To learn a language is not to acquire thoughts that are instances of sentences of the language under analysis, but is in part to acquire the ability to encode one's thoughts in such instances.

Although I defend IVA in Essay 9 above, it appears to be false. Shipley, Smith, and Gleitman report that

Our data show that children make discriminations that are not reflected in the speech. Children whose speech is telegraphic readily obey well-formed commands, and less readily obey telegraphic commands. Thus a description of the child's spontaneous utterances does not do justice to his linguistic organization. In some fairly clear sense, comprehension seems to precede the production of well-formed sentences ... What is truly surprising is that those utterances which a description of natural speech would specify as TYPICAL for the child are just those utterances which are LESS EFFECTIVE to him as commands. (1969: 336–7)

If some of the child's thoughts are to be analysed as sentences of his language under analysis, these sentences are either (1) the telegraphic ones of the sort he spontaneously produces or (2) the well-formed ones of the sort he understands. On alternative (1), the child does not understand what is said by hearing it under analysis. Anyway, it would seem absurd to suggest that the child hears a well-formed sentence as a telegraphic sentence under analysis, since the child has greater difficulty understanding telegraphic sentences than well-formed ones. On the other hand, on alternative (2) the sentences the child spontaneously produces are not, even under analysis, sentences the child thinks in; and speech is not simply a matter of thinking out loud. Neither alternative (1) nor alternative (2) seems consistent with IVA.

The experimental results cited definitely favour CBA. Understanding is a matter of decoding what is said; spontaneous speech is a matter of encoding one's thoughts. Neither of these processes is trivial; and in learning a language, the former process is easier than the latter.

However, even if all this is granted to the code-breaking conception, a defender of the incorporation view will want to claim that the relevant thoughts are language-dependent. If thoughts are not sentences under analysis, i.e. sentences with their LF structures, perhaps they are simply the LF structures themselves without the surface sentences (but with most of the relevant words). Some defenders of the code-breaking conception will want to argue that thoughts are not thus dependent on one's language. Therefore I am led to a second way of stating the incorporation view and the code-breaking conception such that there is a real and nontrivial issue between them.

(IVLF) To understand what is said is to hear what is said as a sentence under analysis. That is because certain of one's thoughts are instances of LF structures of such sentences. Thoughts may be analysed as structures of elements; and the elements can be correlated with sub-scripted words, the structures with LF structures, so that corre-sponding structures of elements and sentences under analysis have the same representational characteristics. To acquire a language is to acquire thoughts that are, at least in part, instances of LF structures of sentences of that language.

(CBLF) In order to understand what is said, one must do more than hear the sentence uttered as having the proper LF structure; one must also interpret that LF structure by decoding it or translating it into the language of thought. The sort of analysis envisaged in IVLF is not possible. To learn a language is not to acquire thoughts that are instances of LF structures of sentences of that language.

Now, consider the following objection, which a defender of CBLF might make to IVLF.

If IVLF were true, thoughts expressed in one language could not be expressed in another, since thoughts are taken to be LF structures of sentences. But an English sentence under analysis can be translated into a French sentence under analysis; and a criterion of good trans-lation is that the translation should express the same thought as the sentence translated. The possibility of good translation shows that the same thoughts can be expressed in different languages. Therefore, IVLF must be false.

One might think it enough to respond to this objection by citing Quine's thesis of the indeterminacy of radical translation. Quine (1960*b*) points out that adequate translation is a matter of pairing sentences from one lan-guage with sentences from another in such a way that the general correla-tion satisfies certain conditions. He claims that, when one considers all reasonable constraints on translation, one discovers that various nonequivalent general schemes of translation will satisfy these conditions. Thus he claims that the translation of one language into another resembles the 'translation' of number theory into set theory, in that there are many different, equally good, nonequivalent ways in which such translation may be carried out.

If Quine were right, it would make no sense to say that two sentences of different languages express the same thought, except relative to one or another general scheme of translation between the two languages. For, although one scheme might count sentence A the translation of sentence B, an alternative, but equally good, scheme would count sentence C as B's translation, where A and C need not express the 'same thought'. Given indeterminacy of radical translation, the possibility of good translation does not establish that the same thoughts can be said to be expressed by different sentences in different languages apart from specification of a general scheme of translation. And to say that relative to a specified scheme of translation the same thoughts are expressed by sentence A and sentence B would not be to say something incompatible with IVLF. If Quine were right, IVLF would seem definitely preferable to CBLF.

Quine (1960*b*) argues that the meaning of a sentence in a single speaker's idiolect is a matter of what sentences he would be disposed to accept or reject as the result of being placed in various perceptual situations. Let me abbreviate this by saying that for Quine meaning is a matter of a speaker's dispositions to accept sentences, where this is meant also to include rejection of sentences. If meaning were only a matter of a speaker's dispositions to accept sentences, then there would almost certainly be indeterminacy of radical translation. For it would seem obvious that there will be many different, equally simple ways to correlate sentences of two different languages which preserve a speaker's dispositions to accept sentences equally well.

The assumption that meaning is essentially a matter of a speaker's dispositions to accept sentences does seem to capture the essence of the approach to the theory of meaning exemplified in the writings of Carnap, Ayer, Lewis, Firth, Hempel, Sellars, and others. This approach seems definitely committed to the indeterminacy of radical translation. But is it obvious that the basic assumption of this approach is correct?

The only argument for the assumption that I have been able to find appears in Harman (1969).

Meaning is not very much a matter of what words a person actually uses. What words he could have used are more relevant. Different people have different ways of speaking, different favorite phrases, etc. This obvious fact does not mean that the sentences of such different people are to be translated differently. To require similarity in actual usage (rather than possible usage) as a criterion of translatability would almost certainly rule out all translation, since any two people use their words differently. I do not mean something different by sentences of set theory from what you mean just because you and I use these sentences differently, e.g. just because I count with the von Neumann numbers while you count with Zermelo's, since I could always do it your way. (18–19)

But this argument is obviously incorrect. Preservation of similarity in actual usage can be a criterion of translation without ruling out all translation on the grounds that people use words differently. Preservation of similarity in belief is a criterion of translation even though no two people believe the same things. It tells us that, other things being equal, we should prefer one general scheme of translation over a second if the first has us ascribe to speakers of another language beliefs that are more similar to our own beliefs than are the beliefs we would have to ascribe to them on the second scheme. A criterion of translation that appeals to similarity in actual usage can be given an analogous formulation: other things being equal, we should prefer one general scheme of translation over a second if translations of things actually said by speakers of another language are more like things we say on the first scheme than on the second. The latter principle would rule out schemes of translation not ruled out by the appeal to a speaker's dispositions to accept sentences. For example, it might rule out a general scheme of translation according to which speakers of another language regularly refer to rabbit stages rather than rabbits, people stages rather than people, etc., in favour of a scheme according to which they regularly refer to rabbits, people, etc., even though both these schemes might be equally good in terms of preservation of dispositions to accept sentences. Furthermore, there is no obvious reason why preservation of similarity of actual usage, so understood, should not be permitted to be just as much a criterion of good translation as preservation of similarity in actual belief. And, if it is allowed as a criterion, Quine's thesis of indeterminacy of radical translation no longer seems obviously true. Therefore, one cannot defend IVLF by appealing to this sort of indeterminacy.

Nevertheless, Quine's overall approach to meaning and translation tends to support IVLF rather than CBLF, even without the indeterminacy thesis. One general scheme of translation is better than another to the extent that it is simpler, preserves dispositions to accept sentences, and preserves similarity of actual usage. Each of these things is a matter of degree, and they can compete with each other. One could achieve perfect correspondence between another person's dispositions to accept sentences and one's own if one were willing to give up on simplicity. And sometimes one gives up the simplest scheme, e.g. the homophonic scheme, in order to preserve more dispositions to accept sentences or to gain more similarity of actual usage. The fit is never perfect; but, let us assume, there is sometimes a best fit—a best general scheme of translation from one language to another.

Since the fit is only a matter of degree, the translation relation is not an 'equivalence relation' in the mathematical sense. It is not transitive. If X is the translation of Y and Y the translation of Z, X need not be the translation of Z. For there may be three languages L, M, and N, such that the best scheme of translation from L to N is not equivalent to the scheme one acts by first translating by the best scheme from L to M and then by the best scheme from M to N. This poses a problem for CBLF, which takes the possibility of good translation to show that the same thoughts can be expressed in different languages. If the thought expressed by X is the same identical thing as that expressed by Y, which is the same as that expressed by Z, the thought expressed by X is the same as that expressed by Z, by the transitivity of identity. On CBLF, the translation relation ought to be an equivalence relation. So, even if Quine's thesis of the indeterminacy of radical translation is not accepted, his theory of translation gives us reason to be sceptical of CBLF, since CBLF implies that thoughts are linguistically neutral states that may be expressed in various languages in a way that is not relative to translation.

IVLF says that certain of one's psychological states may be treated as LF structures of sentences of one's language. This is done by constructing a psychological model in which certain beliefs are represented by the storage in a given place of instances of the appropriate LF structures. Similarly for desires, etc. The acquisition of language is treated in the first instance as the acquisition of a system of representation for the storage of beliefs, desires, etc. I think that IVLF gives the beginnings of the correct account of language learning. It might have been supposed that the possibility of good translation tells against IVLF in favour of a view like CBLF. However, I have argued that this is not so and that, as of now, a view like IVLF looks more promising than one like CBLF.

We cannot say simply whether the code-breaking conception is or is not better than the incorporation view. On the one hand, language learning appears to involve the acquisition of coding and decoding abilities, as is revealed by the child's being better at decoding than he is at coding. CBA is true and IVA is false. On the other hand, the thoughts that a language encodes may themselves be highly dependent on that language, even to the point of being or involving LF structures of sentences of that language. Language learning may involve the incorporation of a system of language-specific LF structures into one's language of thought. In that case IVLF will be true, and CBLF will be false.

11

Meaning and Semantics

Strawson (1952) observes, concerning what he calls statement-making sentences, 'To know the meaning of a sentence of this kind is to know under what conditions someone who used it would be making a true statement; to explain the meaning is to say what these conditions are'. In this essay I want to consider whether such a connection between truth and meaning tells us anything about the nature of meaning or only tells us something about the nature of truth. More specifically, I shall be concerned with the question whether a theory of truth for a language can tell us something about meaning that is not revealed by a method for translating that language into ours. By a theory of truth for a language, I mean a formal theory that implies a statement of truth conditions for every sentence in the language. My question is whether such a theory sheds light on meaning.

The question arises because theories of truth for artificial languages, containing one or another device, often do seem to illuminate meaning. The truth functional analysis of sentential connectives seems to determine the meaning of those connectives. The Frege–Tarski analysis of quantification, which culminates in Tarski's (1956) theory of truth for quantificational languages, appears to give an account of the meaning of the quantifiers. Kripke's (1963) semantics for modal logic and Stalnaker's (1968) analysis of the conditional, both concerned with defining truth conditions in terms of possible worlds, seem to tell us something about meaning (even if not everything we might want to know). Similarly for Davidson's (1967a) analysis of the logical form of action sentences, which explains truth conditions in terms of events. In these cases a formal theory of truth seems to tell us something about meaning that no mere translation scheme could reveal. That is no doubt why there is a use of the term 'semantics' among logicians simply to mean a theory of truth in this sense for a language. So there is empirical evidence that semantics (in this sense) sheds light on meaning.

On the other hand, it is not obvious why. As far as I can see, nothing in the extensive recent discussion of this subject explains why the theories of truth I have mentioned should shed any sort of light on meaning in the way that they do. At the end of this essay, I will suggest a way in which a formal theory of truth can be relevant to the meaning of certain expressions; but, if I am right, the relevance of such a theory to meaning is much more indirect and less central than many philosophers have supposed.

11.1 A THEORY OF TRUTH AS A THEORY OF MEANING

I begin by considering the views of three philosophers who have suggested that a theory of meaning might take the form of a theory of truth—Donald Davidson, David Wiggins (who, however, has doubts about this, as I shall note below), and David Lewis. I start with Davidson, who has argued in a number of places that a theory of meaning should take the form of a formal theory that satisfies a 'convention T', borrowed from Tarski. Roughly speaking, the theory is to imply all relevant instances of the schema 'S is true if and only if P', where what replaces 'S' names a sentence and what replaces 'P' is that very sentence or a translation of that sentence into the metalanguage in which the theory of truth is stated. According to Davidson (1967b), such a theory of truth can be a theory of meaning since 'to give truth conditions is a way of giving the meaning of a sentence. To know the semantic concept of truth for a language is to know what it is for a sentence—any sentence—to be true, and this amounts, in one good sense we can give to the phrase, to understanding the language.'

Wiggins (1972) advocates a similar thesis. He argues that everyone must accept the following 'minimum contention': 'Any satisfactory theory of meaning . . . must entail the following proposition: *To know the sense of an indicative sentence s is to know some condition p which is true if and only if s is true and which is the designated condition for s.*'

Similarly, in the following passage Lewis (1971) complains about theories of meaning that do not mention truth conditions.

My proposals concerning the nature of meanings will not conform to the expectations of those linguists who conceive of semantic interpretation as the assignment to sentences and their constituents of compounds of 'semantic markers' or the like. Semantic markers are symbols: items in the vocabulary of an artificial language we may call Semantic Markerese. Semantic interpretation by means of them amounts merely to a translation algorithm from the object language to the auxiliary language Markerese. But we can know the Markerese translation of an English sentence without knowing the first thing about the meaning of the English sentence: namely, the conditions under which it would be true. Semantics with no treatment of truth conditions is not semantics. Translation into Markerese is at best a substitute for real semantics, relying either on our tacit competence (at some future date) as speakers of Markerese or on our ability to do real semantics at least for the one language, Markerese. Translation into Latin might serve as well, except insofar as the designers of Markerese may choose to build into it useful features— freedom from ambiguity, grammar based on symbolic logic—that might make it easier to do real semantics for Markerese than for Latin.

On the other hand, many philosophers and linguists do not seem to believe that a theory of meaning must involve a theory of truth in any way that is important for the theory of meaning. Of course, everyone would agree that there is some connection between truth and meaning, since whether a sentence is true depends on its meaning. But not everyone would conclude that a theory of meaning should take the guise of a formal theory of truth. There is no suggestion that such a theory of truth might provide a theory of meaning in Katz and Postal (1964), which Lewis refers to. Nor does any such suggestion appear in Katz and Fodor (1964) or Grice (1957).

Even where philosophers explicitly concede the obvious connection between truth and meaning, they do not always suppose that the connection illuminates the theory of meaning. In his comments on Wiggins (1972), Alston (1972) concedes that linguistic rules which give meaning to certain sentences may cite their truth conditions; but he evidently takes this point to have limited significance. And when he developed his own theory in an early introductory text (Alston, 1964), which also surveyed what he took to be the important philosophical theories of meaning, he nowhere mentioned the view that a theory of meaning might be presented as a formal theory of truth. Presumably he did not think that this is one of the important philosophical theories of meaning.

I began this essay with a quotation from Strawson (1952), 'To know the meaning of a sentence of [a statement-making] kind is to know under what conditions someone who used it would be making a true statement; to explain the meaning is to say what these conditions are'. But Strawson (1974*a*) is an attack, with special reference to Davidson's views, on the idea that a formal theory of truth could be a theory of meaning.

In light of such disagreement, it is appropriate to ask what reasons can be given for the supposition that a formal theory of truth—a formal 'semantics'—for a language could be a theory of meaning for that language that reveals anything more about meaning than a translation procedure would. There is, of course, the empirical evidence that I have already mentioned. Partial theories of truth for certain portions of language do seem to shed light on meaning, which mere translation does not. But this evidence does not conclusively establish that a theory of truth is directly relevant to a theory of meaning; perhaps its relevance is indirect. In any event, we want to know *why* a theory of truth should tell us something about meaning.

11.2 ARGUMENTS FOR TRUTH-CONDITIONAL SEMANTICS

Three sorts of argument have been given for the thesis that a formal theory of truth should tell us about meaning. There is, first, an argument that the thesis follows from the fact that knowing the meaning of certain sentences is knowing their truth conditions. Second, there is an argument that appeals to an analogy from what is expected of a theory of meaning and what is expected of a theory of truth. And, third, there is an argument that the normal use of language in communication rests on a background of conventions that correlate sentences with truth conditions. I will discuss each of these arguments in turn and will eventually be led to give my own positive account.

11.2.1 *The Argument from Knowledge of Meaning*

The first argument might be put like this: 'For certain sentences, anyway, to know their meanings is to know their truth conditions and to know their truth conditions is to know their meanings. So, the meanings of these sentences are their truth conditions, and a theory of truth that gives the truth conditions of these sentences amounts to a theory of meaning.'

Two replies can be given to this argument. First, it can be said that whatever is correct about the redundancy theory of truth is sufficient to account for why knowing meaning is knowing truth conditions. Second, it can be said that to specify meaning simply by specifying truth conditions would not seem to require a full-fledged theory of meaning; it would require only a translational theory that specifies the meaning of an expression by providing another expression with the same meaning. Let me elaborate these replies.

11.2.1.1 The redundancy theory of truth

The first reply points to the fact that one can take it to be a remark about the nature of truth, rather than meaning, that knowledge of meaning is knowledge of truth conditions for certain sentences. 'Snow is white' is true if and only if snow is white; and similarly for many other sentences. To understand the meaning of the word 'true' is to understand at least that much. That is what is correct about the redundancy theory of truth.

So, if you understand the sentence 'Snow is white', that is, if you know what the sentence means, and you also understand what truth is, then you can figure out what the truth conditions of the sentence 'Snow is white' are; and similarly for other sentences. But the point has to do with what 'true' means, not with what 'means' means. That is the first reply to the argument that to know meaning is to know truth conditions.

11.2.1.2 Translational theory of meaning

The second reply suggests that there is a sense in which a theory that would explain meaning in terms of truth conditions would be open to Lewis's objection to Katz and Postal's theory of semantic markers. Lewis says, you will recall, 'But we can know the Markerese translation of an English sentence without knowing the first thing about the meaning of an English sentence: namely the conditions under which it would be true'. Similarly, there is a sense in which we can know the truth conditions of an English sentence without knowing the first thing about the meaning of the English sentence. To borrow David Wiggins's (1972) example, we might know that the sentence 'All mimsy were the borogroves' is true if and only if all mimsy were the borogroves. However, in knowing this we would not know the first thing about the meaning of the sentence, 'All mimsy were the borogroves'.

The truth theorist will respond that he envisages stating truth conditions in a metalanguage that is already completely understood. If the sentence, 'All mimsy were the borogroves', is not antecedently understood, it will not be part of this metalanguage, and, if its truth conditions are to be given, it must be translated into terms that are antecedently understood. But then it is not clear how the theory of truth can say anything more about meaning than a straightforwardly translational theory that gives the meanings of sentences in one language by giving translations of those sentences into a language that is antecedently understood. Lewis complains that Katz and Postal give a translational theory of this sort and that they must therefore rely on a tacit and unexplained competence in Markerese; someone who explains meaning in terms of truth conditions similarly relies on a tacit and unexplained competence in the metalanguage.

11.2.2 *Argument from Analogy*

Davidson (1967*b*) argues that a theory of meaning should imply results of the form 'S means P', where what replaces 'S' names a sentence of the object language and what replaces 'P' is that sentence itself or its translation into the metalanguage. Davidson observes that such a condition is similar to Tarski's convention T, which requires of a theory of truth that it should imply relevant instances of 'S is true if and only if P'.

It is easy to see that a theory of meaning in this sense is equivalent to a formal (infinitely axiomatizable) theory of translation. Suppose that we have a formal procedure for translating a language L into our language. Suppose in particular that we have a recursive procedure for recognizing the relevant instances of 'S (in L) translates into our language as T'. Then we can easily formulate a recursive procedure for recognizing relevant instances of 'S (in L) means P' or 'S (in L) is true if and only if P' (where what replaces 'S' is the same name of a sentence as that which replaced 'S' in the previous schema and what replaces 'P' is the sentence named by what replaces 'T' in the previous schema). Then we can treat each of the instances of one of the latter schemas as axioms in a formal theory of meaning or a formal theory of truth, since each of the infinitely many axioms in the theory will be formally specifiable and recognizable. Similarly, given a formal theory of truth or a formal theory of meaning in this sense, we can easily state a formal theory of translation.

Now, the light that is shed on meaning by the theories of truth of Tarski, Kripke, Stalnaker, and Davidson is not due merely to the fact that those theories tell us how to translate sentences of the object language into the metalanguage; so Davidson's analogy gives us no explanation of the fact that these formal theories of truth shed the sort of light they do on meaning.

Perhaps that is why Davidson no longer takes the interest for meaning of a theory of truth to lie only in the T sentences, 'S is true if and only if P'. Davidson (1970) also emphasizes the recursion clauses in a finite theory of truth that implies those T sentences. The unilluminating theories of truth that are equivalent to theories of translation are infinite theories in which all the T sentences are treated as axioms. The theories of truth that do shed light on meaning are finite theories. Our current difficulty is that we do not understand why this should be so. Why should we expect a finite theory of truth to shed light on meaning? Is it just an accident that the theories in question (Tarski's etc.) shed such light? Is it possible that these theories only seem to shed light on meaning? I will return to those questions later.

11.2.3 *Argument from Communicative Conventions*

The third argument that I want to consider asserts that normal linguistic communication exploits conventions that correlate sentences and truth conditions. Lewis (1969) gives a very clear statement of the argument. In brief, he argues that a theory of meaning for a language spoken in some community must be a theory of the linguistic conventions that speakers normally observe; and, he claims, these conventions include in effect the principle that, in certain circumstances, speakers are to try to say what is true in the language in question.

Lewis argues that normal linguistic communication is made possible by the fact that there are certain regularities in the use of the language by speakers and by hearers. People adhere to these regularities because others do and because it is common knowledge that they do. Lewis considers a number of different uses of language, but for our purposes we can confine the discussion to the normal use of language in a situation of communication of information using ordinary statement-making sentences. According to Lewis, it is a relevant background regularity that normally speakers try to observe certain general principles which, if consistently observed in all cases, would have such implications as these: speakers would say 'It is raining' only if it were raining; speakers would say 'It is snowing' only if it were snowing; speakers would say 'Snow is white' only on the condition that snow is white; they would say 'Grass is green' only on the condition that grass is green; and so forth. Furthermore, in gaining information from what has been said, hearers (according to Lewis) normally rely on the fact that speakers normally try to adhere to these regularities. Speakers normally rely on hearers' doing this; and so forth.

Now it may seem that, if Lewis is right about the conventions of a language that are relied on in normal linguistic communication and is also right that a theory of meaning is a theory of these conventions, then a theory of meaning would have to involve something like a theory of truth. For it may seem that the conventional regularities that he is thinking of would have to connect sentences and their truth conditions. And it may seem that the recursion clauses in a finite theory of the conventional regularities would exactly match the recursion clauses in a finite theory of truth in that language. So it may seem that, if Lewis is right, a good way to give an account of the conventions of a particular language L would be, first, to give a theory of truth in L and, second, to say that linguistic communication using L exploits the conventional regularity that speakers normally try to say only what is true in L.

However, it is not obvious that Lewis's theory (even if correct) has this consequence. According to Lewis, the basic convention is that speakers try to say what is true in L. But to try to say what is true is to say what you believe. So, for Lewis, normal linguistic communication in a language L exploits the expectation that a speaker normally says something only if he believes it. What is conventional about language has to do with what sentences express what beliefs. This seems to yield the theory that the meaning of a statement-making sentence depends on the belief it could normally be used to express. Meaning is taken to be a matter of the belief expressed rather than a matter of truth conditions.

Clearly, it is more accurate to say that hearers rely on an expectation that speakers will normally say what they believe than an expectation that speakers will normally say what is true. The expectation that speakers normally say what is true is more optimistic than the expectation that they normally say what they believe. The optimistic expectation would seem to rest not just on an understanding of the conventions of the language but also on an estimate of the reliability of speakers' beliefs.

It is sometimes said that, if speakers did not normally speak the truth, the language could not be learned. We are supposed to conclude that it follows from linguistic conventions that speakers normally say what is true; and such a conclusion would support the idea that meaning is a matter of truth conditions. But such an argument is not compelling. If as a result of false beliefs speakers did not normally speak the truth, the language could still be learned by someone who shared with speakers those false beliefs.

How wrong can we take someone's beliefs to be before we must decide that we have misinterpreted them? It can be and has been argued that the thesis that people are normally right in their beliefs is not an empirical generalization but rather a presupposition of ascribing any beliefs to them at all. However, such an argument could not possibly show that *linguistic conventions* correlate sentences with their truth conditions. For one would have to argue that it follows from linguistic conventions that people are normally right in their beliefs. But the argument would, it seems, apply not only to beliefs that can be expressed in language but also to beliefs, or expectations, or whatever else are analogous to beliefs and expectations, in dumb animals and children who have not yet learned a spoken language. There would be the same sorts of limits to the interpretation of the beliefs, expectations, or what have you of these creatures. So these limits do not seem to be derived from linguistic conventions.

11.3 WHAT LINGUISTIC CONVENTIONS ARE THERE?

Taking the point one step further, observe that there is no general convention among English speakers to say only what one believes. Speakers violate no linguistic conventions when they make suppositions, give examples, joke, tell stories, and so forth. Furthermore, when speakers do such things, they utilize the same linguistic conventions they make use of when they try to say only what is true, and they use these conventions in the same way. Of course, it may be that speakers are supposed to *assert* only what they believe; but that is not a general linguistic convention; it is a particular point about assertion.

The relevant linguistic conventions do not associate sentences only with beliefs but more generally with propositions or, as I shall say, thoughts, which are sometimes believed, sometimes supposed, sometimes just presented for consideration. The meaning of a sentence is determined by the thought with which the sentence is conventionally correlated, that is, the thought which, by convention, speakers would normally intend to communicate to a hearer by using that sentence.

Thoughts in this sense are not mysterious objects; they are just beliefs, hopes, suppositions, and so forth, more generally described. The term 'thought', as I use it here, is simply a more general term than 'belief', 'hope', and 'supposition'. A belief that cigarettes are good for you, a hope that cigarettes are good for you, and a supposition that cigarettes are good for you are all thoughts that cigarettes are good for you, in this sense of 'thought'.

The relevant thoughts are to be identified, not in terms of truth conditions, but rather in terms of their potential role in a speaker's 'conceptual scheme'—the system of concepts constituted by the speaker's beliefs, plans, hopes, fears, and so on, ways the speaker has of modifying his beliefs, plans, hopes, fears, and so on, and ways these modify what the speaker does. I defend a 'functionalist' theory of this sort in Harman (1973), and will say more about it later in this essay and in the following essays. Supposing that such a theory is correct, there is a sense in which meaning depends on role in conceptual scheme. The meaning of a sentence is determined by the role in a conceptual scheme of the thoughts that the sentence would normally be used to express.

Now, to get to the main point, the implications that a thought has are very important to its role in a conceptual scheme; and logical implications are particularly important. Furthermore, logical implication is a matter of truth and logical form. P logically implies Q if and only if, whenever a proposition with the same logical form as P is true, the corresponding proposition with the same logical form as Q is also true. And this, according to me, is how truth is relevant to meaning. It is relevant to the meaning of those syntactic elements of sentences that determine logical form. For the meaning of those elements depends on their role in logical implication; and logical implication is to be defined in terms of truth.

11.4 CONCEPTUAL ROLE SEMANTICS

I say that meaning depends on role in conceptual scheme rather than on truth conditions. That is, meaning has to do with evidence, inference, and reasoning, including the impact sensory experience has on what one believes, the way in which inference and reasoning modify one's beliefs and plans, and the way beliefs and plans are reflected in action. For me, the meaning of the relevant sort of sentence is determined by the thought it would normally express. The nature of that thought is not in the first instance determined by its truth conditions; it is, rather, a matter of psychology. For a thought, as I am using this term, is a psychological state, defined by its role in a system of states that are modified by sensory input, inference, and reasoning, and that have an influence on action. To specify a thought is to specify its role in such a conceptual system. To specify the meaning of a sentence of the relevant sort is to specify a thought, so to specify its meaning is to specify a role in a conceptual scheme.

The idea that meaning is a matter of role in conceptual scheme is not a philosophical novelty. It appears, in simplified form, in verification theories of meaning. Quine's (1960*b*) is a better version because it corrects the mistaken assumption of verificationist theories that evidence can have a direct bearing on individual statements apart from considerations of theory. Although Quine sometimes stresses pragmatism, he often considers only role in relation to sensory experience, evidence, and theoretical inference, leaving the practical side out. Hampshire (1959) takes the practical aspect of role to be important for meaning. Meaning is a matter of role because meaning is a matter of the thought expressed; and a thought is defined by its role in a psychological system that includes not only the effect of sensory stimulation and inference but also the impact on the environment of this system via action.

It would be a mistake to suppose that the relevant thoughts must have an existence independent of the language in which one expresses them. As suggested in the previous two essays, learning a language is not just learning a way to encode thoughts one already has. It is rather in part to acquire the possibility of new thoughts, thoughts that are in that language. That is why a language carries with it aspects of a world view. Learning a language is not to be distinguished from learning a theory. One acquires a new system of representation for thought. One learns a new way of thinking.

Principles of linguistic communication would be difficult to state and harder to learn if they correlated sentences with thoughts that had to be specified independently of each other. But, as a first approximation, the rule is simple: a sentence expresses the thought that one would have if one thought exactly those words. That is only a first approximation because thoughts in words are not just strings of words. They are sentences under an analysis that reveals logical form. They are words with more structure than a string. The thought which a speaker intends to communicate with his words is a complex structure of words. In the normal case, communication is successful if the hearer perceives what is said as having the intended structure. The difference between two possible interpretations of 'Jack dislikes pleasing students' is like the difference between the two interpretations of an ambiguous drawing of a staircase. To hear one interpretation is to hear the sentence as having a particular structure. One does not need to decode the sentence into a completely nonlinguistic thought. The principles of language that are relevant to communication are the principles of grammar that correlate sentences with their underlying logical forms.

But the principles of language that are thus relevant to communication are not the only regularities involving language relevant to meaning. More relevant are regularities concerning the way in which language is used in thought. For example, one may accept a number of basic principles that partially determine the roles and therefore the meanings of various terms. These principles, sometimes misleadingly called 'meaning postulates', might include such things as statements of transitivity for 'more than' and so forth. Furthermore, there will be certain regularities in the way in which beliefs are formed as the result of sensory experience. It is regularities of this sort that are primarily relevant to the roles in belief and therefore the meanings of colour words. And then there will also be some conventional regularities relevant to the meanings of logical words, like 'and', 'or', 'if', 'every', 'some', 'not', and so forth.

11.5 LOGIC, MEANING, AND TRUTH

Principles of logic differ from other general principles in two respects. First, logical principles have a special role in inference (which is not to say that principles of logic are themselves rules of inference—see Essay 1). Second, general logical principles cannot be stated directly in the object language but only indirectly by talking about language and truth. A general logical principle must say that all thoughts of a specified form are true.

The meaning of a logical term is a matter of its role in one's conceptual scheme; and that is a matter of the way such a term is involved in principles of logic which have the special role in inference. Logical principles say that all thoughts of certain specified logical forms are true, where forms are specified with reference to the logical constructions that they involve. A truth of logic can be said to hold by virtue of its form, since any other thought with the same logical form is also true. Logical terms have an important role in logical truths, since the truths hold by virtue of their logical terms. That is why consideration of truth conditions can sometimes tell us something about meaning. It can tell us something about the meanings of logical elements of structure since it can provide an account of the role of such elements in determining what the logical truths are.

I have already mentioned Davidson's idea that what a formal theory of truth tells us about meaning is not given by the T sentences it implies but rather by the recursion clauses of the theory. We can now make sense of that idea, at least as it applies to logical terms. Consider a logical term like 'and', representing logical conjunction. The infinite number of T sentences by themselves tell us nothing about the meaning of 'and' since these T sentences by themselves tell us nothing in particular about the function of 'and'. What is relevant is the clause in a formal theory of truth that says a conjunction is true if and only if both conjuncts are. For that tells us something about conjunction that is relevant to its logical role. Since to specify the meaning of 'and' is to specify this role, the relevant clause of the theory of truth tells us something about the meaning of 'and'.

We can easily envisage formal theories of truth that would tell us nothing about the meaning of 'and', for example the theory that simply took all T sentences as axioms. A theory that sheds light on the meaning of 'and' and other logical terms does not do so simply in virtue of being a theory of truth but rather because it contains specific clauses saying how conjunction and the other logical terms contribute to the truth or falsity of complex sentences.

Now, it seems to me that consideration of those cases in which a theory of truth appears to tell us something about meaning supports my account over the thesis that meaning is generally a matter of truth conditions. For consider some of the examples I have already mentioned: the truth-functional account of the logical connectives, the Frege–Tarski analysis of logical quantification, or Kripke's semantics for operators of modal logic.

Davidson's theory concerning the logical form of action sentences illustrates the point in a different way. Davidson (1967a) does not give clauses in a truth definition for any new logical operator. His aim is rather to argue that the logical form of action sentences can be represented in ordinary quantificational logic on the assumption that these sentences involve disguised quantification over events. Davidson suggests that a sentence like 'John walks' has the logical form,

$(\exists x)$ (John walks x).

The sentence 'John walks in the rain' has the form

$(\exists x)$ (John walks x & x is in the rain).

That the first of these sentences is implied by the second is taken by Davidson to be an instance of a simple implication of ordinary quantificational logic.

Davidson's theory tells us something about meaning because it tells us about logical form, and meaning is partly a matter of logical form. The linguistic conventions that are relevant to meaning include those grammatical conventions that correlate surface forms of sentences with their logical forms. So to say something about the logical form of a sentence is to say something about its meaning. But Davidson's theory does not tell us everything we might want to know about the meaning of action sentences, since the theory sees quantification over events in these sentences. Although a theory of truth can explain the meaning of the quantification, it cannot fully explicate the reference to events. For that, something more is needed, a theory of events along with some indication of how we are to confirm or disconfirm statements about events.

A similar point can be made about Kripke's (1963) semantics for modal logic. It does not fully specify the meaning of 'possible' or 'necessary' because it accounts for truth conditions in terms of quantification over possible worlds. No theory of truth can by itself explain that reference to possible worlds. What is needed is a theory of possible worlds and an indication of how we are to confirm or disconfirm statements about possible worlds.

Recall the sentence, 'All mimsy were the borogroves'. As Wiggins (1972)

remarks, the thing that we lack here is not an understanding of what the relevant clauses in a truth theory would look like (for we know that), but rather an understanding of evidence and inference. I say that this will always be the case for nonlogical terms.

If by 'semantics' we mean a finitely axiomatized formal theory of truth, we must not identify semantics with the theory of meaning. Semantics in this sense can tell us something important about the meanings of logical terms and other aspects of logical structure, but it cannot in the same way illuminate the meaning of nonlogical terms.

(Nonsolipsistic) Conceptual Role Semantics

12.1 WHAT IS (NONSOLIPSISTIC) CONCEPTUAL ROLE SEMANTICS?

In this essay I will defend a nonsolipsistic version of conceptual role semantics. This approach to meaning involves the following four claims:

(1) the meanings of linguistic expressions are determined by the contents of the concepts and thoughts they can be used to express;

(2) the contents of thoughts are determined by their construction out of concepts; and

(3) the contents of concepts are determined by their functional role in a person's psychology, where

(4) functional role is conceived nonsolipsistically as involving relations to things in the world, including things in the past and future.

Thoughts here include beliefs, hopes, desires, fears, and other attitudes, in addition to thoughts properly so called. Functional role includes any special roles a concept may play in perception and in inference or reasoning, including practical reasoning that leads to action.

I include the parenthetical modifier '(nonsolipsistic)' in the title, '(Nonsolipsistic) Conceptual Role Semantics' in order to contrast the present approach with that of authors (Field, 1977b; Fodor, 1980; Loar, 1981) who think of conceptual role solipsistically as a completely internal matter. I put parentheses around 'nonsolipsistic' because, as I will argue below, the term is redundant: conceptual role must be conceived nonsolipsistically.

Commenting on Harman (1982), Loewer (1982) takes this nonsolipsistic aspect to be an important revision in an earlier solipsistic theory. Not so. Conceptual role semantics derives from nonsolipsistic behaviourism. It was originally and has until recently been a nonsolipsistic theory (e.g. Sellars, 1963 (originally 1954); Harman, 1973).

(Nonsolipsistic) conceptual role semantics represents one thing that might be meant by the slogan 'meaning is use'. But a proper appreciation of the point requires distinguishing (at least) two uses of symbols: their use in calculation, as in adding a column of figures, and their use in communication, as in telling someone the result.

12.1.1 *Two Uses of Symbols: Communication and Calculation*

Symbols that are being used in calculation are typically not being used at that time for communication. When you add a column of figures you are not normally communicating anything even to yourself. A similar point holds in reverse. Normally you communicate the results of your calculation to someone else only after you are done calculating. There are, of course, exceptions. You might go through a calculation on the blackboard intending your audience to see how things come out.

(Nonsolipsistic) conceptual role semantics is a version of the theory that meaning is use, where the basic use of symbols is taken to be in calculation, not in communication, and where concepts are treated as symbols in a 'language of thought'. Clearly, the relevant use of such 'symbols', the use of which determines their content, is their use in thought and calculation rather than in communication. If thought is like talking to yourself, it is the sort of talking involved in figuring something out, not the sort of talking involved in communication. Thinking is not communicating with yourself.

However, it would be more accurate to say content is use than to say meaning is use; strictly speaking, thoughts and concepts have content, not meaning.

12.1.2 *The Meaning of 'Meaning'*

I assume, following Grice (1957), that we can distinguish what he calls natural meaning (smoke means fire) from what he calls non-natural meaning (the German word 'Feuer' means fire), and we can also distinguish (non-natural) speaker or user meaning (what a speaker or user of certain symbols means) from what certain words, expressions, or other symbols mean.

Grice proposes to analyse expression meaning in terms of speaker meaning, and he proposes, more controversially, to analyse speaker meaning in terms of a speaker's intentions to communicate something. His second proposal overlooks the meaningful use of symbols in calculation. You might invent a special notation in order to work out a certain sort of problem. It would be quite proper to say that by a given symbol you meant so-and-so, even though you have no intention of using these symbols in any sort of communication.

There is a connection between user meaning and the user's intentions. Suppose you use your special notation to work out a specific problem. You formulate the assumptions of the problem in your notation, do some calculating, and end up with a meaningful result in that notation. It would be correct to say of you that, when you wrote down a particular assumption in your notation, you meant such-and-such by what you wrote; but it would be incorrect to say of you that, when you wrote the conclusion you reached in your notation, you meant so-and-so by what you wrote. This is connected with the fact that, in formulating the assumption as you did in your notation, you intended to express such-and-such an assumption; whereas, in writing down the conclusion you reached in your notation, your intention was not to express such-and-such a conclusion but rather to reach whatever conclusion in your notation followed from earlier steps by the rules of your calculus. This indicates that you mean that so-and-so in using certain symbols if and only if you use those symbols to express the thought that so-and-so, with the intention of expressing such a thought.

Unuttered thoughts (beliefs, fears, desires, etc.) do not have meaning. We would not ordinarily say that in thinking as you did you meant that so-and-so. If thoughts are in a language of thought, they are not always uttered out loud in that language.

Sometimes one does have thoughts in English or some other real language. A language, properly so called, is a symbol system that is used both for communication and thought. If one cannot think in a language, one has not yet mastered it. A symbol system used only for communication, like Morse code, is not a language.

Concepts and other aspects of mental representation have content but not (normally) meaning (unless they are also expressions in a language used in communication). We would not normally say that your concept of redness meant anything in the way that the word 'red' in English means something. Nor would we say that you meant anything by that concept on a particular occasion of its exercise.

12.1.3 *Thoughts and Concepts*

It is sometimes suggested that words have meaning because of the way they are used; the meaning of a word is its use in the language. Ryle (1953, 1961) observes that it is a mistake to extend this idea directly to sentences. There are indefinitely many sentences. Most of them are never used at all, and most sentences that are used are used only once. Sentences do not normally have regular uses in the way that words do. Sentences have meaning because of the words they contain and the way these words are put together. A use theory of meaning has to suppose it is words and ways of putting words together that have meaning because of their uses, not sentences.

Similarly, it is concepts that have uses or functions or roles in thought, not the possible attitudes in which those concepts occur. There are indefinitely many possible attitudes. Most possible attitudes are never taken by anyone, and most attitudes that are at some point taken by someone are taken by someone only once. Possible beliefs, desires, and other attitudes do not normally have regular uses or functions or roles that make them the possible attitudes they are. Consider, for example, what use or role or function there might be for the possible belief of yours that you have bathed in Coca-Cola. This belief would have a certain content, but no obvious use or role or function. The content of a belief does not derive from its own role or function but rather from the uses of the concepts it exercises.

12.1.4 *Are Concepts Literally Parts of Thoughts?*

Loar (1983*a*) objects that this account implies that thoughts literally contain (tokens of) concepts as parts, so that, for example, all conjunctive beliefs share a constituent representing conjunction, and similarly for other concepts. He rejects this view, arguing that our ordinary conception of belief and other attitudes does not require it. He agrees we must suppose that all conjunctive beliefs have something in common, and similarly that all negative beliefs have something in common, but this, he says, is not to suppose that all conjunctive or negative beliefs have a constituent in common. He says that conjunctive or negative beliefs might have certain 'second order properties in common' without having any 'first order, structural properties in common'.

The issue is obscure, like the question of whether the prime factors of a number are really constituents of the number or not. All numbers that have three as a prime factor have something in common. Do they have a first-order structural property in common or only a second-order property? This does not strike me as a well-defined issue, and I feel the same way about Loar's issue. Just as it is useful for certain purposes to think of the prime factors of a number as its constituents, it is also useful for certain purposes to think of attitudes as having concepts as constituents. But it is hard to know what is meant by the question whether concepts are literally constituents of thoughts.

Loar is thinking along something like the following lines. A relation of negation might hold between two beliefs without there being anything that determines which belief is the negative one, and similarly for other concepts. In the case of conjunction, let us say that P has the 'relation of conjunction' to Q and R if and only if Q and R together obviously imply and are obviously implied by P. Belief P might have the relation of conjunction in this sense to Q and R without anything distinguishing the case in which P has the structure 'Q and R' from that in which P does not have that structure, but instead Q and R have the respective structures 'P or S' and 'P or not-S'. Similarly for other concepts.

This may seem a promising way to understand a denial of the claim that thoughts are constructed out of concepts, until one realizes that what is being imagined is simply that equivalent beliefs cannot be distinguished, so that 'not not P' cannot be distinguished from 'P', 'P and Q' cannot be distinguished from 'neither not P nor not Q', and so on. But it is easy to reject this possibility. If the issue is whether there can be two different but logically equivalent beliefs, the answer is obviously 'Yes'. So this cannot be how Loar intends the issue to be understood.

Loar (1983*b*) says that the issue is which of the following possibilities is correct. Is it (1) that the structures of attitudes help to explain functional relations among attitudes? Or is it (2) that the functional relations among the attitudes help to explain why we assign sentence-like structures to the attitudes? But (1) and (2) are not mutually exclusive. Any reasonable theory will allow that people often accept conclusions because the conclusions are instances of generalizations they accept. This is to allow that beliefs can have the quantified structure of generalizations and that this can explain certain functional relations among beliefs. And any reasonable theory will allow that we determine what structures attitudes have by considering functional relations among attitudes. So any reasonable theory will accept both (1) and (2).

In a reply to this, Loar (1983*b*) says to consider what it would be like if a conjunctive belief C(P,Q) were internally represented as a single unstructured symbol R that was linked by particular rules to its conjuncts P and Q, so that R obviously implied and was obviously implied by P and Q although one's recognition of the implication did not depend on thinking of R as the conjunction of P and Q. In other words, the reason why one immediately recognized the implication from R to P would in this case be different from the reason why one immediately recognized the implication from U to S, where U was the conjunction of S and T. The fact that R and U were conjunctions would not be part of the explanation of one's recognition of these implications. And similarly for other logical constants.

But this sort of example is precisely not compatible with our ordinary thinking about belief, since (as I have already observed) we do suppose people often recognize implications because of the relevant formal properties; for example, we think people often accept certain conclusions because the conclusions are instances of generalizations they accept, which is to think that beliefs have a certain internal structure. So this example does not support Loar's scepticism.

12.2 CONTENT AND FUNCTIONAL ROLE

12.2.1 *Types of Role*

Assuming conceptual role semantics as a basic framework, it is plausible that all concepts have a function in reasoning that is relevant to their content. No doubt, some concepts have the content they have primarily because of a special role they play in perception—colour concepts, for example. But the content of even these concepts depends to some extent on inferential role. A given colour concept is the concept of a normally persisting characteristic of objects in the world, a characteristic that can be used both to keep track of objects and as a sign of other things. For example, greenness is a sign of unripeness in certain fruits. Moreover, there are various internal relations among colours. From the premise that an object is red at a certain place at a certain time one can infer that the object is not also green at that place and time.

In the case of concepts of shape and number, inferential connections play a larger role. Perceptual connections are still relevant; to some extent your concept of a triangle involves your notion of what a triangle looks like and your concept of various natural numbers is connection with your ability to count objects you perceive. But the role these notions play in inference looms larger.

The concept expressed by the word 'because' plays an important role in one's understanding of phenomena and has (I believe) a central role in inference, since inference is often inference to the best explanation. This role makes the concept expressed by 'because' the concept it is. Is perception relevant at all here? Perhaps. It may be that you sometimes directly perceive causality or certain explanatory relations, and it may be that this helps to determine the content of the concept you express with the word 'because'. Or perhaps not. Maybe the perception of causality and other explanatory relations is always mediated by inference.

Logical words like 'and', 'not', 'every', and 'some' express concepts whose function in inference seems clearly quite important to their content, which is why it seems plausible to say that these words do not mean in intuitionistic logic and quantum logic what they mean in so-called classical logic, although even here there may be crucial perceptual functions. It may, for example, be central to your concept of negation that you can sometimes perceive that certain things are not so, as when you perceive that Pierre is not in the café, for instance. It may be central to your concept of generality or universal quantification that you can sometimes perceive that everything of a certain sort is so-and-so, for instance that everyone in the room is wearing a hat.

It is possible that there are certain sorts of theoretical term, like 'quark', that play no role in perception at all, so that the content of the concepts they express is determined entirely by inferential role. (But maybe it is important to the concept of a quark that the concept should play a role in the perception of certain pictures or diagrams!)

12.2.2 *Inference and Implication*

Logical words have a function in inference and reasoning because certain implications and inconsistencies depend on them. Inference is, of course, a process of thought which typically culminates in a change in view, a change in your beliefs if it is theoretical reasoning, a change in plans and intentions for practical reasoning. (There is also the limiting case in which you make no change.)

There is as yet no substantial theory of inference or reasoning. To be sure, logic is well developed; but logic is not a theory of inference or reasoning. Logic is a theory of implication and inconsistency.

Logic is relevant to reasoning because implication and inconsistency are. Implication and inconsistency are relevant to reasoning because implication is an explanatory relation and because inconsistency is a kind of incoherence, and in reasoning you try among other things to increase the explanatory coherence of your view (Harman, 1986*a*). Particularly relevant are relations of immediate or obvious psychological implication and immediate or obvious psychological inconsistency.

These notions, of immediate implication and inconsistency for a person S, might be partly explained as follows. If P and R immediately imply Q for S, then, if S accepts P and R and considers whether Q, S is strongly disposed to accept Q too, unless S comes to reject P or R. If U and V are immediately inconsistent for S, S is strongly disposed not to accept both, so that, if S accepts the one, S is strongly disposed not to accept the other without giving up the first.

I should stress that these dispositions are only dispositions or tendencies which might be overridden by other factors. Sometimes one has to continue to believe things one knows are inconsistent, because one does not know of any good way to resolve the inconsistency. Furthermore, the conditions I have stated are at best only necessary conditions. For example, as Scott Soames has pointed out to me, U and 'I do not believe U' satisfy the last condition without being inconsistent. Soames has also observed that the principles for implication presuppose there is not a purely probabilistic rule of acceptance for belief. Otherwise one might accept P and Q without accepting their conjunction, which they obviously imply, on the grounds that the conjuncts can have a high probability without the conjunction having such a high probability. I have elsewhere argued against such a purely probabilistic rule (Harman, 1986*a*).

Now, if logical concepts are entirely fixed by their functions in reasoning, a concept C expresses logical conjunction if it serves to combine two thoughts P and Q to form a third thought C(P,Q), where the role of C can be characterized in terms of the principles of 'conjunction introduction' and 'conjunction elimination'. In other words, P and Q obviously and immediately imply, and are immediate obvious psychological implications of, C(P,Q). Similarly, a concept N expresses logical negation if it applies to a thought P to form a second thought N(P) and the role of N can be characterized as follows: N(P) is obviously inconsistent with P and is immediately implied by anything else that is obviously inconsistent with P and vice versa, that is, anything obviously inconsistent with N(P) immediately implies P. (I am indebted to Scott Soames for pointing out that this last clause is needed.) In the same way, concepts express one or another type of logical quantification if their function can be specified by relevant principles of generalization and instantiation. To repeat, this holds only on the assumption that logical concepts are determined entirely by their role in reasoning and that any role in perception they might have is not essential or derives from their role in reasoning.

12.2.3 *Logical Form*

Accounts of the logical forms of sentences of a natural language can shed light on meaning to the extent that they indicate aspects of language on which implications may depend, since this is to indicate something about the inferential role played by the concepts expressed by those aspects of language.

Presumably, such accounts of logical form should be relevant to or perhaps even part of a grammatical analysis of the relevant sentences. Here is an area where there may be useful interaction between what philosophers do and what linguists do. However, as Chomsky (1980) observes, distinctions that are important for linguistics may not coincide with the distinctions that are important for philosophers. Or, to put the point in another way, the factors that determine relations of implication may not all be of the same sort. Some may be aspects of what Chomsky calls 'sentence grammar', others may not. And some aspects of 'sentence grammar' that function syntactically like logical features may not be directly connected with implication. For example, Chomsky suggests that the rules of grammar that determine how quantifiers are understood, which are of course crucial in determining what the logical implications of the sentence are, may be the same as the rules that determine such things as the 'focus' of a sentence, something which seems not to affect the logical implications of a sentence but only its 'conversational implicatures'.

12.2.4 *Indeterminacy*

There are apparently competing analyses of the logical forms of sentences. Where one analysis sees modal logic or tense logic, another sees reference to possible worlds or times; where one analysis sees reference to events, another analysis invokes an adverbial logic; and so on. Similarly, there are apparently competing grammatical theories: Montague grammar, Chomsky's framework in terms of rules of government and binding, and many other variations. What are we to make of all this?

Quine (1960b) argues plausibly that, even given all possible evidence about a language, that may not decide between various locally incompatible 'analytical hypotheses', where by 'analytical hypotheses' he means hypotheses about logical or grammatical form of the sort just mentioned. There has been considerable dispute as to exactly how Quine's claim should be interpreted, whether it is true, and what the implications of its truth might be. It has been said (falsely) that all Quine's thesis amounts to is the claim that a theory is underdetermined by the evidence. It has also been said (correctly, I believe) that whatever valid point Quine may be making, it does not involve any significant difference between the 'hard sciences', like physics, and the study of language.

One issue suggested by Quine's argument is this. Suppose you have a theory, of physical reality or of language, which you think is true. Even though you think the theory is true, you can go on to consider what aspects of the theory correspond to reality and what aspects are instead mere artefacts of the notation in which the theory is presented. A true geographical description of the Earth will mention longitudes as well as cities and mountains, but longitudes do not have geographical reality in the way that cities and mountains do. It is true that Greenwich, England, is at zero degrees longitude, but this truth is an artefact of our way of describing the Earth, since there are other equally true ways of describing the geography of the Earth that would assign Greenwich other longitudes. Similarly, there are various true physical descriptions of the world which assign a given space-time point different coordinates. It may be true that under a particular description a particular point has the special coordinates $(0,0,0,0)$, but that is an artefact of the description which, by itself, does not correspond to anything in reality, and the same is true as regards grammars and theories of logical form. Even if a given account of grammar or logical form is true, there is still a question what aspects of the account correspond to reality and what aspects are merely artefacts of that particular description. It is quite possible that several different, locally incompatible accounts might all be true, just as several different, locally incompatible assignments of longitudes and latitudes to places on Earth might all be true.

This might be put in another way. Reality is what is invariant among true complete theories. Geographical reality is what is invariant in different true complete geographical descriptions of the world. Physical reality is what is invariant in different true complete physical descriptions of the universe. What worries Quine is that he has a fairly good sense of physical and geographical reality but little or no sense of grammatical reality or of the reality described by accounts of logical form. Indeed, Quine is inclined to think that there are only two relevant levels of reality here:

(1) physical reality at the level of neurophysiology, and
(2) behavioural reality, including dispositions to behave in various ways.

An alternative view is that there are other, functionally defined levels of reality between the two levels Quine acknowledges. I see no other way to investigate this issue except by seeing where current investigation of grammar and logical form ultimately leads. Of course, from a heuristic point of view, it is probably best to suppose that different accounts of grammar and logical form make conflicting claims about reality unless there is some reason to think otherwise (Harman, 1986c).

The possibility of indeterminacy allows an interpretation of the question, raised by Loar (1983a) and discussed above, as to whether thoughts really contain concepts as parts. Suppose there are many different sets of 'analytical hypotheses' that account for the facts. On one set of hypotheses, Q would be a simpler belief than P, and P would be the explicit negation of Q. On a different set of analytical hypotheses, things would be reversed and Q would be the explicit negation of P. Nothing would determine which belief really contained the explicit negation independently of one or another set of hypotheses. If this should prove to be so, which I doubt, it would show that a particular assignment of structure to a given thought was an artefact of a given way of describing thoughts. It would of course also be true that, relative to a given set of analytical hypotheses, a given thought would truly consist in a particular structure of concepts.

12.2.5 *Meaning and Truth Conditions*

Davidson (1967b), Lewis (1971), and others have argued that an account of the truth conditions of sentences of a language can serve as an account of the meanings of those sentences. But, as noted in Essay 11, above, this seems wrong. Of course, if you know the meaning in your language of the sentence S, and you know what the word 'true' means, then you will also know something of the form 'S is true if and only if . . .'; for example, '"Snow is white" is true if and only if snow is white' or '"I am sick" is true if and only if the speaker is sick at the time of utterance'. But this is a trivial point about the meaning of 'true', not a deep point about meaning.

There are well-known difficulties with the view that a theory of truth might provide even part of a theory of meaning (e.g., Foster, 1976). For one thing, how are the truth conditions to be specified? There seem to be two possibilities. The first is that truth conditions are assigned to beliefs by virtue of the theory's implying clauses of the form 'Belief B is true if and only if C'. Then the problem is that the same theory will also imply indefinitely many results of the form 'C if and only if D', where 'C' and 'D' are not synonymous, so the theory will imply indefinitely many 'incorrect' clauses of the form 'Belief B is true if and only if D'. The problem is, in other words, that specifying truth conditions in this way does not distinguish among beliefs that are equivalent in relation to the principles of the theory.

The other possibility is to allow that equivalent beliefs might have different truth conditions. The trouble with this possibility is that it treats truth conditions as very much like meanings or contents which are no longer specifiable by the usual Tarski-type theories of truth. It is unclear how this appeal to truth conditions might offer any benefit to the theory of content beyond the tautology that a theory of content must include an account of content.

This is not to deny that attempts to develop theories of truth adequate for certain aspects of natural language may well shed light on meaning. Examples might include the truth-functional analysis of 'and', 'not', and 'or'; the Frege–Tarski analysis of quantification; Davidson's analysis of action sentences; and the possible-worlds account of modality. But in all these cases the analyses help specify implications among sentences. Their bearing on meaning may be due entirely to that, apart from anything further necessary to having a theory of truth, although this, of course, allows that there may also be a heuristic point to attempting to develop theories of truth (Harman, 1972).

12.2.6 *Probabilistic Semantics*

Field (1977*b*) suggests that inferential role might be captured in terms of a probability distribution. This would yield at best a theory of probabilistic implication or coherence, not a theory of inference in the relevant sense involving (normally) a certain sort of change in view. Furthermore, people do not and could not operate probabilistically, since keeping track of probabilities involves memory and calculating capacities which are exponentially exploding functions of the number of logically unrelated propositions involved (Harman, 1985, 1986*a*).

For the most part you have to accept propositions in an all or nothing way. Conservatism is important. You should continue to believe as you do in the absence of any special reason to doubt your views, and in reasoning you should try to minimize change in your initial opinions in attaining other goals of reasoning. Such other goals include explanatory coherence and, of course, practical success in satisfying your needs and desires. But these points are vague and do not take us very far. Furthermore, something ultimately needs to be said about practical reasoning (Harman, 1986*a*, 1987).

12.3 CONCEPTUAL ROLE AND EXTERNAL WORLD

In the most elementary cases, possession of a concept of something is connected with perceiving that thing and acting appropriately towards it.

What one perceives the thing as is reflected in the way one acts. For example, an animal perceives something as food if it treats what it perceives as food, for example by eating what it perceives. Of course, there are complications to this simple story and things can go wrong. But this represents the most elementary case and more complex cases must be conceived in terms of it. So, for example, we can describe a creature as mistakenly thinking that something is food when it tries to treat it as food. In so describing the animal, we appeal to a conception of what happens in the normal case when nothing goes wrong and there is no mistake.

In Harman (1973) I emphasize how the appeal to a background of normality figures in all identifications of representational states, even those in an artefact such as a radar aimer. A radar aimer interprets data from radar and calculates where to fire guns in order to shoot down enemy planes. We can describe the device as representing the present and future locations of the planes because radar waves reflected from the planes are received and interpreted to form a representation of the future locations of the planes, and that representation is used in the aiming and firing of the guns that shoot down the planes. We can describe the device as representing the locations of planes even if something goes wrong and the guns miss, because we have a conception of the normal operation of the radar aimer. We can even treat the device as representing enemy planes when it is being tested in the laboratory, unconnected to radar and guns, since in our testing we envisage it as connected in the right way. However, given a different conception of normal context, we could not describe the device as representing planes at all.

The moral is that (nonsolipsistic) conceptual role semantics does not involve a 'solipsistic' theory of the content of thoughts. There is no suggestion that content depends only on functional relations among thoughts and concepts, such as the role a particular concept plays in inference. Of primary importance are functional relations to the external world in connection with perception, on the one hand, and action, on the other. The functions of logical concepts can be specified 'solipsistically', in terms of the inner workings of one's conceptual system, without reference to things in the 'external world'. But this is not true for the functions of other concepts.

Concepts include individual concepts and general concepts, where an individual concept functions in certain contexts to pick out a particular object in the external world to which a general concept applies, in the simplest case to enable one to handle the object as a thing of the appropriate sort (cf. Strawson, 1974a: 42–51). To repeat an earlier example, it is an important function of the concept of food that in certain circumstances one can recognize particular stuff as food, this recognition enabling one to treat that thing appropriately as food by eating it (Dennett, 1969: 73). What makes something the concept red is in part the way in which the concept is involved in the perception of red objects in the external world. What makes something the concept of danger is in part the way in which the concept is involved in thoughts that affect action in certain ways.

12.3.1 *The Division of Linguistic Labour*

The content of certain concepts appears to depend crucially on functional relations between those concepts and certain words in a public language. You might have a concept of an oak tree by virtue of which you have thoughts about oak trees where the crucial functional relation is a relation between your concept and the word 'oak' in English. You might, for example, wonder whether there were any oak trees in your back yard even if you cannot distinguish oak trees from elm trees and do not know any of the distinguishing properties of these two sorts of trees (Putnam, 1975; Kripke, 1972).

(Nonsolipsistic) conceptual role semantics asserts that an account of the content of thoughts is more basic than an account of communicated meaning and the significance of speech acts. In this view, the content of linguistic expressions derives from the contents of thoughts they can be used to express. However, allowance must also be made for cases in which the content of your thoughts depends in part on the content of certain words, such as 'oak' and 'elm'.

Of course, in this case there are other people who can recognize oaks and distinguish them from elms and who know various distinguishing properties of the trees. These other people may have a concept of an oak tree which has functional roles that are sufficient to make it the concept of an oak tree apart from any relations the concept has with the word 'oak'. It is plausible

(1) that their concept acquires its content from this aspect of its functional role, i.e. its role apart from its relation to the word 'oak',

(2) that the word 'oak' as they use it has the meaning it has because of its connection with their concept of an oak tree,

(3) that the word 'oak' as used by a more ignorant person can have the same reference by virtue of connections between that person's ignorant use of the word and the expert's use, and

(4) the content of the more ignorant person's concept of an oak tree

derives from its connection to his or her use of the word and its meaning as he or she uses it.

Of course, the content of the more ignorant person's concept of an oak tree is not as rich as, so not the same as, the content of the expert's concept. But the ignorant person's concept is still a concept of an oak tree, by virtue of its connection with the word 'oak'.

12.3.2 *Twin Earth*

Putnam (1975) imagines a world, which he calls 'Twin Earth', which is just like Earth except for certain minor differences. There are on Twin Earth duplicates of all the people on Earth and the people on Twin Earth speak the same languages as on Earth, using expressions in the same way, except that, because of the minor differences between Earth and Twin Earth, they sometimes refer to different things by their words. In particular, the main difference between Twin Earth and Earth is that where there is water on Earth there is on Twin Earth a liquid with the same macro properties as water but a different chemical structure, which Putnam calls 'XYZ'.

Comparing Earth in 1750 (before the micro-structure of water has been investigated) with Twin Earth at the corresponding time, we find that the English word 'water' means something different in the two places, simply because the word is used on Earth to refer to what is in fact H_2O and is used on Twin Earth to refer to what is in fact XYZ. Similarly, where Earthlings think about H_2O, Twin Earthlings think about XYZ. This difference is not in 1750 reflected in any difference in dispositions to react to various perceptual situations, in any difference in inferences that people in the respective places would make, nor in any differences in the actions which people undertake as the result of thoughts involving the relevant concept.

The difference is also not simply a difference in context of utterance or context of thought. Suppose an Earthling were to travel by spaceship and land on an ocean of XYZ in Twin Earth. Looking around, the Earthling comes to believe there is water all around. This belief is false, since the Earthling's concept of water is a concept of something that is in fact H_2O. The Earthling's concept of water remains a concept of the same thing that is referred to by 'water' on Earth even though the Earthling is now located in a different context. The context of the thoughts of the Earthling and the context of the thoughts of the Twin Earthlings are now the same; but the latters' thoughts are about XYZ where his are still about water. So this difference in the content of the thoughts of Earthlings and Twin Earthlings cannot be simply a difference in the context in which they have their thoughts.

The difference is due rather to the fact that the content of a person's concept is determined by its functional role in some normal context. The normal context for an Earthling's thoughts about what he or she calls 'water' is here on Earth, while the normal context for a Twin Earthling's thoughts about what he or she calls 'water' is on Twin Earth.

The normal context can change. If the traveller from Earth to Twin Earth stays on, after a while the normal context for the concepts he or she uses will be properly taken to be the Twin Earth contexts. Thoughts about what he or she calls 'water' will be properly considered thoughts about XYZ rather than H_2O. There is, of course, a certain amount of arbitrariness in any decision about when this change has occurred. It will sometimes be possible with equal justice to consider a given thought a thought about H_2O or a thought about XYZ.

A similar arbitrariness would arise concerning a person created spontaneously in outer space as the improbable result of random events at the quantum level, supposing the person were saved from space-death by a fortuitously passing spaceship, and supposing the person spoke something that sounded very much like English. Suppose, indeed, that this person is a duplicate of you and also (of course) of your Twin Earth counterpart. When the person has thoughts that he or she would express using the term 'water', are these thoughts about water (H_2O) or thoughts about XYZ? If we interpret this person's thoughts against a normal background on Earth, we will interpret the relevant thoughts as thoughts about water. If we take the normal background to be Twin Earth, they are thoughts about XYZ. Clearly it is quite arbitrary what we say here.

12.3.3 *Qualia*

According to (nonsolipsistic) conceptual role semantics, then, the content of a thought is not a matter of the 'intrinsic nature' of either that thought or other mental states and experiences but is rather a matter of how mental states are related to each other, to things in the external world, and to things in a context understood as a normal context. There is a familiar objection (Block and Fodor, 1972; Nagel, 1974) to this which claims that content is not determined always by such functions or relations. In this view the intrinsic qualities or 'qualia' of certain experiences are sometimes relevant. It is said that your concept of red involves your notion of what it is like to see something red, where what it is like to see something red is not just a matter of the functional or relational characteristics of the relevant experience but of its intrinsic character as well.

One argument for this is that it is possible to imagine a person whose spectrum was inverted with respect to yours, so that the quality of experience you have in seeing something red is the quality this other person has in seeing something green, the quality of experience you have in seeing something blue is the quality this other person has in seeing something yellow, and similarly for other colours, although in all relevant respects your colour experiences function similarly, so that each of you is just as good as the other in applying the public colour words to coloured objects. According to this argument, the two of you would have different concepts which you would express using the word 'red', although it might be difficult or even impossible to discover this difference, since it is not a functional difference.

I speak of an 'argument' here, although (as Lewis (1980) observes in a similar context), the 'argument' really comes down simply to denying the functionalist account of the content of concepts and thoughts, without actually offering any reason for that denial. This makes the 'argument' difficult to answer. All one can do is look more closely at a functionalist account of the content of colour concepts in order to bring out the way in which, according to functionalism, this content does not depend on the intrinsic character of experiences of colour.

How could you imagine someone whose spectrum was inverted with respect to yours? One way would be to imagine this happening to yourself. Suppose there were colour-inverting contact lenses. You put on a pair of lenses and the colours things seem to have are reversed. The sky now looks yellow rather than blue, ripe apples look green, unripe apples look red, and so on. Suppose you keep these lenses on and adapt your behaviour. You learn to say 'green' rather than 'red' when you see something that looks the way red things used to look; you learn to treat what you used to consider a green appearance of apples as a sign of ripeness, and so on. The years pass and your adaptation becomes habitual. Would not this be an intelligible case in which someone, the imagined future you, has a notion of what it is like to have the experience of seeing something to which the term 'red' applies, where the notion functions in exactly the way in which your notion of what such an experience is like functions, although your notions are different? The functionalist must deny this and say that the imagined you associates the same concept with the word 'red' as the actual you does now and indeed sees the world as you now do.

Consider an analogous case. There actually exist lenses that are spatially inverting. With these lenses on, things that are up look down and vice versa. At first it is very difficult to get around if you are wearing such lenses, since things are not where they seem to be. But after a while you begin to adapt. If you want to grab something that looks high, you reach low, and vice versa. If you want to look directly at something that appears in the bottom of your visual field you raise your head, and so on. Eventually, such adaptation becomes more or less habitual.

Now, functionalism implies that if you become perfectly adapted to such space-inverting lenses, then your experience will be the same as that of someone who is not wearing the inverting lenses (who has adapted to not wearing them if necessary), because now the normal context in relation to which your concepts function will have become a context in which you are wearing the inverting lenses. And in fact, people who have worn such lenses do say that, as they adapt to the lenses, the world tends to look right side up again (Taylor, 1962; Pitcher, 1971; Thomas, 1978).

Similarly, functionalism implies that if you become perfectly adapted to colour-inverting lenses, the world will come to look to you as it looked before, in the sense that given such perfect adaptation the normal context in which your colour concepts function will be a context in which you are wearing the colour-inverting lenses. According to functionalism, the way things look to you is a relational characteristic of your experience, not part of its intrinsic character.

In order to get a feel for this seemingly paradoxical aspect of (nonsolipsistic) conceptual role semantics, it may be useful to consider certain further cases. Consider Inverted Earth, a world just like ours, with duplicates of us, with the sole difference that there the actual colours of objects are the opposite of what they are here. The sky is yellow, ripe apples are green, etc. The inhabitants of Inverted Earth speak something that sounds like English, except that they say the sky is 'blue', they call ripe apples 'red', and so on. Question: what colour does their sky look to them? Answer: it looks yellow. The concept they express with the word 'blue' plays a relevantly special role in the normal perception of things that are actually yellow.

Suppose there is a distinctive physical basis for each different colour experience. Suppose also that the physical basis for the experience of red is the same for all normal people not adapted to colour-inverting lenses, and similarly for the other colours. According to (nonsolipsistic) conceptual role semantics this fact is irrelevant. The person who has perfectly adapted to colour-inverting lenses will be different from everyone else as regards the physical basis of his or her experience of red, but that will not affect the quality of his or her experience.

Consider someone on Inverted Earth who perfectly adapts to colour-inverting lenses. Looking at the sky of Inverted Earth, this person has an experience of colour whose physical basis is the same as that of a normal person on Earth looking at Earth's sky. But the sky looks yellow to the person on Inverted Earth and blue to normal people on Earth. What makes an experience the experience of something's looking the colour it looks is not its intrinsic character and/or physical basis, but rather its functional characteristics within an assumed normal context.

Consider a brain spontaneously created in space as the improbable result of random events at the quantum level. The physical events in the brain happen to be the same as those in you on Earth looking at the sky on a clear day and also the same as those in a person adapted to colour-inverting lenses looking at the sky of Inverted Earth. What is it like for the brain? Is it having an experience of yellow or of blue? According to (nonsolipsistic) conceptual role semantics, there is no nonarbitrary way to answer this question; it depends on what is taken as the normal context for assessing the functional role of events in that brain. If the normal context is taken to be the normal context for perception of colour on Earth, the brain is having an experience of blue. If the normal context is taken to be the normal context for a wearer of inverted lenses on Inverted Earth, the brain is having an experience of yellow. (The possibility of an inverted spectrum is discussed further in Essay 14, below.)

12.3.4 *Inner and Outer Aspects of Conceptual Role*

It is sometimes suggested that we need to distinguish inner and outer aspects of conceptual role, counting only the inner solipsistically specifiable side as conceptual role proper, taking the outer aspects to be part of context (Field, 1977b; Loar, 1981). The suggestion is that a theory of the content of attitudes must have two parts: (1) a theory of conceptual role proper, solipsistically conceived, and (2) a theory of context that would indicate how content is a function of inner conceptual role and outer context.

But the distinction is unmotivated and the suggestion is unworkable. The distinction is unmotivated because there is no natural border between inner and outer. Should the inner realm be taken to include everything in the local environment that can be perceived, or should it stop at the skin, the nerve ends, the central nervous system, the brain, the central part of the brain, or what? The suggestion is unworkable because, for most concepts, inner conceptual role can only be specified in terms of conceptual role in a wider sense, namely the function a concept has in certain contexts in relation to things in the so-called 'external world' (Harman, 1973: 62–5).

To be sure, there are cases of illusion in which one mistakes something else for food. From a solipsistic point of view, these cases may be quite similar to veridical cases, but clearly the cases of mistake are not cases that bring out the relevant function of the concept of food. They are cases of misfunctioning. We can see these as cases of mistake precisely because the function of the concept of food is specified with reference to real and not just apparent food.

Mental states and processes are functional states and processes, that is, they are complex relational or dispositional states and processes, and it is useful to consider simpler dispositions, like fragility or solubility. Water solubility cannot be identified with possession of a particular molecular structure, because (a) different sorts of molecular structure underlie the water solubility of different substances and, more importantly, (b) attributions of water solubility are relative to a choice of background or normal context. Rate of dissolving is affected by such things as the presence or absence of electrical, magnetic, or gravitational fields, the amount of vibration, varying degrees of atmospheric pressure, the purity and temperature of the water, and so forth. Whether it is proper to say a given substance is water soluble will depend on what the normal set of conditions for mixing the substance with water is taken to be. A substance is soluble in water if it would dissolve at a fast enough rate if mixed with water in a certain way under certain conditions. Solubility is a relational state of a substance, relating it to potential external things—water and various conditions of mixture and the process of dissolving under those conditions.

Notice that we cannot say that for a substance to be water soluble is for it to be such that, if it receives certain 'stimuli' at its surface, it reacts in a certain way. We must also mention water and various external conditions. There is a moral here for Quine's (1960*b*) account of language in terms of 'stimulus meaning' and of the related later attempts to develop a purely solipsistic notion of conceptual role.

We are led to attribute beliefs, desires, and so on to a creature only because the creature is able to attain what we take to be its goals by being able to detect aspects of its environment. In the first instance, we study its capacity for mental representation by discovering which aspects of the environment it is sensitive to. Only after that can we investigate the sorts of mistakes it is capable of that might lead to inappropriate behaviour. This gives us further evidence about the content of its concepts. But we could never even guess at this without considering how the creature's mental states are connected with things in the outside world.

The point is not merely one of evidence, since concepts have the content they have because of the way they function in the normal case in relation to an external world. If there were no external constraints, we could conceive of anything as instantiating any system of purely solipsistic 'functional' relations and processes. We could think of a pane of glass or a pencil point as instantiating Albert Einstein or George Miller, solipsistically conceived. But that does not count. Concepts really must be capable of functioning appropriately. No one has ever described a way of explaining what beliefs, desires, and other mental states are except in terms of actual or possible relations to things in the external world (Dennett, 1969: 72–82; Harman, 1973: 62–5; Bennett, 1976: 36–110).

The most primitive psychological notions are not belief and desire but rather knowledge and successful intentional action. Belief and intention are generalizations of knowledge and success that allow for mistake and failure. We conceive a creature as believing things by conceiving it as at least potentially knowing things, and similarly for intention.

Does this show that a theory of truth plays a role in semantics? To be sure, in my view the content of a concept is determined by the way in which the concept functions in paradigm or standard cases in which nothing goes wrong. In such cases, one has true beliefs that lead one to act appropriately in the light of one's needs and other ends. But an account of correct functioning is not itself a full account of the truth of beliefs, since beliefs can be true by accident in cases where there is some misfunctioning. And there are no serious prospects for a theory of content that significantly involves an account of truth conditions.

12.4 MEANING AND SPEECH ACTS

It may be an exaggeration to say that all aspects of linguistic meaning derive from the use of language to express concepts with corresponding contents. Certain aspects of meaning seem to derive directly from the use of language in speech acts and communication. (Nonsolipsistic) conceptual role semantics may therefore have to allow for this, attempting (of course) to treat it as a minor and relatively peripheral phenomenon. On the other hand, it may be that no such concession needs to be made. Here are brief reflections on some of the issues involved.

12.4.1 *Greetings*

The cases that may seem clearest here concern expressions which are used primarily in greetings and salutations, words like 'hello' and 'goodbye', for example. The meanings of these words do not seem to derive from any use they might have to express single concepts that play a distinctive role in calculation and thought. It is true that you might, on occasion, 'greet' a new idea or precept with the thought, 'Hello! What's this?' But this seems to be a case in which the content of your thought derives from the use of the word 'hello' to greet people and begin conversations rather than the other way round.

However, it may be that such words can be analysed as expressing a combination of concepts which individually have contents that are connected with distinctive conceptual roles. For example, perhaps 'hello' means something like 'I acknowledge your presence', or sometimes maybe 'Let us talk', and analogously for 'goodbye' and other words and phrases of this sort. If so, the issue becomes whether the aspect of meaning expressed by the imperative in 'Let us talk' and the performative aspect of the meaning of 'I acknowledge your presence' derive irreducibly from the use of words in speech acts or ultimately derive instead from the use of language to express concepts whose content is determined by their role in calculation and thought. These are complex issues which we must consider in a moment. As for the question whether this is the right way to analyse 'hello', 'goodbye', and so on, I am not very sure what to think. The analyses I have suggested seem to leave something out, but this might be accommodated by better analyses.

12.4.2 *Words of Politeness*

Before turning to imperatives and performatives, we might consider words and phrases which function as forms of deference and politeness, words and phrases like 'please' and 'thank you', for example. The use of such words and phrases seems to presuppose some sort of social interaction, rather than simply expressing concepts with a content determined by the way these concepts function in thought and calculation. It is true that you might say 'please' or 'thank you' to yourself, in thought, if you were speaking to yourself as an instructor or coach might. But this seems a very special case, which itself presupposes the social use of these expressions.

Again, in this case, it might be argued that in this use 'please' means the same as some longer expression, like 'if you please', i.e. 'if it pleases you to do so', and 'thank you' means something like 'I hereby thank you'. If so, the issue would become whether the meaning of the term 'you' derives entirely from its use to express concepts whose content is determined by their distinctive function in calculation or thought, an issue we need to discuss. There is, of course, also again here the question whether the performative element in 'I hereby thank you' carries a meaning which at least in part is irreducibly connected with speech acts, another issue we will be coming to in a moment. As for the question whether such polite phrases can always be analysed in this sort of way, I am not sure what to say.

12.4.3 'You'

What about the meaning of the word 'you'? It is plausible that this word means something like 'the person(s) I am now addressing' and each of the words in this phrase is plausibly held to have a meaning that depends on the concept the word is used to express, where the concept in question has the content it has by virtue of the way it functions in thought and calculation. So, even though the word 'you' has the distinctive function in speech acts and communication of designating the intended audience, this function can plausibly be explained in terms of the functional roles in thought of the concepts the word is used to express.

12.4.4 *Imperative and Interrogative Mood*

The use of the imperative mood in English seems to carry a certain meaning, connected with the giving of directions of some sort. This does not by itself imply that this meaning does not derive from the content of certain concepts with a distinctive use in thought and calculation. Indeed, something in your thoughts functions to distinguish your beliefs from your plans and intentions, which are directions of a sort. So there is a sense in which the upshot of practical reasoning is a modification of certain directions one intends to follow. Perhaps the imperative mood serves to express the concept which functions in thought to thus distinguish practical or directing thoughts from theoretical thoughts.

Similar remarks apply to the interrogative mood. Indeed, questions are not unlike requests for information, so that the interrogative mood is plausibly analysed in terms of the imperative mood. In any event, questions obviously have a function in thinking. You pose a problem to yourself and work out the answer, perhaps by posing various sub-questions and answering them.

12.4.5 *Performatives*

Consider next explicit performatives, like 'I promise to be there' and 'I hereby apologize for my rude behaviour'. It seems part of the meaning of such sentences that they are used not to describe the speaker as promising or apologizing but actually to do the promising or apologizing. Furthermore, it is plausible that promising or apologizing to yourself is not a typical or normal case of promising or apologizing and is rather the sort of case which is to be understood in relation to more typical or normal cases in which you promise someone else something or apologize to another person.

On the other hand, each of the words in a sentence like 'I promise to be there' has a meaning which expresses a concept whose content is arguably determined by its functional role in calculation and thought. And it is possible that the meaning of the whole sentence, including whatever gives the sentence its performative function of being appropriate for actually promising, arises from the meaning of the words used in a regular way. Given what the words in the sentence mean and given the way these words are put together, it may be predictable that the sentence has a performative use (Bach, 1975).

Suppose we adopted the convention that promises have to be made in some special way, for example by writing down the content of the promise in purple chalk on a special promise board that is not used for any other purpose. The convention would be that nothing else is to count as a promise. In such a case, the words 'I promise to be there' could not be used to promise you will be there. Would this be a way to pry off the performative meaning of 'I promise' from that aspect of its meaning that derives from its use to express concepts whose content is determined by their functional role in thought? Not obviously. For one thing, this might change the concept of promising in a significant way. The word 'promise' might not mean what it means when a promise can be made by saying 'I promise'. It could be argued that if 'I promise' means what it ordinarily means, then it follows from the concepts expressed by the words 'I promise' that these words can be used to promise.

Alternatively, it might be said that, even if the word 'promise' would retain (enough of) its usual meaning when promising was restricted by such a convention, the example is like one in which a special convention is adopted that an utterance of the sentence 'The sky is blue' is not to be interpreted as an assertion that the sky is blue but rather as a question asking whether it rained last week. This would not show that there is any aspect of the meaning of an ordinary assertion of the sentence 'The sky is blue', as we use it now without such a bizarre convention, which does not derive from the way the words in the sentence are used to express concepts that have the content they have because of their functional role in thought.

12.4.6 *Conversational Implicature*

Grice (1961, 1975) argues that the implications of an utterance do not always correspond directly to the meanings of the linguistic expressions used, even in quite ordinary cases. He suggests in particular that what seem to be aspects of meaning may be due to 'conversational implicature', i.e. to conclusions the audience is intended to reach by reflecting on the speaker's reasons for saying what is said, assuming the speaker is trying to be helpful. For example, if you use 'either . . . or', as in 'Albert is in either Boston or New York', you normally imply you do not know which. This does not have to be taken as showing something special about the meaning of 'either . . . or', a difference in the meaning of this ordinary expression as compared with what the logician takes it to mean. Instead we can suppose this implication is due to the natural assumption that normally, if you know which city Albert is in, you will say which it is. To take another example, the apparent difference in meaning between 'Mary closed the door and turned on the light' and 'Mary turned on the light and closed the door' does not have to be explained by supposing that the English word 'and' sometimes means 'and then'. The suggestion is that the difference can be explained by supposing that a helpful speaker will normally relate events in an orderly way, so that a hearer is normally justified in supposing that the order in which the speaker relates the events is to be understood as the order in which they occurred. Similarly, Grice suggests that certain aspects of presupposition might be explained by considering the normal expectations of speakers and hearers.

However, some of these phenomena can occur in thinking to oneself, where they are presumably not due to conversational implicature. Calculation and reasoning often involve various presuppositions. One will normally want descriptions used in reasoning to relate events in an orderly way, so the same phenomenon with the word 'and' may occur. On the other hand, it is doubtful that use of an 'either . . . or' proposition in thought normally carries the implication that one does not know which alternative is the case; so this phenomenon may really occur only at the level of conversation.

12.4.7 *Figurative Language*

Metaphor and simile occur in thinking. I am inclined to think irony does not. I am not sure about hyperbole.

12.5 CONCLUSION

To summarize: there are two uses of symbols, in communication and speech acts and in calculation and thought. (Nonsolipsistic) conceptual role semantics takes the second use to be the basic one. The ultimate source of meaning or content is the functional role symbols play in thought.

The content of a concept depends on its role in inference and sometimes in perception. Particularly important for inference are a term's implications. Implication is relevant to inference and therefore to meaning, because implication is explanatory and inference aims at explanatory coherence. Accounts of truth conditions can shed light on meaning to the extent that they bring out implications; it is doubtful whether such accounts have any further bearing on meaning, although they may have heuristic value for studies of logical form. Probabilistic semantics does not provide an adequate conceptual role semantics, because people do not and cannot make much use of probabilistic reasoning.

Allowance must be made for various connections between concepts and the external world. Some concepts have the content they have because of the words they are associated with, although (according to conceptual role semantics) this content ultimately always derives from someone's use of concepts. The content of concepts is often relative to a choice of a normal context of functioning. This is true of colour concepts, despite the unargued view of some philosophers that these concepts depend on the intrinsic character of experience.

Finally, it is not clear whether any aspects of meaning derive directly from the use of language in speech acts in a way not reducible to the expression of concepts whose content is independently determined. In any event, many phenomena often taken to be particularly connected with speech acts and conversation also occur in calculation and thought.

PART IV

Mind

13

Wide Functionalism

Psychological explanation is a kind of functional explanation (Fodor, 1968; Putnam, 1967*a*, 1967*b*) in the way that some biological explanation is. We explain the maintenance of bodily functions by appeal to processes involving heart, blood, lungs, arteries, veins, nerves, brain, stomach, and other organs. Organs are defined by their function, not their shape or physical constitution. A heart is an organ that pumps a creature's blood: it need not be any particular shape, nor does it have to be made from any particular material, as long as it serves that function. Similarly, psychological events and states can be physically realized in different ways in different creatures, as long as they play the relevant functional role in those creatures' psychology. Pain is not to be identified with a particular physical event, such as the stimulation of C-fibres (Place, 1956), because other sorts of physical event might function as pain does, for example as a kind of alarm system indicating that something wrong is going on at a particular place in the organism. Beliefs and desires have distinctive functions, beliefs recording information about the world, desires specifying the goals of the system. Both sorts of states can be physically realized in various ways, perhaps even as states of intelligent machines.

I claim that psychological explanations are typically *wide* functional explanations. That is, I claim that such explanations typically appeal to an actual or possible environmental situation of the creature whose activity is being explained. A *narrow* functional explanation appeals only to internal states of the creature and says nothing about how the creature functions in relation to an actual or possible environment. I claim that there are few (if any) narrowly functional psychological explanations of this latter sort.

In arguing for this, I disagree with Fodor (1980) and others who hold that the relevant psychological explanations are always narrow functional explanations.

I begin with a short history of the issue. Then I say why most psychological explanations are wide functional explanations. Finally I indicate why twin-earth arguments do not show that all such explanations must be narrowly functional.

13.1 HISTORY OF THE ISSUE

Functionalism emerged from a behaviourism that identified psychological states and events with dispositions to respond in an appropriate way to appropriate stimuli, where a stimulus was usually conceived as a perceivable aspect of the environment and a response was usually identified with behaviour appropriately affecting the environment (Morris, 1946). Such dispositions were 'functionally' defined in the sense that they were compatible with various physical bases for the relevant stimulus/response relations. Since stimulus and response were usually defined partly in terms of events in the environment, behaviouristic theories tended to be instances of wide functionalism.

Functionalism allows also psychological explanations that refer to internal states and events that mediate perceptual input and behavioural output. Many versions of functionalism retain the wide characteristic of behaviourism by continuing to conceive of the relation between perceptual inputs and behavioural outputs in terms of actual or possible environmental occurrences.

For example, Wilfrid Sellars (1963) argued that we can think of the relevant intervening states and events as analogous to linguistic acts. He distinguished three sorts of functional 'transitions' involving mental states and events: entry transitions from events outside the system to states and events of the system, exit transitions from states and events in the system to outside events, and purely internal transitions between states and events of the system. The entry transitions represented the influence of perception on the system, the exit transitions represented the influence of the system on action, and the purely internal transitions represented inferences. All transitions were to be governed by rules of a Mentalese language game that a person has been conditioned to follow. Rules for entry into the system and exit from it referred explicitly to the environment. For example, a person might be conditioned to think 'That's red' on seeing something red under standard conditions, or a person might be conditioned to interpose a pawn on having the thought 'I shall interpose my pawn now!'

In 1969, Daniel Dennett argued that psychological explanation is explanation within an 'Intentional system' and 'for any system to be called Intentional it must be capable of discriminating and reacting to fairly complex features of its environment'. For example, an animal has thoughts about food only if the perception of food under certain conditions can lead it to act appropriately toward the food, by eating it (Dennett, 1969: 72–3). In Harman (1973), I endorsed this claim of Dennett's and remarked on the way in which the attribution of psychological states makes implicit reference to a 'normal case'. (I observed that the point applies also to representational states of artificial devices such as a radar aimer used for shooting at enemy planes.) I also argued that animals' mental representations must in part represent the satisfaction of their needs by means of appropriate behaviour, so 'those representations involve representation of a public world'.

In 1976 Jonathan Bennett argued in elegant detail that the only likely strategy for explicating psychological notions like belief and desire takes the following form (Bennett, 1976; also Taylor, 1964). We start with the notion of a teleological system. Such a system has an associated goal. To say that the system has such a goal is to say that the laws or principles of the system are such that it does what it can to ensure that the goal is secured.

Next, we need to observe that a system may or may not 'register' certain information in its environment concerning what changes are needed in the environment to achieve its goals. The system will not do what is needed to ensure that its goal is secured unless it registers the information that this is needed to ensure that the goal is secured. To say that the system can register such information is to say that there are states of the system (1) that arise from the environment's being such that a certain action is needed in order to achieve the system's goal, and (2) that lead the system to act in the required way.

Finally, we need to consider further complications. For example, a system will make mistakes when a state that normally would register a certain environmental situation is caused in an abnormal way and the system might therefore act in ways that will not satisfy its goals but would if the environment were as the system takes it to be. A system can have more than one goal at a time. And so on. Bennett argues that a system has states that are more and more like beliefs and desires as these and other complications are allowed for.

For present purposes, we can ignore the complications. What concerns us is Bennett's claim that psychological notions ultimately must be understood by appeal to concepts of teleology and registration that make reference to an actual or possible environment.

Robert Stalnaker (Stalnaker, 1984; also Stampe, 1977) defends a similar account using a notion of 'indication' that resembles Bennett's 'registration'. Stalnaker stresses that such an account presupposes a notion of 'normal conditions'. The perceptual belief that P is a state that occurs under normal conditions only if it true that P. And other writers have advocated similar ideas with varying emphases. For example, Fred Dretske's theory (Dretske, 1981) places stress mostly on the input or information side.

On the other hand, several writers have opted for a narrower function-alism. Quine (1960*b*) advocated a narrow behaviourism that identified a stimulus with a pattern of stimulation of sensory nerves. In a series of papers shortly afterward, Hilary Putnam (1960, 1964, 1967*a*, and 1967*b*) argued for a nonbehaviouristic narrow functionalism, which identified systems of mental states first with something like Turing machines possessing paper tape input and output and then, more realistically, with probabilistic automata possessing 'motor outputs and sensory inputs'.

Putnam soon abandoned this narrow functionalism because of its commitment to what he called 'methodological solipsism'. According to Putnam,

When traditional philosophers talked about psychological states or 'mental' states, they made an assumption which we may call the assumption of methodological solipsism. This assumption is the assumption that no psychological state, properly so called, presupposes the existence of any individual other than the subject to whom that state is ascribed . . . This assumption is pretty explicit in Descartes, but it is implicit in just about the whole of traditional philosophical psychology. (1975: 220)

Putnam then rejected methodological solipsism with the enigmatic remark that 'the three centuries of failure of mentalistic psychology is tremendous evidence against this procedure in my opinion' (220).

Jerry Fodor (1980) commented, 'I suppose this is intended to include everybody from Locke and Kant to Freud and Chomsky. I should have such failures'. Fodor also suggested that Putnam himself had provided an argument for methodological solipsism, roughly, the notorious twin-earth argument to be considered below. For that and other reasons Fodor claimed that mental states and processes are 'computational', where computational operations are both *symbolic* and *formal*, 'symbolic because they are defined over representations and . . . formal because they apply to representation in virtue of (roughly) the syntax of the representations . . . Formal operations are the ones that are specified without reference to such semantic properties of representations as, for example, truth, reference, and meaning' (226–7). The upshot is a narrowly functionalistic psychology.

Acceptance of methodological solipsism has led several writers to advocate so called 'two-level' theories of meaning. These theories attempt to give an account of meaning by combining 'conceptual role semantics' with a specification of conditions of truth and reference. Conceptual role semantics holds that the content of mental representations is partly or wholly determined by the functional role the representations play in the perception–inference–action language game of thought. The theory takes different forms depending on whether functional role is conceived widely or narrowly. Those who conceive functional role widely (Sellars, 1963; Harman, 1973 and Essay 12, above) argue that meaning can be identified with functional role. Other writers suppose that functional role must be conceived narrowly and therefore cannot account for all of the content of mental states. These writers include Hartry Field (1977*a*), Brian Loar (1981), Stephen Schiffer (1981), and William G. Lycan (1984).

13.2 CONSIDERATIONS FAVOURING WIDE FUNCTIONALISM

Wide functionalism is more plausible on its face than narrow functionalism. Ordinary psychological explanations are not confined to reports of inner states and processes. They often refer to what people perceive of the world and what changes they make to the world. Although some ordinary explanations refer to sensory input and some refer to motor output—a hallucination, an attempt to move that fails—even in these cases there is normally implicit reference to a possible environment. A hallucination of a pink elephant is a hallucination of something in the environment. An unsuccessful attempt to pick up the telephone is an attempt to move something in the environment. Furthermore, the explanation of someone's reaction to a hallucination is normally parasitic on explanations of how people react to veridical perception. And explaining why someone made an unsuccessful attempt to do something is normally parasitic on explanations of successful action. (It is true that a person can have a hallucination without being taken in by it, and a person can try to do something that he knows he will not succeed in doing. But these are special cases that require a certain amount of sophistication.)

Consider the hand–eye coordination involved in drawing a picture. This involves a complex interplay between perception and action. What is done next depends on the perception of what has been done so far as well as the perception of hand and pencil. No explanation of what the agent is doing can avoid reference to the effects the agent's act has on the world and the agent's perception of these effects.

Functional explanations in perceptual psychology often appeal to relations between sense organs and the environment, for example when certain systems of neurones in the eye are identified as 'edge detectors'. The relevant explanation appeals to facts about edges in the external world, in particular, facts about the way light is differentially reflected to the eye from differently oriented surfaces that meet in an edge.

Fodor (1968) compares psychological explanation to automotive explanation. If we explain how an automobile works by appealing to valve lifter, carburettor, throttle, brakes, speedometer, and so forth, we appeal to parts of the automobile that are functionally defined. For present purposes it is useful to notice that some of these parts have a relatively internal function within the system, for example, the valve lifter and the carburettor, whereas others have a function in relation to things outside the system, for example, the brakes are used to stop the automobile, and the speedometer functions to indicate to the driver what the speed is. This parallels the psychological case, in which edge detectors have a function in relation to external things and pain has a more internal function.

Functional explanations of automobiles and of people require the wide view. You do not understand what an automobile is and how it functions if you know only its internal operation independently of the fact that automobiles are vehicles that travel on roads to get people from one place to another, that the accelerator is pressed in order to make the car move, that the brake pedal is pressed in order to stop the car, that the gearshift is moved to a certain position in order to put the car into reverse so that it goes backwards, and so forth. Similarly, you do not understand how people operate psychologically unless you see how their mental states are related to perception of the environment and to action that modifies the environment. You do not understand what is going on in the eye unless you understand that the eye is an organ of perception, that certain systems of neurones in the eye function as edge detectors, and so on. If you understand only the uninterpreted program indicating the flow of information or energy in the system without saying what information is flowing, then you do not understand what is going on in the eye or in the brain.

Consider the following uninterpreted program: there are three possible input states, A, B, and C. A leads to output X and C leads to output Y; B has no effect. Do you understand what is going on? No. You need to know how this system is functioning. In fact, the system is a thermostatically controlled air-conditioner. A is normally the result of a temperature greater than 72 degrees Fahrenheit. B is normally the result of a temperature between 68 and 72 degrees. C is normally the result of a temperature below 68 degrees. The output signal X turns on the air-conditioner if it is not already on. Otherwise it leaves it on. The output of Y turns off the air-conditioner if it is on. Otherwise it leaves the air-conditioner turned off. In order to understand this system you need to know the wide functional story. The narrow functional story is insufficient. This is not to deny that there is a narrow story. It is merely to observe that story is insufficient for understanding how the system functions.

Psychology is concerned to provide a functional understanding of people and other animals. Such an understanding requires the wider view. Otherwise, the relevant function of various aspects of the system is not sufficiently specified. This is not to deny the existence of a corresponding narrow story, an uninterpreted program. It is merely to observe that the narrow story is insufficient for psychology.

If you want to understand how a radio receiver works, you need to know that the receiver is designed to pick up signals sent by a transmitter and to convert them into audible sounds that can be heard by listeners. Just knowing how electrical currents flow through the system is not enough. You need to know that certain parts of the system are there in order to tune into signals transmitted at a certain frequency, part of the system functions to retrieve the frequency of the message from signal as it is encoded in a carrier frequency, part functions to screen out competing signals of nearby carrier frequencies, a different part functions to screen out interference from aeroplanes, and so forth. (Smart (1968) suggests that understanding how people work is like understanding how a radio receiver works and that biology and psychology are therefore more like applied engineering than basic physical science.)

A purely narrow functionalism is methodologically incoherent. All sorts of currents flow in a radio receiver, only some of which are relevant to its functioning. Others are from that point of view merely leaks, of no importance. If something goes wrong, there may be short circuits. This classification into proper flow of current, leaks, and misfunctions such as short circuits depends on taking the wide functional view of the radio receiver. Nothing about its internal operation, narrowly conceived, dictates these distinctions. Narrow functionalism is not really *functionalism*, since it has no way to capture the relevant functions.

Methodological solipsism is similarly incoherent in psychology. There is no hope of isolating the relevant psychological components of a creature without considering how these components function in enabling the creature to deal with its environment. For example, it is necessary to identify certain parts of the creature as organs of perception. Without the wide view, there is no way to think of internal workings of the creature as a functional system, because there is no way to distinguish functional parts of the system from irrelevant parts and no way to distinguish cases in which something is functioning properly from cases of misfunction. Hallucination involves some sort of misfunction, but there is no way to capture this point within a narrow functionalism. Narrow functionalism is not an intelligible option in the philosophy of mind.

13.3 TWIN EARTH

Consider an agent Albert whose actions we wish to explain. Consider also all possible duplicates of Albert from the surface in who are in various possible environments. Some of these duplicates would be on Putnam's 'Twin Earth' (Putnam, 1975), which would resemble Earth except that their 'water' would not be H_2O but would have a complex chemical structure that Putnam abbreviates as XYZ. These duplicates would not be in the same wide functional states as Albert. For example, Albert believes that water is wet; his duplicate on Twin Earth would not. The Twin-Earth duplicate would believe that what he called 'water' was wet, but what he called 'water' would not be water, since it would be XYZ rather than H_2O. Similarly, Albert sees a tree; one possible duplicate would hallucinate a tree; another would see a tree illusion.

Although Albert's duplicate on Twin Earth would not believe that water is wet, he would have a corresponding belief. His belief would function internally in exactly the same way that Albert's belief does. So we can say that Albert's duplicate on Twin Earth would be in the same belief state as Albert, in the sense that it would have the same narrow belief. Indeed, each of Albert's possible duplicates would be in a state corresponding to Albert's belief that water is wet. Each would be in the same narrow belief state; they would all have the same narrow belief. Similarly, for each of Albert's other psychological states there would be a corresponding psychological state in every possible duplicate. Albert's duplicates would share narrow belief states with Albert.

Furthermore, whatever Albert does in response to sensory input will be exactly the same as what his various duplicates would do in response to the same sensory input. In whatever way that Albert's reaction is to be explained in terms of his psychological states, there would be analogous explanations of the reactions of his duplicates in terms of their corresponding psychological states.

Some writers (e.g. Lycan, 1984) see this as an argument for methodological solipsism. They infer that only Albert's narrow psychological states are responsible for his reaction. His wide states are irrelevant, so his narrow psychological states rather than his wide psychological states are the relevant states for psychological explanation.

This is like saying that Charles's pushing Bob out of the boat was not the cause of Bob's drowning, since Bob would have drowned no matter who had pushed him out of the boat. In an official investigation of the cause of Bob's death, it is more relevant that Charles pushed him out of the boat than simply that someone pushed him out of the boat or that his body was subject to a force that pushed him out of the boat. The narrowest explanation is not always the relevant explanation. This is as true for psychology as it is for a court of inquiry into the cause of Bob's drowning. As I have already argued, psychological explanation is functional explanation and that specification of functions typically makes reference to an actual or possible environment.

Many possible duplicates of Albert would think they were seeing water when they were not. Some would be hallucinating. Others would be brains in vats receiving the same sensory stimulation that Albert is receiving. But I claim that an understanding of what happens in such a case is parasitic on an understanding of what happens in veridical perception.

Although we can test the functioning of automobiles and radio receivers in the laboratory even though they are not functioning to drive people from one place to another or to receive broadcasts from radio transmitters, our understanding of the functioning of the tested automobiles and receivers depends on our envisaging them in the relevant context, namely, the context in which they are used to transport people or to receive broadcasts. Similarly, we understand the functioning of a brain in a vat by envisaging it as part of a person in the relevant environment.

13.4 CONCLUSION

Psychological explanation is wide functional explanation, because only a wide functionalism gives the understanding sought for in psychological explanations. It is possible to introduce a notion of narrow psychological function by abstraction from the notion of wide psychological function. But an autonomous narrow psychological functionalism would be incoherent, because only a wide psychological functionalism can motivate appropriate distinctions between aspects of a system, irrelevant side effects, and misfunctions.

14

The Intrinsic Quality of Experience

14.1 THE PROBLEM

Many theorists accept a broadly functionalist view of the relation between mind and body, for example, viewing the mind in the body as something like a computer in a robot, perhaps with massively parallel processing (as in Rumelhart and McClelland, 1986). Other theorists object that functionalism must inevitably fail to account for the most important part of mental life, namely, the subjective feel of conscious experience. In this essay I reply to that objection.

The computer model of mind represents one version of functionalism, although it is not the only version. In its most general form, functionalism defines mental states and processes by their causal or functional relations to each other and to perceptual inputs from the world outside and behavioural outputs expressed in action. According to functionalism, it is functional relations that are important, not the intrinsic qualities of the stuff in which these relations are instanced. Just as the same computer programs can be run on different computers made out of different materials, so functionalism allows for the same mental states and events in beings with very different physical constitutions, since the same functional relations might be instantiated in beings with very different physical makeup. According to functionalism, beliefs, desires, thoughts, and feelings are not limited to beings that are materially like ourselves. Such psychological states and events might also occur, for example, in silicon-based beings, as long as the right functional relations obtained.

Functionalism can allow for the possibility that something about silicon makes it impossible for the relevant relations to obtain in silicon-based beings, perhaps because the relevant events could not occur fast enough in silicon. It is even conceivable that the relevant functional relations might obtain only in the sort of material that makes up human brains (Thagard, 1986; Dennett, 1987: ch. 9). Functionalism implies that in such a case the material is important only because it is needed for the relevant functional relations and not because of some other more mysterious or magical connection between that sort of matter and a certain sort of consciousness.

Various issues arise within the general functionalist approach. There is a dispute about how to identify the inputs to a functional system. Should inputs be identified with events in the external environment, as argued in Essays 12 and 13 above, or should they instead be identified with events that are more internal such as the stimulation of an organism's sensory organs (Block, 1986)? There is also the possibility of disagreement as to how causally deterministic the relevant functional relations have to be. Do they have to be completely deterministic, or can they be merely probabilistic? Or might they even be simply nondeterministic, not even associated with definite probabilities (Harman, 1973: 51–3)?

I will not be concerned with these issues here. Instead, I will concentrate on the different and more basic issue that I have already mentioned, namely, whether this sort of functionalism, no matter how elaborated, can account for the subjective feel of experience, for 'what it is like' (Nagel, 1974) to undergo this or that experience. Furthermore, I will not consider the general challenge, 'How does functionalism account for X?' for this or that X. Nor will I consider negative arguments against particular functionalist analyses. I will instead consider three related arguments that purport to demonstrate that functionalism cannot account for this aspect of experience. I will argue that all three arguments are fallacious. I will say little that is original and will for the most part merely elaborate points made many years ago (Quine, 1960*a*: 235; Anscombe, 1965; Armstrong, 1961, 1962, and especially 1968; Pitcher, 1971), points that I do not think have been properly appreciated.

The three arguments are these:

(1) When you attend to a pain in your leg or to your experience of the redness of an apple, you are aware of an intrinsic quality of your experience, where an intrinsic quality is a quality something has in itself, apart from its relations to other things. This quality of experience cannot be captured in a functional definition, since such a definition is concerned entirely with relations: relations between mental states and perceptual input, relations among mental states, and relations between mental states and behavioural output. 'An essential feature of [Armstrong's functionalist] analysis is that it tells us nothing about the intrinsic nature of mental states . . . He never takes seriously the natural objection that we must know the

intrinsic nature of our own mental states since we experience them directly' (Nagel, 1970).

(2) A person blind from birth could know all about the physical and functional facts of colour perception without knowing what it is like to see something red. So what it is like to see something red cannot be explicated in purely functional terms (Nagel, 1974; Jackson, 1982, 1986).

(3) It is conceivable that two people should have similarly functioning visual systems despite the fact that things that look red to one person look green to the other, things that look yellow to the first person look blue to the second, and so forth (Lycan, 1973; Shoemaker, 1982). This sort of spectrum inversion in the way things look is possible but cannot be given a purely functional description, since by hypothesis there are no functional differences between the people in question. Since the way things look to a person is an aspect of that person's mental life, this means that there is an important aspect of a person's mental life that cannot be explicated in purely functional terms.

14.2 INTENTIONALITY

In order to assess these arguments, I begin by remarking on what is sometimes called the intentionality of experience. Our experience of the world has content— that is, it represents things as being in a certain way. In particular, perceptual experience represents a perceiver as in a particular environment, for example, as facing a tree with brown bark and green leaves fluttering in a slight breeze.

One thing that philosophers mean when they refer to this as the intentional content of experience is that the content of the experience may not reflect what is really there. Although it looks to me as if I am seeing a tree, that may be a clever illusion produced with tilted mirrors and painted backdrops. Or it may be a hallucination produced by a drug in my coffee.

There are many other examples of intentionality. Ponce de León searched Florida for the Fountain of Youth. What he was looking for was a fountain whose waters would give eternal youth to whoever would drink them. In fact, there is no such thing as a Fountain of Youth, but that does not mean Ponce de León wasn't looking for anything. He was looking for something. We can therefore say that his search had an intentional object.

But the thing that he was looking for, the intentional object of his search, did not (and does not) exist.

A painting of a unicorn is a painting of something; it has a certain content. But the content does not correspond to anything actual; the thing that the painting represents does not exist. The painting has an intentional content in the relevant sense of 'intentional'.

Imagining or mentally picturing a unicorn is usefully compared with a painting of a unicorn. In both cases the content is not actual; the object pictured, the intentional object of the picturing, does not exist. It is only an intentional object. This is not to suppose that mentally picturing a unicorn involves an awareness of a mental picture of a unicorn. I am comparing mentally picturing something with a picture of something, not with a perception of a picture. An awareness of a picture has as its intentional object a picture. The picture has as its intentional object a unicorn. Imagining a unicorn is different from imagining a picture of a unicorn. The intentional object of the imagining is a unicorn, not a picture of a unicorn.

It is very important to distinguish between the properties of a represented object and the properties of a representation of that object. Clearly, these properties can be very different. The unicorn is pictured as having four legs and a single horn. The painting of the unicorn does not have four legs and a single horn. The painting is flat and covered with paint. The unicorn is not pictured as flat or covered with paint. Similarly, an imagined unicorn is imagined as having legs and a horn. The imagining of the unicorn has no legs or horn. The imagining of the unicorn is a mental activity. The unicorn is not imagined as either an activity or anything mental.

The notorious sense-datum theory of perception arises through failing to keep these elementary points straight. According to that ancient theory, perception of external objects in the environment is always indirect and mediated by a more direct awareness of a mental sense datum. Defenders of the sense-datum theory argue for it by appealing to the so-called argument from illusion. This argument begins with the uncontroversial premise that the way things are presented in perception is not always the way they are. Eloise sees some brown and green. But there is nothing brown and green before her; it is all an illusion or hallucination. From this the argument fallaciously infers that the brown and green Eloise sees is not external to her and so must be internal or mental. Since veridical, nonillusory, nonhallucinatory perception can be qualitatively indistinguishable from illusory or hallucinatory perception, the argument concludes that in all cases of perception Eloise is directly aware of something inner and mental and only indirectly aware of external objects like trees and leaves.

An analogous argument about paintings would start from the premise that a painting can be a painting of a unicorn even though there are no unicorns. From this it might be concluded that the painting is 'in the first instance' a painting of something else that is actual, for example, the painter's idea of a unicorn.

In order to see that such arguments are fallacious, consider the corresponding argument applied to searches: 'Ponce de León was searching for the Fountain of Youth. But there is no such thing. So he must have been searching for something mental.' This is just a mistake. From the fact that there is no Fountain of Youth, it does not follow that Ponce de León was searching for something mental. In particular, he was not looking for an idea of the Fountain of Youth. He already had the idea. What he wanted was a real Fountain of Youth, not just the idea of such a thing.

The painter has painted a picture of a unicorn. The picture painted is not a picture of an idea of a unicorn. The painter might be at a loss to paint a picture of an idea, especially if he is not familiar with conceptual art. It may be that the painter has an idea of a unicorn and tries to capture that idea in his painting. But that is to say his painting is a painting of the same thing that his idea is an idea of. The painting is not a painting of the idea, but a painting of what the idea is about.

In the same way, what Eloise sees before her is a tree, whether or not it is a hallucination. That is to say, the content of her visual experience is that she is presented with a tree, not with an idea of a tree. Perhaps Eloise's visual experience involves some sort of mental picture of the environment. It does not follow that she is aware of a mental picture. If there is a mental picture, it may be that what she is aware of is whatever is represented by that mental picture; but then that mental picture represents something in the world, not something in the mind.

Now, we sometimes count someone as perceiving something only if that thing exists. So if there is no tree before her and Eloise is suffering from a hallucination, we might describe this either by saying that Eloise sees something that is not really there or by saying that she does not really see anything at all but only seems to see something. There is not a use of 'search for' corresponding to this second use of 'see' that would allow us to say that, because there was and is no such thing as the Fountain of Youth, Ponce de León was not really searching for anything at all.

But this ambiguity in perceptual verbs does not affect the point I am trying to make. To see that it does not, let us use 'see†' ('see-dagger') for the sense of 'see' in which the object seen might not exist, as when Macbeth saw a dagger before him.

Is this a dagger which I see before me,
The handle toward my hand? Come let me clutch thee.
I have thee not, and yet I see thee still.
Art thou not, fatal vision, sensible
To feeling as to sight? or art thou but
A dagger of the mind, a false creation,
Proceeding from the heat-oppressed brain?
                    . . . I see thee still;
And on thy blade and dudgeon gouts of blood,
Which was not so before. There's no such thing;
It is the bloody business which informs
Thus to mine eyes. (Shakespeare, *Macbeth*, Act II, scene i)

Let us use 'see*' ('see-star') for the sense of 'see' in which only things that exist can be seen. Macbeth saw† a dagger but he did not see* a dagger.

The argument from illusion starts from a case in which Eloise 'sees' something brown and green before her, although there is nothing brown and green before her in the external physical world. From this, the argument infers that the brown and green she sees must be internal and mental. Now, if 'see' is 'see†' here, this is the fallacy already noted, like that of concluding that Ponce de León was searching for something mental from the fact that there is no Fountain of Youth in the external world. On the other hand, if 'see' is 'see*' here, then the premise of the argument simply begs the question. No reason at all has so far been given for the claim that Eloise sees* something brown and green in this case. It is true that her perceptual experience represents her as visually presented with something brown and green; but that is to say merely that she sees† something brown and green, not that she sees* anything at all. (From now on I will suppress the † and * modification of perceptual verbs unless indication of which sense is meant is crucial to the discussion.)

Here, some philosophers (e.g. Jackson, 1977) would object as follows:

> You agree that there is a sense in which Eloise sees something green and brown when there is nothing green and brown before her in the external world. You are able to deny that this brown and green thing is mental by taking it to be a nonexistent and merely intentional object. But it is surely more reasonable to suppose that one is in this case aware of something mental than to suppose that one is aware of something that does not exist. How can there be anything that does not exist? The very suggestion is a contradiction in terms, since 'be' simply means 'exist', so that you are really saying that there exists

something that does not exist (Quine, 1953*a*). There are no such
things as nonexistent objects!

In reply, let me concede immediately that I do not have a well-worked-out
theory of intentional objects. Parsons (1980) offers one such theory,
although I do not mean to express an opinion as to the success of Parson's
approach. Indeed, I am quite willing to believe that there are not really any
nonexistent objects and that apparent talk of such objects should be analysed away somehow. I do not see that it is my job to resolve this issue.
However the issue is resolved, the theory that results had better end up
agreeing that Ponce de León was looking for something when he was looking for the Fountain of Youth, even though there is no Fountain of Youth,
and the theory had better not have the consequence that Ponce de León was
looking for something mental. If a logical theory can account for searches
for things that do not, as it happens, exist, it can presumably also allow for
a sense of 'see' in which Macbeth can see something that does not really exist.

Another point is that Eloise's visual experience does not just present a
tree. It presents a tree as viewed from a certain place. Various features that
the tree is presented as having are presented as relations between the viewer
and the tree; for example, features the tree has from here. The tree is presented as 'in front of' and 'hiding' certain other trees. It is presented as fuller
on 'the right'. It is presented as the same size 'from here' as a closer smaller
tree, which is not to say that it really looks the same in size, only that it is
presented as subtending roughly the same angle from here as the smaller
tree. To be presented as the same in size from here is not to be presented as
the same in size, period.

I do not mean to suggest that the way the tree is visually presented as
being from here is something that is easily expressed in words. In particular, I do not mean to suggest that the tree can thus be presented as subtending a certain visual angle only to someone who understands words like
'subtend' and 'angle' (as is assumed in Peacocke, 1983: ch. 1). I mean only
that this feature of a tree from here is an objective feature of the tree in relation to here, a feature to which perceivers are sensitive and which their
visual experience can somehow represent things as having from here.

Now, perhaps, Eloise's visual experience even presents a tree as seen by
her, that is, as an object of her visual experience. If so, there is a sense after
all in which Eloise's visual experience represents something mental: it represents objects in the world as objects of visual experience. But this does
not mean that Eloise's visual experience in any way reveals to her the intrinsic properties of that experience by virtue of which it has the content it has.

I want to stress this point, because it is very important. If we suppose that Eloise is aware of the tree as a tree that she is now seeing, we can suppose she is aware of some features of her current visual experience. In particular, she is aware that her visual experience has the feature of being an experience of seeing a tree. That is to be aware of an intentional feature of her experience: she is aware that her experience has a certain content. On the other hand, I want to argue that she is not aware of those intrinsic features of her experience by virtue of which it has that content. Indeed, I believe that she has no access at all to the intrinsic features of her mental representation that make it a mental representation of seeing a tree.

Things are different with paintings. In the case of a painting Eloise can be aware of those features of the painting that are responsible for its being a painting of a unicorn. That is, she can turn her attention to the pattern of the paint on the canvas by virtue of which the painting represents a unicorn. But in the case of her visual experience of a tree, I want to say that she is not aware of, as it were, the mental paint by virtue of which her experience is an experience of seeing a tree. She is aware only of the intentional or relational features of her experience, not of its intrinsic nonintentional features.

Some sense-datum theorists will object that Eloise is indeed aware of the relevant mental paint when she is aware of an arrangement of colour, because these sense-datum theorists assert that the colour she is aware of is inner and mental and not a property of external objects. But this sense-datum claim is counter to ordinary visual experience. When Eloise sees a tree before her, the colours she experiences are all experienced as features of the tree and its surroundings. None of them are experienced as intrinsic features of her experience. Nor does she experience any features of anything as intrinsic features of her experience. And that is true of you too. There is nothing special about Eloise's visual experience. When you see a tree, you do not experience any features as intrinsic features of your experience. Look at a tree and try to turn your attention to intrinsic features of your visual experience. I predict you will find that the only features there to turn your attention to will be features of the presented tree, including relational features of the tree 'from here'.

The sense-datum theorists' view about our immediate experience of colour is definitely not the naive view; it does not represent the viewpoint of ordinary perception. The sense-datum theory is not the result of phenomenological study; it is rather the result of an argument, namely, the argument from illusion. But that argument is either invalid or question-begging, as we have seen.

It is very important to distinguish what are experienced as intrinsic features of the intentional object of experience from intrinsic features of the experience itself. It is not always easy to distinguish these things, but they can be distinguished. Consider the experience of having a pain in your right leg. It is very tempting to confuse features of what you experience as happening in your leg with intrinsic features of your experience. But the happening in your leg that you are presented with is the intentional object of your experience; it is not the experience itself. The content of your experience is that there is a disturbance of a certain specific sort in your right leg. The intentional object of the experience is an event located in your right leg. The experience itself is not located in your right leg. If the experience is anywhere specific, it is somewhere in your brain.

Notice that the content of your experience may not be true to what is actually happening. A slipped disc in your back may press against your sciatic nerve making it appear that there is a disturbance in your right leg when there really is not. The intentional object of your painful experience may not exist. Of course, that is not to say there is no pain in your leg. You do feel something there. But there is a sense in which what you feel in your leg is an illusion or hallucination.

It is true that, if Melvin hallucinates a pink elephant, the elephant that Melvin sees does not exist. But the pain in your leg resulting from a slipped disc in your back certainly does exist. (Here I am indebted to Sydney Shoemaker.) The pain is not an intentional object in quite the way the elephant is. The pain in your leg caused by the slipped disc in your back is more like the after-image of a bright light. If you look at a blank wall, you see the image on the wall. The image is on the wall, the pain is in your leg. There is no physical spot on the wall, there is no physical disturbance in your leg. The after-image exists, the pain exists. When we talk about after-images or referred pains, some of what we say is about our experience and some of what we say is about the intentional object of that experience. When we say the pain or after-image exists, we mean that the experience exists. When we say that the after-image is on the wall or that the pain is in your leg, we are talking about the location of the intentional object of that experience.

14.3 ASSESSMENT OF THE FIRST OBJECTION

We are now in a position to reject the first of the three arguments against functionalism, which I now repeat:

When you attend to a pain in your leg or to your experience of the redness of an apple, you are aware of an intrinsic quality of your experience, where an intrinsic quality is a quality something has in itself, apart from its relations to other things. This quality of experience cannot be captured in a functional definition, since such a definition is concerned entirely with relations: relations between mental states and perceptual input, relations among mental states, and relations between mental states and behavioural output.

We can now see that this argument fails through confounding a quality of the intentional object of an experience with a quality of the experience itself. When you attend to a pain in your leg or to your experience of the redness of an apple, you are attending to a quality of an occurrence in your leg or a quality of the apple. Perhaps this quality is presented to you as an intrinsic quality of the occurrence in your leg or as an intrinsic quality of the surface of the apple. But it is not at all presented as an intrinsic quality of your experience. And, since you are not aware of the intrinsic character of your experience, the fact that functionalism abstracts from the intrinsic character of experience does not show it leaves out anything you are aware of.

To be sure, there are possible complications. Suppose David undergoes brain surgery which he watches in a mirror. Suppose that he sees certain intrinsic features of the firing of certain neurones in his brain and suppose that the firing of these neurones is the realization of part of the experience he is having at that moment. In that case, David is aware of intrinsic features of his experience. But that way of being aware of intrinsic features of experience is not incompatible with functionalism. Given a functionalist account of David's perception of trees, tables, and the brain processes of other people, the same account applies when the object perceived happens to be David's own brain processes. The awareness David has of his own brain processes is psychologically similar to the awareness any other sighted perceiver might have of those same brain processes, including perceivers constructed in a very different way from the way in which David is constructed.

According to functionalism, the psychologically relevant properties of an internal process are all functional properties. The intrinsic nature of the process is relevant only inasmuch as it is responsible for the process's having the functional properties it has. I have been considering the objection that certain intrinsic features of experience must be psychologically relevant properties apart from their contribution to function, since these are properties we are or can be aware of. The objection is not just that we can become aware of intrinsic features of certain mental processes in the way just mentioned, that is, by perceiving in a mirror the underlying physical processes that realize those mental processes. That would not be an objection to functionalism. The objection is rather that all or most conscious experience has intrinsic aspects of which we are or can be aware in such a way that these aspects of the experience are psychologically significant over and above the contribution they make to function.

Of course, to say that these aspects are psychologically significant is not to claim that they are or ought to be significant for the science of psychology. Rather, they are supposed to be psychologically significant in the sense of mentally significant, whether or not this aspect of experience is susceptible of scientific understanding. The objection is that any account of our mental life that does not count these intrinsic properties as mental or psychological properties leaves out a crucial aspect of our experience.

My reply to this objection is that it cannot be defended without confusing intrinsic features of the intentional object of experience with intrinsic features of the experience. Apart from that confusion, there is no reason to think that we are ever aware of the relevant intrinsic features of our experiences.

There are other ways in which one might be aware of intrinsic features of our experience without that casting any doubt on functionalism. For example, one might be aware of intrinsic features of experience without being aware of them as intrinsic features of experience, just as Ortcutt can be aware of a man who, as it happens, is a spy, without being aware of the man as a spy. When Eloise sees a tree, she is aware of her perceptual experience as an experience with a certain intentional content. Suppose that her experience is realized by a particular physical event and that certain intrinsic features of the event are in this case responsible for certain intentional features of Eloise's experience. Perhaps there is then a sense in which Eloise is aware of this physical process and aware of those intrinsic features, although she is not aware of them as the intrinsic features that they are.

Even if that is so, it is no objection to functionalism. The intrinsic features that Eloise is aware of in that case are no more psychologically significant than is the property of being a spy to Ortcutt's perception of a man who happens to be a spy. The case gives no reason to think that there is a psychologically significant difference between Eloise's experience and the experience of any functional duplicate of Eloise that is made of different stuff from what Eloise is made of.

Similarly, if Eloise undertakes the sort of education recommended by

Paul Churchland (1985), so that she automatically thinks of the intentional aspects of her experience in terms of their neurophysiological causes, then she may be aware of intrinsic features of her experience as the very features that they are. But again that would be no objection to functionalism, since it gives no reason to think that there is a psychological difference between Eloise after such training and a robot who is Eloise's functional duplicate and who has been given similar training (Shoemaker, 1985). The duplicate now wrongly thinks of certain aspects of its experience as certain features of certain neurological processes—wrongly, because the relevant processes in the duplicate are not neurological processes at all.

Observe, by the way, that I am not offering a positive argument that Eloise and her duplicate must have experiences that are psychologically similar in all respects. I am only observing that the cases just considered are compatible with the functionalist claim that their experiences are similar.

The objections to functionalism that I am considering in this essay claim that certain intrinsic properties of experience so inform the experience that any experience with different intrinsic properties would have a different psychological character. What I have argued so far is that this objection is not established by simple inspection of our experience.

14.4 PERCEPTION AND UNDERSTANDING

Now, let me turn to the second objection, which I repeat:

> A person blind from birth could know all about the physical and functional facts of colour perception without knowing what it is like to see something red. So what it is like to see something red cannot be explicated in purely functional terms.

In order to address this objection, I need to say something about the functionalist theory of the content of mental representations and, more particularly, something about the functionalist theory of concepts. I have to do this because to know what another person's experience is like is to know how to translate that person's experience into your own experience (see Essay 15). You can know what it is like for someone to see something red only if you are able in the right way to represent to yourself something's being red. You can do that only if you have the relevant concept of what it is for something to be red. A blind person who lacks the full concept of redness that a sighted person has cannot fully represent what it is for a sighted person to see something red. Therefore, the blind person cannot be said to know what it is like to see something red.

According to the functionalist account of mental representation discussed in Essays 12 and 13, mental representations are constructed from concepts, where the content of a representation is determined by the concepts it contains and the way these concepts are put together to form that representation. In this view, what it is to have a given concept is functionally determined. Someone has the appropriate concept of something's being red if and only if the person has available a concept that functions in the appropriate way. The relevant functioning may involve connections with the use of other concepts, connections to perceptual input, and/or connections to behavioural output. In this case, connections to perceptual input are crucial. If the concept is to function in such a way that the person has the full concept of something's being red, the person must be disposed to form representations involving that concept as the natural and immediate consequence of seeing something red. Since the blind person lacks any concept of this sort, the blind person lacks the full concept of something's being red. Therefore, the blind person does not know what it is like to see something red.

It is not easy to specify the relevant functional relation precisely. Someone who goes blind later in life will normally retain the relevant concept of something's being red. Such a person has a concept that he or she would be able to use in forming such immediate visual representations except for the condition that interferes in his or her case with normal visual perception. So the right functional relation holds for such a person. I am supposing that the person blind from birth has no such concept; that is, the person has no concept of something's being red that could be immediately brought into service in visual representations of the environment if the person were suddenly to acquire sight.

We are now in a position to assess the claim that the person blind from birth could know all the physical and functional facts about colour perception without knowing what it is like to see something red. I claim that there is one important functional fact about colour perception that the blind person cannot know, namely, that there is a concept that is appropriately activated when a normal perceiver sees something red in good lighting conditions. (That is, there is a concept R such that when a normal perceiver sees something red in good lighting conditions, the perceiver has a visual experience with a representational structure containing this concept R.) The person blind from birth does not know that fact, because in order to know it the person needs to be able to represent that fact to him or herself, which requires having the relevant concepts. A key concept needed to represent that fact is the concept of something's being red, because the fact in question is a fact about what happens when a normal perceiver sees something red. Since the person blind from birth does not have the full concept of something's being red, the person cannot fully understand that fact and so cannot know that fact.

The blind person might know something resembling this, for example, that there is a concept that is appropriately activated when a normal perceiver sees something that reflects light of such-and-such a frequency. But that is to know something different. The person blind from birth fails to know what it is like to see something red because he or she does not fully understand what it is for something to be red, that is, because he or she does not have the full concept of something's being red. So, contrary to what is assumed in the second objection, the person blind from birth does not know all the functional facts, since he or she does not know how the concept R functions with respect to the perception of things that are red.

This response to the second objection appeals to a functionalism that refers to the functions of concepts, not just to the functions of overall mental states. There are other versions of functionalism that try to make do with references to the functions of overall mental states, without appeal to concepts. Some of these versions identify the contents of such states with sets of possible worlds (or centred possible worlds). These versions of functionalism cannot respond to the objection in the way that I have responded. It is unclear to me whether any satisfactory response is possible on behalf of such theories. For example, Lewis (1983) is forced to say that although the person blind from birth lacks certain skills, e.g., the ability to recognize red objects just by looking at them in the way that sighted people can, this person lacks no information about visual perception. I am not happy with that response, since it is clearly false to say that the person blind from birth does not lack any information.

14.5 INVERTED SPECTRUM

I now turn to the third objection to functionalism, which I repeat:

> It is conceivable that two people should have similarly functioning visual systems despite the fact that things that look red to one person look green to the other, things that look yellow to the first person look blue to the second, and so forth. This sort of spectrum inversion in

the way things look is possible but cannot be given a purely functional description, since by hypothesis there are no functional differences between the people in question. Since the way things look to a person is an aspect of that person's mental life, this means that there is an important aspect of a person's mental life that cannot be explicated in purely functional terms.

In order to discuss this objection, I need to say something more about how perceptual states function. In particular, I have to say something about how perceptual states function in relation to belief.

Perceptual experience represents a particular environment of the perceiver. Normally, a perceiver uses this representation as his or her representation of the environment. That is to say, the perceiver uses it in order to negotiate the furniture. In still other words, this representation is used as the perceiver's belief about the environment. This sort of use of perceptual representations is the normal case, although there are exceptions when a perceiver inhibits his or her natural tendency and refrains from using a perceptual representation (or certain aspects of that representation) as a guide to the environment, or as a belief about the surroundings. The content of perceptual representation is functionally defined in part by the ways in which this representation normally arises in perception and in part by the ways in which the representation is normally used to guide actions (Armstrong, 1961, 1968; Dennett, 1969; Harman, 1973).

The objection has us consider two people, call them Alice and Fred, with similarly functioning visual systems but with inverted spectra with respect to each other. Things that look red to Alice look green to Fred, things that look blue to Alice look yellow to Fred, and so on. We are to imagine that this difference between Alice and Fred is not reflected in their behaviour in any way. They both call ripe strawberries 'red' and call grass 'green' and they do this in the effortless ways in which normal perceivers do who have learned English in the usual ways.

Consider what this means for Alice in a normal case of perception. She looks at a ripe strawberry. Perceptual processing results in a perceptual representation of that strawberry, including a representation of its colour. She uses this representation as her guide to the environment, that is, as her belief about the strawberry, in particular, her belief about its colour. She expresses her belief about the colour of the strawberry by using the words, 'It is red'. Similarly for Fred. His perception of the strawberry results in a perceptual representation of the colour of the strawberry that he uses as his belief about the colour and expresses with the same words, 'It is red'.

Now, in the normal case of perception, there can be no distinction between how things look and how they are believed to be, since how things look is given by the content of one's perceptual representation and in the normal case one's perceptual representation is used as one's belief about the environment. The hypothesis of the inverted spectrum objection is that the strawberry looks different in colour to Alice and to Fred. Since everything is supposed to be functioning in them in the normal way, it follows that they must have different beliefs about the colour of the strawberry. If they had the same beliefs while having perceptual representations that differed in content, then at least one of them would have a perceptual representation that was not functioning as his or her belief about the colour of the strawberry, which is to say that it would not be functioning in what we are assuming is the normal way.

A further consequence of the inverted spectrum hypothesis is that, since in the normal case Alice and Fred express their beliefs about the colour of strawberries and grass by saying 'It is red' and 'It is green', they must mean something different by their colour words. By 'red' Fred means the way ripe strawberries look to him. Since that is the way grass looks to Alice, what Fred means by 'red' is what she means by 'green'.

It is important to see that these really are consequences of the inverted spectrum hypothesis. If Alice and Fred meant the same thing by their colour terms, then either (a) one of them would not be using these words to express his or her beliefs about colour, or (b) one of them would not be using his or her perceptual representations of colour as his or her beliefs about colour. In either case, there would be a failure of normal functioning, contrary to the hypothesis of the inverted spectrum objection.

According to functionalism, if Alice and Fred use words in the same way with respect to the same things, then they mean the same things by those words (assuming also that they are members of the same linguistic community and their words are taken from the common language). But this is just common sense. Suppose Alice and Humphrey are both members of the same linguistic community, using words in the same way, etc. Alice is an ordinary human being and Humphrey is a humanoid robot made of quite a different material from Alice. Common sense would attribute the same meanings to Humphrey's words as to Alice's, given that they use words in the same way. Some sort of argument is needed to conclude otherwise. No such argument has been provided by defenders of the inverted spectrum objection.

Shoemaker (1982) offers a different version of the inverted spectrum objection. He has us consider a single person, call him Harry, at two different times, at an initial time of normal colour perception and at a later time after Harry has suffered through a highly noticeable spectrum inversion (perhaps as the result of the sort of brain operation described in Lycan, 1973, in which nerves are switched around so that red things now have the perceptual consequences that green things used to have, etc.), and has finally completely adapted his responses so as to restore normal functioning. Shoemaker agrees that Harry now has the same beliefs about colour as before and means the same things by his colour words, and he agrees that there is a sense in which strawberries now look to Harry the same as they looked before Harry's spectrum inversion. But Shoemaker takes it to be evident that there is another sense of 'looks' in which it may very well be true that things do not look the same as they looked before, so that in this second sense of 'looks' red things look the way green things used to look.

In other words, Shoemaker thinks it is evident that there may be a psychologically relevant difference between the sort of experience Harry had on looking at a ripe strawberry at the initial stage and the experience he has on looking at a ripe strawberry at the final stage (after he has completely adapted to his operation). That is, he thinks it is evident that there may be a psychologically relevant difference between these experiences even though there is no functional difference and no difference in the content of the experiences.

Now, this may seem evident to anyone who has fallen victim to the sense-datum fallacy, which holds that one's awareness of the colour of a strawberry is mediated by one's awareness of an intrinsic feature of a perceptual representation. But why should anyone else agree? Two perceptual experiences with the same intentional content must be psychologically the same. In particular, there can be nothing one is aware of in having the one experience that one is not aware of in having the other, since the intentional content of an experience comprises everything one is aware of in having that experience.

I suggest that Shoemaker's inverted spectrum hypothesis will seem evident only to someone who begins with the prior assumption that people have an immediate and direct awareness of intrinsic features of their experience, including those intrinsic features that function to represent colour. Such a person can then go on to suppose that the intrinsic feature of experience that represents red for Alice is the intrinsic feature of experience that represents green for Fred, and so forth. This prior assumption is exactly the view behind the first objection, which I have argued is contrary to ordinary experience and can be defended only by confusing qualities of the intentional objects of experience with qualities of the experience itself. Shoemaker's inverted spectrum hypothesis therefore offers no independent argument against functionalism. (I should say that Shoemaker himself does not offer his case as an objection to what he calls functionalism. He claims that his version of functionalism is compatible with his case. But I am considering a version of functionalism that is defined in a way that makes it incompatible with such a case.)

14.6 CONCLUSION

To summarize briefly, I have described and replied to three related objections to functionalism. The first claims that we are directly aware of intrinsic features of our experience and argues that there is no way to account for this awareness in a functional view. To this, I reply that when we clearly distinguish properties of the object of experience from properties of the experience, we see that we are not aware of the relevant intrinsic features of the experience. The second objection claims that a person blind from birth can know all about the functional role of visual experience without knowing what it is like to see something red. To this I reply that the blind person does not know all about the functional role of visual experience; in particular, the blind person does not know how such experience functions in relation to the perception of red objects. The third objection claims that functionalism cannot account for the possibility of an inverted spectrum. To this I reply that someone with the relevant sort of inverted spectrum would have to have beliefs about the colours of things that are different from the beliefs others have and would have to mean something different by his or her colour terms, despite being a functionally normal colour perceiver who sorts things by colour in exactly the way others do and who uses colour terminology in the same way that others do. Functionalism's rejection of this possibility is commonsensical and is certainly not so utterly implausible or counterintuitive that these cases present an objection to functionalism. On the other hand, to imagine that there could be relevant cases of inverted spectrum without inversion of belief and meaning is to fall back onto the first objection and not to offer any additional consideration against functionalism.

Immanent and Transcendent
Approaches to Meaning
and Mind

15.1 BACKGROUND: THE NEED FOR *DAS VERSTEHEN* IN THE SOCIAL SCIENCES

A philosophical tradition from Dilthey (1989) to Nagel (1986) sees an important distinction between the methods of the natural sciences and the methods of the social sciences, where the phrase 'social sciences' is broadly interpreted so as include sociology, economics, political theory, anthropology, literary criticism, history, and psychology. According to this tradition, the natural sciences explain phenomena by exhibiting them as instances of orderly patterns, hierarchies of classification, and laws, whereas the social sciences typically require something more, namely, an understanding of meaning, including what actions and experience mean to a person from the inside. We can understand physics or chemistry without knowing what it is like to be an electron, but we cannot fully understand what people are doing or saying unless we have an understanding of how things are for them.

The required subjective empathetic understanding, which Dilthey calls *Das Verstehen*, cannot in this view be arrived at solely through the methods of the natural sciences. Suppose, for example, that we discover a regularity in the behaviour of some social group. Every day at about six o'clock each member of the group stands up and turns in a circle five times. Even if we can predict this with great confidence, that is not yet to understand what they are doing. Is it a religious ritual? A moderate form of callisthenics? A method for getting water out of their ears? We have to know what meaning this action has for them, which is not just to place the action under one or another general principle.

In contrast with the theorists of *Das Verstehen*, philosophical positivists deny that the understanding of social phenomena requires a special kind of empathy not needed in the natural sciences. Positivists argue that the significance an action has to its agents is a psychological fact about the agent, where a psychological fact is a fact about the person's behaviour and internal states that can be understood from the completely objective point of view characteristic of natural science.

Some positivists have argued for a reductionist behaviouristic psychology (Hempel, 1949). Others have proposed a mind–body identity theory (Smart, 1959; Lewis, 1966), a functionalism that may involve a computer model of mind (Sellars, 1963; Putnam, 1967*a*; Armstrong, 1968), or an instrumentalism according to which the attribution of beliefs, desires, and other mental states is a useful device for predicting what rational beings will do. Dennett (1987) compares such an instrumentalist use of psychological attributions to predictions of the stability of a physical system based on where its centre of gravity lies. In some respects Quine (1960*b*) argues for a similar instrumentalism, but, as I will argue, his emphasis on translation in the philosophy of language makes him more akin to a theorist of *Das Verstehen* than to a strict positivist.

Defenders of the method of empathetic subjective understanding assert in opposition to positivism that a strictly objective account of behaviour, behavioural dispositions, inner physical and functional states, and instrumentally effective attributions of intentional states must fail to account for the inner subjective feel of psychological experience and the nonderivative intentionality of beliefs and desires. No amount of objective scientific research will allow a blind person to know what it is like to see something red (Nagel, 1970, 1974, 1986; Jackson, 1982, 1986).

15.2 THE ROLE OF TRANSLATION IN THE THEORY OF LANGUAGE

The same issue exists in the theory of language. We can distinguish two distinct approaches to reference and meaning depending on the role translation plays in the approach. In order to characterize the competing approaches, I will borrow the terms 'transcendent' and 'immanent' from Quine's distinction between transcendent and immanent linguistic notions (Quine, 1986: 19). An immanent notion is explained only for one particular language. A transcendent notion is explained for all languages. The notion 'a sequence of sounds lasting more than five seconds' is a transcendent notion, since it applies to relevant auditory tokens of any language. On the other hand, Tarski's (1956) definition of truth yields an immanent notion that applies only to the particular language for which the definition is given; it does not provide a transcendent definition of truth in L for variable L. Quine gives the example of *der* words in German as an immanent notion, defined only for words in German. On the other hand, the notion of a word is a transcendent notion, since it makes sense to ask for any language what the words of that language are.

Suppose we introduce a notion of meaning via the schema: 'E' means E. Instances of this schema include 'rabbit' means rabbit, 'eat' means eat, 'not' means not. Such an account would explain the verb 'to mean' only as an immanent notion. We might go on to explain a transcendent notion of meaning by appeal to translation: X means E if and only if the translation of X into our language means E.

More precisely, we first define an immanent notion, meaning$_i$, using the schema: 'E' means$_i$ E. We then define a transcendent notion, meaning$_t$, as follows: X in L means$_t$ E if and only if a translation from language L into our own language means$_i$ E.

The transcendent notion, meaning$_t$, can be applied to sentences of our own language on the assumption that a translation of our language into itself translates each expression by that same expression. So, we have 'not' in our language means$_t$ not, 'rabbit' in our language means$_t$ rabbit, and 'hop' in our language means$_t$ hop.

The theory of *Das Verstehen* says that certain aspects of psychological and social phenomena can only be understood by imaginatively putting oneself in the other person's position. An immanent approach to the theory of meaning says that at least sometimes the meaning of an expression in another language cannot be appreciated except by discovering what expression in our language best translates the expression in the other language. These are clearly closely related ideas.

15.3 MEANING$_I$ AND LOGICAL FORM

The suggested account of meaning$_i$ is not so far a full account because it leaves unclear the logical form of a statement using 'means$_i$'. It does not determine whether the statement '"rabbit" means$_i$ rabbit' logically implies the statement, '"rabbit" means$_i$ something'. If there is such an implication, the suggested account does not indicate what the something in question is. Is it a word ('rabbit'), a kind of animal (a rabbit), a property (rabbithood), a concept, an intension, or what?

The simplest and most natural way of further developing an immanent approach to meaning might be to suppose that the something in question is the very word 'rabbit'. Or, rather, 'means$_i$' might be taken to abbreviate a certain relational predicate 'S' together with a pair of quotation marks surrounding what follows, so that 'X means$_i$ . . .' is equated with 'X S " . . .",', where 'S' is such that 'X S X' is true for every expression X of our language.

This will not handle all contexts of interest. Barry Stroud has pointed out to me ambiguous instances of '"E" means E', such as '"nothing" means$_i$ nothing'. The two senses in this case might be represented as (a) '"nothing" S "nothing"', which is true, and as (b) '"nothing" S nothing', in other words, 'It is not the case there is something X such that "nothing" S X', which is false. The second, false, sense represents an additional use of 'means', over and above its use to abbreviate 'S " . . .",', so, we have to distinguish two cases: (a) cases in which 'means$_i$ . . .' abbreviates 'S . . .' and (b) certain cases involving a quantified variable 'X' in which 'means$_i$ X' abbreviates 'S X'.

A number of variations on this theme are possible, depending on whether the word involved is identified with a particular token of a word or with one or another type of word. In the statement '"rabbit" S "rabbit"', the second 'rabbit' might be taken to refer to the particular occurrence or token used on the occasion of making the statement (cf. Davidson, 1968). Or it might be taken to refer to the word-type whose tokens are all tokens of the word 'rabbit' in English that are used in the relevant sense. Or it might be taken to refer to the word-type whose tokens are all tokens of the word with that sense, either in English, or any other language (Sellars, 1974).

The restriction to types whose tokens all have the same sense in these last two proposals prevents the account from assigning the same meaning$_i$, i.e. the same word-type, to different senses of the word 'rabbit'. This may introduce an unwelcome circularity into these accounts, an issue to which we will return.

15.4 IMPLICATIONS OF INDETERMINACY OF TRANSLATION

Quine (1960b) takes an immanent approach to meaning and then goes on to undermine the objectivity of the transcendent notion of meaning via his thesis of the indeterminacy of radical translation.

If translation is indeterminate, an expression Y in our language is a translation of an expression X of language L only relative to some parameter P, where the parameter P determines a unique translation manual between L and our language. In that case an immanent approach must take transcendent reference to be also relative to the parameter P and a relativized transcendental notion of meaning can be defined as follows: X means$_t$ Y in relation to parameter P if and only if the translation of L into our language in relation to P means$_i$ Y.

Of course, even if translation is indeterminate, the immanent notion, meaning$_i$, is not relativized to choice of parameter P—only the transcendent notion is, meaning$_t$. On the other hand, the transcendent notion, meaning$_t$, has to be relativized to choice of parameter P even for expressions in our language, the 'home language'. Given sufficient indeterminacy of translation, it may fail to be determined whether 'rabbit' in our language means$_t$ rabbit independent of choice of parameter. Nevertheless, it will still be determinate that 'rabbit' in our language means$_i$ rabbit apart from any choice of parameter. When Quine (1969) famously says, rather obscurely, '[W]e end the regress of background languages . . . by acquiescing in our mother tongue and taking its words at face value', I interpret him to be saying the words of our language have an objective meaning$_i$, not that they have an objective meaning$_t$.

In what follows, I ignore complications that arise from possible indeterminacy of translation. (In any event, Essay 10 raises doubts about the indeterminacy of radical translation.)

15.5 UNTRANSLATABLE EXPRESSIONS

What is it for a linguistic expression to be meaningful? Naively, we might suppose that an expression is meaningful if it has a meaning. If we can quantify over meanings (that is, if we can quantify with respect to the position of the complement of the verb 'means'), we can say that an expression is meaningful if and only if it means something.

In all immanent approach to meaning, 'means' can be either 'means$_i$' or 'means$_t$', so we can say either that a linguistic expression is 'meaningful$_i$' or that it is 'meaningful$_t$'. What can be meaningful$_i$? That depends on what can replace 'E' in the schema: 'E' means$_i$ E. It seems that any word of our language ought to be allowed and perhaps also phrases, clauses, and sentences. But we don't want to allow any arbitrary string of words to count, because then we would have to say that any arbitrary string of words in our language is meaningful$_i$. For example, we do not want to allow as an instance of our meaning$_i$ schema: 'there in all different in but' means$_i$ there in all different in but.

It would be circular to explain meaningfulness$_i$ in terms of meaning$_i$ and then to explain meaning$_i$ by taking as axioms all meaningful$_i$ instances of our schema. But perhaps we could specify the relevant instances by enumerating the allowable words and allowable grammatical constructions.

Turning now to the transcendental notion meaning$_t$, we get the result that for an expression in another language to be meaningful$_t$ is for it to have a meaningful translation in our language. This implies the thesis of the universality of our language: our language is capable of expressing anything meaningful (Searle, 1969; Katz, 1972).

But there are at least three reasons to think that our language is not universal in this sense. Our language lacks the resources to express (1) certain semantic concepts, (2) certain scientific concepts, and (3) certain perceptual concepts.

First, it is necessary to observe that there is a sense in which we all have somewhat different languages. We speak different dialects. Each of us has his or her own particular 'idiolect'. In order to fix on a particular language, let us take my present language—my present idiolect of English, as it is right now. Then, to take up the first point, consider a metalanguage for my idiolect that includes translations of all indicative sentences of my idiolect and also contains a truth predicate for my idiolect satisfying Tarski's convention T (Tarski, 1956). That is, the truth predicate T satisfies the schema 'X is true if and only if P', for every indicative sentence X in my idiolect, where P is a translation of X into the metalanguage. That truth predicate cannot be translated into my idiolect on pain of contradiction, since that would yield the liar paradox. (There will be an indicative sentence S in my language that says of itself that it is not true, where 'true' represents the translation into my idiolect of T. But this is impossible. If S is true, it is not true, so S cannot be true. But if S is not true, it must be true. So S must be true. The assumptions imply that S is both true and not true, a contradiction.)

Second, consider an expression used in a science that I have not yet mastered, for example, the expression 'quantum number' as used in quantum physics. I strongly suspect that this expression cannot be translated into my idiolect. I do not know how to use the phrase 'quantum number' in the way it is used in quantum physics; it does not have the same meaning for me that it has for physicists. Furthermore, it is extremely unlikely that there is any complex expression in my language that means to me what 'quantum number' means to physicists.

Someone might explain the meaning of 'quantum number' to me in such a way that I come to understand what the phrase means, and that explanation will have to be in terms that I understand. But that explanation would not necessarily provide a translation into my current idiolect of the phrase 'quantum number'. It is not enough for me to memorize an explanation of this phrase. I have to acquire new abilities. The explanation works only if I learn how to use the phrase 'quantum number' as physicists use it. I will have to learn some physics, that is, I may have to learn how to use the notion quantum number in solving certain sorts of problems. Once that is done, my language will have changed; I will have a new concept that I did not have before.

Third, consider the idiolect of the five-year-old blind speaker of English studied by Landau and Gleitman (1985). Although this child's idiolect contains colour words like 'red' and 'green', it is clear that these words do not have the meaning in her idiolect that they have in mine. Indeed, no expressions of her idiolect can mean what my word 'red' means, because she has no way of knowing what it is for something to be red. In the same way, if there is a creature that directly perceives aspects of the world which I do not perceive in the way I perceive colour, and if that creature can speak of these aspects of the world as I can speak of colour, then it is likely that there is no way to translate such talk into my language, my current idiolect.

It seems that each of us must allow for meaningful expressions that cannot be translated into our language. So a strict immanent approach must fall. We must either weaken the immanent approach or abandon it. To weaken the approach we have to allow for meaningful expressions that we cannot now translate into our language. We might say, for example, that such expressions can be meaningful because they are sufficiently similar in usage to expressions in our language, perhaps because we can imagine our own language changing so as to allow such translation. I can conceive of myself modifying my current idiolect by adding a truth predicate for it that applies only to the old part of my new idiolect. I can imagine learning physics. I can allow for the possibility that I gain new ways of talking about the world by acquiring new perceptual abilities. I cannot now understand the meaning of that truth predicate, that concept from physics, or that perceptual term, but I can understand how there can be expressions that are used in a way that I cannot now understand.

This might still be counted as an immanent approach to semantics to the extent that it takes the basic case of meaning to be the immanent notion, meaning$_i$, which applies only to expressions of one's present language. This basic notion is then extended to a transcendent notion, meaning$_t$, that applies to expressions in other languages that can be translated into one's language. It is further extended to expressions in one's language in the past and future and to various possible languages that one could imagine speaking. And it is extended to expressions in other languages that could be translated into a language one could imagine oneself speaking. Further extensions may be possible also, although someone who takes an immanent approach must presumably suppose that the intelligibility of the extensions drops off with the distance from one's present language.

So we have found two problems for an immanent approach to semantics. One problem concerns the logical form of statements like '"not" means$_i$ not'. If we suppose that such a statement abbreviates a statement of the form '"not" S "not"', that leaves the question of what the second 'not' refers to. If it refers to a type of expression, it seems that this expression type must be semantically specified (as including all tokens used with a certain sense or meaning), which makes the account circular.

The other problem is to allow for the meanings$_t$ of expressions in other languages that have no counterparts in our language.

15.6 QUINE ON THE PROBLEM OF MEANING IN LINGUISTICS

The solution in Quine (1953b) is to give up talk of meanings as when we say that an expression 'has meaning' or that two expressions 'have the same meaning'. We should stop trying to relate these two notions and should instead introduce two separate notions of significance and synonymy.

Recall the suggestion considered above that there are two uses of 'means$_i$ . . . ', one as an abbreviation of 'S " . . . "', the other, for the case in which ' . . . ' is a bound variable of quantification, where 'means$_i$ ...' is treated as an abbreviation of 'S . . . '. We could expand this idea by understanding 'S' as 'is synonymous with'. Then the second use of 'means$_i$ . . . ' suggests defining 'is significant' as 'is synonymous with itself'.

15.7 A TRANSCENDENT APPROACH: CONCEPTUAL ROLE SEMANTICS

The rest of Quine's (1953b) idea is that the notions of synonymy and significance should be explained directly in terms of behaviour or linguistic usage. If such explanations can be given, they will be explanations of transcendental notions of synonymy and significance, since they will apply to expressions in any language, not just our own.

If we are going to appeal to usage to explain synonymy and significance, why can we not ignore Quine's suggestion to ignore meaning and develop a use theory of meaning? If the meaning of an expression is its use, then we can say that an expression is a significant expression in a language if it has a use in the language and that two expressions are synonymous to the extent that they have the same use. Let us explore this idea.

How might the meaning of an expression be explained in terms of the way the expression is used? There are various possibilities. One idea is to appeal to speakers' intentions. In this view, speakers intend that words be associated with certain concepts or meanings and they intend that when expressions are combined with certain grammatical constructions the result should be associated with concepts or meanings that are derived in specified ways from the concepts or meanings of the expressions figuring in that grammatical construction. This would require a theory of abstract concepts or meanings, e.g. in terms of possible objects, situations, and/or worlds (Lewis, 1971; Parsons, 1980; Barwise and Perry, 1983). Such an approach might be combined with a Gricean top level: when a sentence meaning M is used to make a statement, the speaker (normally) intends that the audience should come to think that M by virtue of their recognition of the speaker's intention (Grice, 1957, 1968, 1982; Schiffer, 1972).

In this view, people can intend to associate an expression with a certain abstract concept or meaning, if there is a good enough chance that others will recognize that they have that intention. It helps for it to be common knowledge that they or people in their group use the expression with that intention, but new uses are possible too, since a speaker can often count on his audience to grasp what new word–meaning association he has in mind.

So far, this approach does not really explain meaning in terms of use, because it takes the relevant use to be: using an expression to mean something. A different approach would have a more serious role for use. For example, a person uses the word 'and' so as to treat a conjunction, 'P and Q', as a sentence that immediately implies each of its conjuncts, 'P' and 'Q', and is immediately implied by both taken together (Harman, 1986*b*). That use of 'and' distinguishes it from 'or' and, for that matter, from the logically equivalent construction that would combine two sentences 'P' and 'Q' into the compound 'not both not-P and not-Q'. (The latter compound implies but does not immediately imply 'P'.) The indicated use of 'and' gives it its meaning. Another expression is synonymous with 'and' only if it is used in the same way.

In one specific version of this approach, a 'conceptual role semantics' might be adopted, as in Essay 12, above. In this view, concepts are items used in thought (in contrast with abstract contents or intensions). People associate concepts with words, and concepts are distinguished by the way the concepts are used. What makes a certain concept the concept of conjunction is that it combines two thoughts, its conjuncts, in such a way that the combination immediately implies each of its conjunctions and is immediately implied by the conjunctions taken together.

15.8 CAUSAL THEORY OF REFERENCE

The meanings of some expressions may have something to do with causal relations between those expressions and certain things in the world (Kripke, 1972). For example, I sometimes use the name 'Van' as the name of one of my neighbours in Princeton. What makes it true that I have this use of the name while other people do not has to do with causal relations that hold between my uses of the name 'Van' and my neighbour, Van Williams.

Perhaps it would be better to say this: I use the name 'Van' to pick out, refer to, a certain person, so that I can say something about him, for example, 'Van lives across the street from me'. In saying this I am talking about Van Williams, not about Van Quine. The causal theory is therefore a theory about the thought I am trying to express in these words, the thought I am trying to communicate. What makes the thought a thought about a particular person is due in part to certain causal relations between that person and my thought (Devitt, 1981).

A thought and the corresponding communication tend to rely on a causal relation between the person and his name. You are now in a position to have thoughts about Van (i.e. Van Williams, my neighbour) primarily because of your newly acquired causal relation between him and the name. I have many neighbours, so it is not just the description 'my neighbour' that gets you to Van. It is 'my neighbour named "Van"'. If I have more than one neighbour named 'Van', your thoughts are about the one I was referring to, the one causally connected in the relevant way with my utterance.

Putnam (1975) defends a similar view of common names of natural kinds like 'tiger' and 'gold'. In such cases there is a perception (involving a causal relation) of an instance of the natural kind coupled with the introduction of the name. Later uses of the name derive in part from causal relations to earlier uses and their causal relations via perception to the substance in question.

Perhaps this can be extended to various features and attributes of things.

It might even be argued that 'red' means what it does because of causal relations between this word and the redness of red things. In that case, a blind person could use the term 'red' to designate redness just as you can now use the name 'Van' to ask me whether my neighbour has any children (Tawil, 1987). It might be argued that a number word like 'twelve' has meaning in part because of causal relations to manifestations of twelveness. In this view, a small child who has not learned to count can still use the word 'twelve' to mean what we mean.

But there is an additional element of meaning in words like 'red' and 'twelve'. A blind person cannot use the word 'red' with the full meaning a sighted person assigns to this word. A person who has not learned to count may fail to mean by number words all that we mean who have learned to count.

Furthermore, it is clear that something other than mere causal relation has to be relevant to what a term names, since the term will have causal relations to irrelevant things. There are causal relations of various sorts between my use of the term 'Van' and my neighbour's house, his children, his telephone, my wife Lucy (who gives me a message from Van), my daughter Olivia (who tells me about Van's new car), certain issues of a Princeton paper called *Town Topics* (with a story mentioning Van), and so forth. I do not use 'Van' as a name of any of these other things.

Similarly, Quine (1960*b*) observes that the use of a native term 'gavagai' might be equally connected causally to rabbits, rabbit (meat), undetached rabbit parts, rabbithood, and other things as well. For 'gavagai' to be used as a name of rabbits, it must play a certain role in counting, identity statements, and quantification.

Perhaps we can accommodate the role of causation in meaning by taking use to be the use of a word in one's interactions with other things in the world, as discussed in Essays 12–13, above.

15.9 PIECEMEAL VERSUS HOLISTIC THEORIES
OF MEANING

A piecemeal transcendent account of meaning tries to characterize the meaning of an expression entirely in terms of the use of that expression (or of the concept it expresses). A more holistic account would allow that the use of other expressions can also be relevant, e.g. in distinguishing the mass term 'rabbit' from the count term 'rabbit'.

Whether a term has the meaning of classical or intuitionistic negation may depend in part on whether there is a different expression in the language representing classical or intuitionistic negation that interacts in relevant ways with the former term. Whether a construction represents objectual quantification may not be determinable merely by looking at the use of that construction by itself; it may also be necessary to look at how names are used in relation to that construction, whether there is a relation that can be interpreted as expressing identity, whether there is a predicate meaning exists, and so on (Quine, 1974).

What a proper name refers to may depend not just on causal relations but on the use of other predicates that you combine with that name. What makes 'Van' a name of my neighbour rather than a name of his teeth, his hair, his individual concept, or his lawn has something to do with the way I use the terms 'neighbour' and 'person' in contrast to 'teeth', 'part', 'concept', 'lawn', and so forth, since I introduce the term 'Van' as the name of a person, that is, in relation to my concept or our concept of a person, which is connected with how I and we use the word 'person'. (On the other hand, I may acquire a term from John Pollock thinking that it refers to a person, although he uses it to refer to a computer program, 'Oscar'.)

Holistic theories sometimes appeal to a Principle of Charity, holding that expressions have those meanings that are assigned by the best interpretation of speakers of the language, where the best interpretation might be the interpretation that maximizes the truth of what speakers say subject to certain other constraints.

Verificationism is a form of conceptual role semantics that equates the meaning of a predicate with procedures for deciding whether the predicate applies or not. This tends toward holism, given the Duhem–Quine thesis about confirmation, namely, that evidence does not confirm or disconfirm sentences taken one at a time. If a test fails, that does not guarantee that the predicate does not apply, since something may be wrong with measuring instruments or with some other aspect of the experimental design, or some other auxiliary assumption may be wrong, etc. (Duhem, 1906; Quine, 1953c).

15.10 IMMANENT VERSUS TRANSCENDENT HOLISTIC APPROACHES

Quine (1960b) adopts an immanent holistic approach to transcendent meaning. In Quine's view, what expressions in L mean is determined by the translation from L into our language that maximizes our agreement with speakers of L (subject to certain constraints). Davidson (1973*b*) advocates a transcendent holistic approach. In his view, what expressions in L mean is determined by the best theory of truth for L that maximizes the truth of what they say and believe (subject to certain constraints).

These approaches involve two distinct 'Principles of Charity'. As practical guides, the two principles will normally coincide because, trivially, our beliefs represent our view of what is true, so it would be unusual for us to be in a position to suppose that, subject to the relevant constraints, interpretation A maximizes agreement with our beliefs whereas interpretation B maximizes the truths that they believe. But it is clearly possible that there could be two such interpretations, A and B, even if we would have trouble establishing that this is so for those interpretations. In that case, A will be the correct interpretation according to Quine's approach and B will be the correct interpretation according to Davidson's approach, even though (to repeat) we may not recognize this in any given instance.

Grandy (1973) points out that both Principles of Charity are over crude. We will not want to attribute certain beliefs to speakers of L if we cannot understand how they could have acquired that information. For example, it might be possible to map certain of their opinions into truths or beliefs of ours about a place with which they have had no contact, but that would not be a reasonable interpretation. We should say instead that speakers of L have those beliefs it would be reasonable for them to have given their epistemic situation.

15.11 LIMITATIONS OF A TRANSCENDENT APPROACH

Simply learning what the rules are for the use of an expression (or for the use of the concept expressed) does not always bring an understanding of meaning with it. Consider the suggested description of the use of a certain connective mentioned above: the connective is used to combine two sentences in such a way that the combination immediately implies each of these sentences and is immediately implied by the two sentences taken together. Someone could understand this description of the use of the connective without realizing what the connective means (namely, *and*).

Suppose that N is a one-place sentential operator that can be applied to a sentence A to get a result N(A). N is used in such a way that A and N(A) immediately exclude each other and each is immediately implied by anything that immediately excludes the other. What does N mean? I am inclined to think that N means *not* or *it is not the case that* (Harman, 1986*b*), but I do not think this is at all obvious from this description of the use of N. Scott Soames pointed out to me that a somewhat different account of use that I had initially accepted was actually more appropriate for intuitionistic negation than for (the classical) not.

A description of use is not enough to give understanding. What is needed, it seems, is a translation of the expression into our language, a translation that associates the expression with something in our language with the same use. We need to know the use 'from the inside'. Consider learning the meaning of intuitionistic connectives. In my experience, a description of their use (e.g. in terms of rules of immediate implication and exclusion) is not all that useful. One way to understand intuitionistic connectives is to learn to use them in such a way that this use is second nature. That is the way we learn concepts in physics or chemistry or mathematics. We learn to use those concepts. It is not enough to have that usage described if we can't go on to use the concepts for ourselves. The usage has to be internalized. So we need an immanent approach. We can try for as much as we can get of a transcendent approach, i.e. of objective descriptions of usage, but that is going to tell us about meaning only to the extent it allows us to do translation.

This is the same point that Dilthey and Nagel make in their appeal to *Das Verstehen* and an understanding of 'what it is like' to experience something. Because a blind child does not know what it is like to experience something as red, the child lacks an understanding of what the word 'red' means.

We need to combine an immanent approach with a transcendent approach to semantics. We cannot restrict ourselves to a purely immanent approach because we need an independent transcendent characterization of similarity in usage (or synonymy). We cannot restrict ourselves to a purely transcendent account because that leaves us with no account of what expressions mean.

BIBLIOGRAPHY

ALSTON, W. (1964). *The Philosophy of Language.* Englewood Cliffs, NJ: Prentice-Hall.

—— (1972). 'How Does One Tell if a Word has One, Several, or Many Senses?' In D. D. Steinberg and L. A. Jakobovits (eds.), *Semantics*, 35–47. Cambridge: Cambridge University Press.

—— (1989). *Epistemic Justification: Essays in the Theory of Knowledge.* Ithaca, NY: Cornell University Press.

ANGLUIN, D. C., and SMITH, C. H. (1983). 'Inductive Inference: Theory and Methods.' *Computing Surveys*, 15: 237–69.

ANSCOMBE, G. E. M. (1965). 'The Intentionality of Sensation: A Grammatical Feature.' In R. J. Butler (ed.), *Analytical Philosophy, Second Series.* Oxford: Basil Blackwell.

ARMSTRONG, D. M. (1961). *Perception and the Physical World.* London: Routledge & Kegan Paul.

—— (1962). *Bodily Sensations.* London: Routledge & Kegan Paul.

—— (1968). *The Materialist Theory of Mind.* London: Routledge & Kegan Paul.

AYER, A. J. (1936). *Language, Truth, and Logic.* London: Gollancz.

—— (1940). *The Foundations of Empirical Knowledge.* London: Macmillan.

BACH, K. (1975). 'Performatives Are Statements, Too.' *Philosophical Studies*, 28: 229–36.

BARWISE, J., and PERRY, J. (1983). *Situations and Attitudes.* Cambridge, Mass.: MIT Press.

BENACERRAF, P. (1965). 'What Numbers Could Not Be.' *Philosophical Review*, 74: 47–73.

BENNETT, J. (1959). 'Analytic–Synthetic.' *Proceedings of the Aristotelian Society*, 59: 163–88.

—— (1966). *Kant's Analytic.* Cambridge: Cambridge University Press.

—— (1976). *Linguistic Behaviour.* Cambridge: Cambridge University Press.

—— (1990). 'Why is Belief Involuntary?' *Analysis*, 50: 87–107.

BLACK, M. (1958a). 'Necessary Statements and Rules.' *Philosophical Review*, 67: 313–41.

—— (1958b). 'Self Supporting Inductive Arguments.' *Journal of Philosophy*, 55: 718–25.

BLOCK, N. (1986). 'Advertisement for a Semantics for Psychology.' *Midwest Studies in Philosophy*, 10: 615–78.

—— and Fodor, J. A. (1972). 'What Psychological States are Not.' *Philosophical Review*, 81: 159–81.

BLOOMFIELD, L. (1933). *Language*. New York: Holt.

—— (1955). 'Linguistic Aspects of Science.' *International Encyclopedia of Unified Science*. Chicago, Ill.: University of Chicago Press.

BLUM, L., and BLUM, M. (1975). 'Toward a Mathematical Theory of Inductive Inference.' *Information and Control*, 28: 125–55.

BLUM, M. (1967). 'A Machine-Independent Theory of the Complexity of Recursive Functions.' *Journal of the Association for Computing Machinery*, 14: 322–36.

BOGHOSSIAN, P. (1996). 'Analyticity Reconsidered.' *Nous*, 30: 360–91.

BOLINGER, D. (1965). 'The Atomization of Meaning.' *Language*, 41: 555–73.

BONJOUR, L. (1992). 'Problems of Induction.' In J. Dancy and E. Sosa (eds.), *A Companion to Epistemology*, 391–5. Oxford: Basil Blackwell.

BRATMAN, M. (1987). *Intention, Plans, and Practical Reason*. Cambridge, Mass.: Harvard University Press.

CARNAP, R. (1936). 'Testability and Meaning', Pt. 1. *Philosophy of Science*, 3: 419–71.

—— (1937). 'Testability and Meaning', Pt. 2. *Philosophy of Science*, 4: 1–40.

—— (1950). 'Empiricism, Semantics, and Ontology.' *Revue internationale de philosophie*, 4: 20–40.

—— (1956). 'Meaning and Synonymy in Natural Languages.' In his *Meaning and Necessity*, 2nd edn. Chicago, Ill.: University of Chicago Press, 233–47.

—— (1966). *Philosophical Foundations of Physics*, ed. M. Gardner. New York: Basic Books.

CARTWRIGHT, N. (1983). *How the Laws of Physics Lie*. Oxford: Oxford University Press.

CHISHOLM, R. (1982). *The Foundations of Knowing*. Minneapolis, Minn.: University of Minnesota Press.

CHOMSKY, N. (1964). 'Current Issues in Linguistic Theory.' In J. Fodor and J. Katz (eds.), *The Structure of Language*. Englewood Cliffs, NJ: Prentice-Hall.

—— (1966). *Cartesian Linguistics*. New York: Harper & Row.

—— (1980). *Reflections on Language*. New York: Columbia University Press.

CHRISTENSEN, D. (1991). 'Clever Bookies and Coherent Beliefs.' *Philosophical Review*, 100: 229–47.

CHURCHLAND, P. (1985). 'Reduction, Qualia, and the Direct Introspection of Mental States.' *Journal of Philosophy*, 82: 8–28.

COHEN, J. (1981). 'Can Human Irrationality Be Experimentally Demonstrated?' *Behavioral and Brain Sciences*, 4: 317–70.

CONEE, E. (1992). 'The Truth Connection.' *Philosophy and Phenomenological Research*, 52: 657–69.

DAVIDSON, D. (1965). 'Theories of Meaning and Learnable Languages.' In Y. Bar-Hillel (ed.), *Logic, Methodology and Philosophy of Science: Proceedings of the 1964 International Congress*. Amsterdam: North-Holland.

—— (1967a). 'The Logical Form of Action Sentences.' In N. Rescher (ed.), *The Logic of Decision and Action*. Pittsburgh, Pa.: University of Pittsburgh Press.

—— (1967*b*). 'Truth and Meaning.' *Synthese*, 17: 304–23.

—— (1968). 'On Saying That.' *Synthese*, 19: 130–46.

—— (1970). 'Semantics for Natural Languages.' In *Linguaggi nella societa e nella tecnica*. Milan: Edizione di Comunita.

—— (1973*a*). 'Freedom to Act.' In T. Honderich (ed.), *Essays on Freedom of Action*. London: Routledge & Kegan Paul.

—— (1973*b*). 'Radical Interpretation.' *Dialectica*, 27: 313–28.

—— MCKINSEY, J. J. C., and SUPPES, P. (1955). 'Outlines of a Formal Theory of Value.' *Philosophy of Science*, 22: 140–60.

DENNETT, D. C. (1969). *Content and Consciousness*. London: Routledge & Kegan Paul.

—— (1971). 'Intentional Systems.' *Journal of Philosophy*, 68: 87–106.

—— (1987). *The Intentional Stance*. Cambridge, Mass.: MIT Press.

DESCARTES, R. (1637). *Discours de la méthode*. In *Philosophical Works of Descartes*, trans. E. S. Haldane and G. R. T. Ross. Cambridge: Cambridge University Press, 1967.

DEVITT, M. (1981). *Designation*. New York: Columbia University Press.

DILTHEY, W. (1989). *Introduction to the Human Sciences*, ed. and trans. R. A. Makkreel and F. Rodi. Princeton, NJ: Princeton University Press. (Originally published as *Einleitung in die Geisteswissenschaften*, 1883.)

DRETSKE, F. (1981). *Knowledge and the Flow of Information*. Cambridge, Mass.: MIT Press.

DUHEM, P. (1906). *La Théorie physique: Son object et sa structure*. Paris: Chevalier & Rivière.

FIELD, H. (1977*a*). 'Logic, Meaning, and Conceptual Role.' *Journal of Philosophy*, 74: 379–409.

—— (1977*b*). 'Probabilistic Semantics.' *Journal of Philosophy*, 74: 63–73.

FODOR, J. A. (1965). 'Explanations in Psychology.' In M. Black (ed.), *Philosophy in America*. Ithaca, NY: Cornell University Press.

—— (1968). *Psychological Explanation: An Introduction to the Philosophy of Psychology*. New York: Random House.

—— (1980). 'Methodological Solipsism as a Research Strategy in Psychology.' *Behavioral and Brain Sciences*, 3: 63–73.

FOLEY, R. (1983). 'Epistemic Conservatism.' *Philosophical Studies*, 43: 165–82.

—— (1987). *The Theory of Epistemic Rationality*. Cambridge, Mass.: Harvard University Press.

FOSTER, J. A. (1976). 'Meaning and Truth Theory.' In G. Evans and J. McDowell (eds.), *Truth and Meaning: Essays in Semantics*. Oxford: Oxford University Press.

FRANKLIN, B. (1817). *Private Correspondence*, vol. i. London: Colburn.

GÄRDENFORS, P. (1988). *Knowledge in Flux*. Cambridge, Mass.: MIT Press.

GAZDAR, G., KLEIN, E., PULLUM, G., and SAG, I. (1985). *Generalized Phrase Structure Grammar*. Cambridge, Mass.: Harvard University Press.

GINSBERG, M. (ed.) (1987). *Readings in Nonmonotonic Reasoning.* Los Altos, Calif.: Morgan Kaufmann.

GLYMOUR, C. (1980). *Theory and Evidence.* Princeton, NJ: Princeton University Press.

GOLD, E. M. (1967). 'Language Identification the Limit.' *Information and Control,* 10: 447–74.

GOLDMAN, A. (1967). 'A Causal Theory of Knowing.' *Journal of Philosophy,* 64: 357–71.

—— (1986). *Epistemology and Cognition.* Cambridge, Mass.: Harvard University Press.

—— (1992). *Liaisons: Philosophy Meets the Cognitive Sciences.* Cambridge, Mass.: MIT Press.

GOODMAN, N. (1965). *Fact, Fiction and Forecast,* 2nd edn. Indianapolis, Ind.: Bobbs-Merrill.

—— (1966). 'Constructive Definition.' In his *Structure of Appearance,* 2nd edn. Indianapolis, Ind.: Bobbs-Merrill.

GOULD, S. J. (1985). *The Flamingo's Smile.* New York: W. W. Norton.

GRANDY, R. (1973). 'Reference, Meaning, and Belief.' *Journal of Philosophy,* 70: 439–52.

GRICE, H. P. (1957). 'Meaning.' *Philosophical Review,* 66: 377–88.

—— (1961). 'The Causal Theory of Perception.' *Proceedings of the Aristotelian Society Supplementary Volume,* 35: 121–52.

—— (1968). 'Utterer's Meaning, Sentence Meaning, and Word Meaning.' *Foundations of Language,* 4: 225–42.

—— (1969). 'Utterer's Meaning and Intentions.' *Philosophical Review,* 78: 147–77.

—— (1972). *Intention and Uncertainty.* Oxford: Oxford University Press.

—— (1975). 'Logic and Conversation.' In D. Davidson and G. Harman (eds.), *The Logic of Grammar.* Encino, Calif.: Dickenson.

—— (1982). 'Mutual Knowledge.' In N. Smith (ed.), *Meaning Revisited.* London: Academic Press.

—— and STRAWSON, P. F. (1956). 'In Defense of a Dogma.' *Philosophical Review,* 65: 141–58.

HAHN, H. (1959). 'Logic, Mathematics, and Knowledge of Nature.' In A. J. Ayer (ed.), *Logical Positivism.* New York: Free Press.

HAMPSHIRE, S. (1959). *Thought and Action.* London: Chatto & Windus.

HARMAN, G. (1963). 'Generative Grammars without Transformation Rules: A Defense of Phrase Structure.' *Language,* 39: 597–616.

—— (1966). 'What an Adequate Grammar Could Do.' *Foundations of Language,* 2: 134–6.

—— (1967a). 'Psychological Aspects of the Theory of Syntax.' *Journal of Philosophy,* 64: 75–87.

—— (1967b). 'Quine on Meaning and Existence, I: The Death of Meaning.' *Review of Metaphysics,* 21: 124–51.

—— (1967*c*). 'Quine on Meaning and Existence, II.' *Review of Metaphysics*, 21: 343–67.

—— (1968). 'Knowledge, Inference, and Explanation.' *American Philosophical Quarterly*, 3: 164–73.

—— (1969). 'An Introduction to Translation and Meaning: Chapter Two of Word and Object.' In D. Davidson and J. Hintikka (eds.), *Words and Objections: Essays on the Work of W. V. Quine*, 14–26. Dordrecht: Reidel.

—— (1972). 'Logical Form.' *Foundations of Language*, 9: 38–65.

—— (1973). *Thought*. Princeton, NJ: Princeton University Press.

—— (1976). 'Practical Reasoning.' *Review of Metaphysics*, 29: 431–63.

—— (1978). 'Meaning and Theory.' *Southwestern Journal of Philosophy*, 9: 9–19.

—— (1982). 'Conceptual Role Semantics.' *Notre Dame Journal of Formal Logic*, 28: 242–56.

—— (1985). 'Problems with Probabilistic Semantics.' In A. Orenstein *et al.* (eds.), *Developments in Semantics*. New York: Haven.

—— (1986*a*). *Change in View: Principles of Reasoning*. Cambridge, Mass.: MIT Press.

—— (1986*b*). 'The Meanings of Logical Constants.' In E. LePore (ed.), *Truth and Interpretation*, 125–34. Oxford: Basil Blackwell.

—— (1986*c*). 'Quine's Grammar.' In P. Schilpp (ed.), *The Philosophy of W. V. Quine*. La Salle, Ill.: Open Court.

—— (1987). 'Willing and Intending.' In R. Grandy and R. Warner (eds.), *Philosophical Grounds of Rationality: Intentions, Categories, Ends*, 363–80. Oxford: Oxford University Press.

—— (1990). 'Immanent versus Transcendent Approaches to the Theory of Meaning.' In R. Gibson and R. B. Barrett (eds.), *Perspectives on Quine*, 144–57. Oxford: Basil Blackwell.

—— (1993*a*). 'Desired Desires.' In R. Frey and C. Morris (eds.), *Value, Welfare, and Morality*, 138–57. Cambridge: Cambridge University Press.

—— (1993*b*). 'Meaning Holism Defended.' *Grazer Philosophische Studien*, 46: 163–71.

—— (1994*a*). 'Doubts about Conceptual Anaysis.' In M. Michael and J. O'Leary-Hawthorne (eds.), *Philosophy in Mind: The Place of Philosophy in the Study of Mind*, 43–8. Dordrecht: Kluwer.

—— (1994*b*). 'Simplicity as a Pragmatic Criterion for Deciding what Hypotheses to Take Seriously.' In D. Stalker (ed.), *Grue: The New Riddle of Induction*, 153–71. Peru, Ill.: Open Court.

—— (1995). 'Rationality.' In E. E. Smith and D. N. Osherson (eds.), *Thinking: Invitation to Cognitive Science*, iii. 175–211. Cambridge, Mass.: MIT Press.

—— (1996). 'Explaining Objective Color in Terms of Subjective Reactions.' In E. Villanueva (ed.), *Perception: Philosophical Issues*, 7: 1–17. Atascadero, Calif.: Ridgeview.

—— (1997). 'Pragmatism and Reasons for Belief.' In C. B. Kulp (ed.), *Realism/ Antirealism and Epistemology*, 123–47. Lanham, Md.: Rowman & Littlefield.

HEMPEL, C. G. (1949). 'The Logical Analysis of Psychology.' In H. Feigl and W. Sellars (eds.), *Readings in Philosophical Analysis*, 373–84. New York: Appleton-Century-Crofts.

—— (1965*a*). *Aspects of Scientific Explanation and Other Essays in the Philosophy of Science*. New York: Free Press.

—— (1965*b*). 'Inductive Inconsistencies.' In Hempel (1965*a*).

HORTY, J. F., and THOMASON, R. H. (1991). 'Conditionals and Artificial Intelligence.' *Fundamenta Informaticae*, 15: 301–23.

JACKSON, F. (1977). *Perception: A Representative Theory*. Cambridge: Cambridge University Press.

—— (1982). 'Epiphenomenal Qualia.' *Philosophical Quarterly*, 32: 127–32.

—— (1986). 'What Mary Didn't Know.' *Journal of Philosophy*, 83: 291–5.

—— (1994). 'Armchair Metaphysics.' In M. Michael and J. O'Leary-Hawthorne (eds.), *Philosophy in Mind*. Dordrecht: Kluwer.

KATZ, J. (1964). 'Analyticity and Contradiction in Natural Language.' In J. Fodor and J. Katz (eds.), *The Structure of Language*. Englewood Cliffs, NJ: Prentice-Hall.

—— (1966*a*). 'Mentalism in Linguistics.' *Language*, 40: 124–37.

—— (1966*b*). *The Philosophy of Language*. New York: Harper & Row.

—— (1967). 'Some Remarks on Quine on Analyticity.' *Journal of Philosophy*, 64: 35–52.

—— (1972). *Semantic Theory*. New York: Harper & Row.

—— and FODOR, J. (1964). 'The Structure of a Semantic Theory.' In J. Fodor and J. Katz (eds.), *The Structure of Language*. Englewood Cliffs, NJ: Prentice-Hall.

—— and POSTAL, P. (1964). *An Integrated Theory of Linguistic Description*. Cambridge, Mass.: MIT Press.

KELLEY, H. H. (1967). 'Attribution Theory in Social Psychology.' *Nebraska Symposium on Motivation*, 14: 192–241.

KRIPKE, S. A. (1963). 'Semantical Considerations on Modal Logic.' *Acta Philosophica Fennica*, 16: 83–94.

—— (1972). 'Naming and Necessity.' In D. Davidson and G. Harman (eds.), *Semantics of Natural Language*. Dordrecht: Reidel.

KUGEL, P. (1977). 'Induction, Pure and Simple.' *Information and Control*, 35: 276–336.

LANDAU, B., and GLEITMAN, L. R. (1985). *Language and Experience*. Cambridge, Mass.: Harvard University Press.

LEVI, I. (1967). *Gambling with Truth*. New York: Knopf.

LEWIS, D. (1966). 'An Argument for the Identity Theory.' *Journal of Philosophy*, 63: 17–25.

—— (1969). *Convention*. Cambridge, Mass.: Harvard University Press.

—— (1971). 'General Semantics.' In D. Davidson and G. Harman (eds.), *Semantics of Natural Language*. Dordrecht: Reidel.

—— (1980). 'Mad Pain and Martian Pain.' In N. Block (ed.), *Readings in Philosophy of Psychology*. Cambridge, Mass.: Harvard University Press.

—— (1983). 'Postscript to "Mad Pain and Martian Pain".' In his *Philosophical Papers*, i. 130–2. New York: Oxford University Press.

LOAR, B. (1981). *Mind and Meaning*. Cambridge: Cambridge University Press.

—— (1983*a*). 'Must Beliefs Be Sentences?' In P. D. Asquith and T. Nickles (eds.), *PSA 1982*, ii. 627–43. East Lansing, Mich.: Philosophy of Science Association.

—— (1983*b*). 'Reply to Fodor and Harman.' In P. D. Asquith and T. Nickles (eds.), *PSA 1982*, ii. 662–6. East Lansing, Mich.: Philosophy of Science Association.

LOEWER, B. (1982). 'The Role of "Conceptual Role Semantics".' *Notre Dame Journal of Formal Logic*, 23: 305–22.

LYCAN, W. G. (1973). 'Inverted Spectrum.' *Ratio*, 15.

—— (1984). *Logical Form in Natural Language*. Cambridge, Mass.: MIT Press.

MCCAWLEY, J. D. (1970). 'Where do Noun Phrases Come From?' In P. S. Rosenbaum (ed.), *Readings in English Transformational Grammar*. Waltham, Mass.: Ginn.

MEILAND, J. (1980). 'What Ought we to Believe, or the Ethics of Belief Revisited.' *American Philosophical Quarterly*, 17: 15–24.

MILLER, G. A., GALANTER, E., and PRIBRAM, K. H. (1960). *Plans and the Structure of Behavior*. New York: Holt, Rinehart & Winston.

MILLER, R. W. (1992). *Moral Differences: Truth, Justice and Conscience in a World of Conflict*. Princeton, NJ: Princeton University Press.

MORAVCSIK, J. M. E. (1965). 'The Analytic and the Nonempirical.' *Journal of Philosophy*, 62: 421–3.

MORRIS, C. (1946). *Signs, Language, and Behavior*. New York: Braziller.

NAGEL, T. (1970). 'Armstrong on the Mind.' *Philosophical Review*, 79: 395–403.

—— (1974). 'What is it Like to Be a Bat?' *Philosophical Review*, 83: 435–50.

—— (1986). *The View From Nowhere*. New York: Oxford University Press.

NEWTON-SMITH, W. H. (1981). *The Rationality of Science*. Boston, Mass.: Routledge & Kegan Paul.

NOZICK, R. (1993). *The Nature of Rationality*. Princeton, NJ: Princeton University Press.

PAP, A. (1958). *Semantics and Necessary Truth*. New Haven, Conn.: Yale University Press.

PARSONS, C. (1965). 'Frege's Concept of Number.' In M. Black (ed.), *Philosophy in America*. Ithaca, NY: Cornell University Press.

PARSONS, T. (1980). *Nonexistent Objects*. New Haven, Conn.: Yale University Press.

PASCAL, B. (1995). *Pensées*. New York: Penguin.

PEACOCKE, C. (1983). *Sense and Content*. Oxford: Oxford University Press.

PEIRCE, C. S. (1955). 'Some Consequences of Four Incapacities.' In J. Buchler (ed.), *Philosophical Writings of Peirce*. New York: Dover.

PITCHER, G. (1971). *A Theory of Perception*. Princeton, NJ: Princeton University Press.

PLACE, U. T. (1956). 'Is Consciousness a Brain Process?' *British Journal of Psychology*, 47: 44–50.

POJMAN, L. P. (1985). 'Believing and Willing.' *Canadian Journal of Philosophy*, 15: 37–55.

POLLOCK, J. (1979). 'A Plethora of Epistemological Theories.' In G. Pappas (ed.), *Justification and Knowledge*. Dordrecht: Reidel: 93–114.

—— (1991), 'OSCAR: A General Theory of Rationality.' In R. Cummins and J. Pollock (eds.), *Philosophy and AI: Essays at the Interface*, 189–213. Cambridge, Mass.: MIT Press:

PRICHARD, H. A. (1949). *Moral Obligation*. Oxford: Oxford University Press.

PUTNAM, H. (1960). 'Minds and Machines.' In S. Hook (ed.), *Dimensions of Mind*. New York: NYU Press.

—— (1962a). 'The Analytic and the Synthetic.' In H. Feigl and G. Maxwell (eds.), *Minnesota Studies in the Philosophy of Science*, 3: 358–97. Minneapolis, Minn.: University of Minnesota Press.

—— (1962b). 'It Ain't Necessarily So.' *Journal of Philosophy*, 59: 658–71.

—— (1964). 'Robots: Machines or Artificially Created Life.' *Journal of Philosophy*, 61: 668–91.

—— (1967a). 'The Mental Life of Some Machines.' In H. Castañeda (ed.), *Intentionality, Minds, and Perception*. Detroit: Wayne State University Press.

—— (1967b). 'Psychological Predicates.' In W. H. Capitan and D. D. Merrill (eds.), *Art, Mind, and Religion*. Pittsburgh, Pa.: University of Pittsburgh Press.

—— (1975). 'The Meaning of Meaning.' In his *Mind, Language, and Reality: Philosophical Papers*, vol. ii. Cambridge: Cambridge University Press.

QUINE, W. V. (1936). 'Truth by Convention.' In O. H. Lee (ed.), *Philosophical Essays for A. N. Whitehead*, 90–124. New York: Longman.

—— (1953a). 'On What There Is.' In his *From a Logical Point of View*. Cambridge, Mass.: Harvard University Press.

—— (1953b). 'The Problem of Meaning in Linguistics.' In his *From a Logical Point of View*. Cambridge, Mass.: Harvard University Press.

—— (1953c). 'Two Dogmas of Empiricism.' In his *From a Logical Point of View*. Cambridge, Mass.: Harvard University Press.

—— (1960a). 'Carnap and Logical Truth.' *Synthese*, 12: 350–74.

—— (1960b). *Word and Object*. Cambridge, Mass.: MIT Press.

—— (1966). 'Necessary Truth.' In his *The Ways of Paradox*. New York: Harper & Row.

—— (1967). 'On a Suggestion of Katz.' *Journal of Philosophy*, 64: 52–4.

—— (1969). 'Ontological Relativity.' In his *Ontological Relativity and Other Essays*. New York: Columbia University Press.

—— (1974). *The Roots of Reference*. LaSalle, Ill.: Open Court.

—— (1986). *Philosophy of Logic*, 2nd edn. Cambridge, Mass.: Harvard University Press.

QUINTON, A. (1963). 'The A Priori and the Analytic.' *Proceedings of the Aristotelian Society*, 64: 31–54.

RUMELHART, D. E., and MCCLELLAND, J. L. (1986). *Parallel Distributed Processing*, 2 vols. Cambridge, Mass.: MIT Press.

RYLE, G. (1949). *The Concept of Mind*. London: Hutchinson.

—— (1953). 'Ordinary Language.' *Philosophical Review*, 62: 167–86.

—— (1961). 'Use, Usage, and Meaning.' *Proceedings of the Aristotelialian Society Supplementary Volume*, 35: 223–30.

SCHELLING, T. (1960). *The Strategy of Conflict*. Cambridge, Mass.: Harvard University Press.

—— (1966). *Arms and Influence*. New Haven, Conn.: Yale University Press.

SCHIFFER, S. (1972). *Meaning*. Oxford: Oxford University Press.

—— (1981). 'Truth and the Theory of Content.' In H. Parret and J. Bouveresse (eds.), *Meaning and Understanding*, 204–22. Berlin: W. de Gruyter.

SCRIVEN, M. (1958). 'Definitions, Explanations, and Theories.' In H. Feigl, M. Scriven, and G. Maxwell (eds.), *Minnesota Studies in the Philosophy of Science*, 2: 99–195. Minneapolis, Minn.: University of Minnesota Press.

—— (1966). *Primary Philosophy*. New York: McGraw-Hill.

SEARLE, J. (1969). *Speech Acts*. Cambridge: Cambridge University Press.

—— (1983). *Intentionality*. Cambridge: Cambridge University Press.

SELLARS, W. (1963). 'Some Reflections on Language Games.' In his *Science, Perception, and Reality*. London: Routledge & Kegan Paul.

—— (1966). 'Fatalism and Determinism.' In K. Lehrer (ed.), *Freedom and Determinism*. New York: Random House.

—— (1974). 'Meaning as Functional Classification.' *Synthese*, 27: 417–38.

SHIPLEY, E., SMITH, C. S., and GLEITMAN, L. R. (1969). 'A Study in the Acquisition of Language.' *Language*, 45: 322–42.

SHOEMAKER, S. (1982). 'The Inverted Spectrum.' *Journal of Philosophy*, 79: 357–81.

—— (1985). 'Churchland on Reduction, Qualia, and Introspection.' *PSA 1984*, ii. 799–809. East Lansing, Mich.: Philosophy of Science Association.

—— (1994). 'Phenomenal Character.' *Nous*, 28: 357–81.

SKYRMS, B. (1980). 'Higher-Order Degrees of Belief.' In D. H. Mellor (ed.), *Prospects for Pragmatism*, 118–20. Cambridge: Cambridge University Press.

—— (1987). 'Coherence.' In N. Rescher (ed.), *Scientific Inquiry in Philosophical Perspective*, 222–42. Pittsburgh, Pa.: University of Pittsburgh Press.

SMART, J. J. C. (1959). 'Sensations and Brain Processes.' *Philosophical Review*, 68: 141–56.

—— (1968). *Between Science and Philosophy: An Introduction to the Philosophy of Science*. New York: Random Houe.

SOBER, E. (1975). *Simplicity*. Oxford: Oxford University Press.

—— (1988). *Reconstructing the Past*. Cambridge, Mass.: MIT Press.

—— (1990). 'Let's Razor Ockham's Razor.' In D. Knowles (ed.), *Explanation and its Limits*. Cambridge: Cambridge University Press.

SOLOMONOFF, R. J. (1964). 'A Formal Theory of Inductive Inference.' *Information and Control*, 7: 1–22, 224–54.

STALNAKER, R. (1968). 'A Theory of Conditionals.' In Rescher, N. (ed.), *Studies in Logical Theory*. Oxford: Oxford University Press.

—— (1984). *Inquiry*. Cambridge, Mass.: MIT Press.

STAMPE, D. (1977). 'Toward a Causal Theory of Linguistic Representation.' *Midwest Studies in Philosophy*, 2: 42–63.

STRAWSON, P. F. (1952). *Introduction to Logical Theory*. London: Methuen.

—— (1974a). 'Meaning and Truth.' In his *Logico-Linguistic Papers*. London: Methuen.

—— (1974b). *Subject and Predicate in Logic and Grammar*. London: Methuen.

TARSKI, A. (1956). 'The Concept of Truth in Formalized Languages.' In his *Logic, Semantics, Metamathematics*. Oxford: Oxford University Press.

TAWIL, N. (1987). 'Reference and Intentionality.' Ph.D. Dissertation, Princeton University.

TAYLOR, C. (1964). *The Explanation of Behaviour*. London: Routledge.

TAYLOR, J. G. (1962). *The Behavioral Basis of Perception*. New Haven, Conn.: Yale University Press.

TELLER, P. (1973). 'Conditionalization and Observation.' *Synthese*, 26: 218–58.

THAGARD, P. (1986). 'Parallel Computation and the Mind-Body Problem.' *Cognitive Science*, 10: 301–18.

THOMAS, S. (1978). *The Formal Mechanics of Mind*. Ithaca, NY: Cornell University Press.

TURNEY, P. D. (1988). 'Inductive Inference and Stability.' Ph.D. Dissertation, Department of Philosophy, University of Toronto.

VALIANT, L. G. (1979). 'The Complexity of Enumeration and Reliability Problems.' *SIAM Journal of Computing*, 8: 410–21.

VAN FRAASSEN, B. (1980). *The Scientific Image*. Oxford: Oxford University Press.

—— (1984). 'Belief and the Will.' *Journal of Philosophy*, 81: 235–56.

—— (1989). *Laws and Symmetry*. Oxford: Oxford University Press.

VON NEUMANN, J., and MORGENSTERN, O. (1944). *Theory of Games and Economic Behavior*. Princeton, NJ: Princeton University Press.

WHITE, M. (1950). 'The Analytic and the Synthetic: An Untenable Dualism.' In S. Hook (ed.), *John Dewey: Philosopher of Science and Freedom*. New York:

WIGGINS, D. (1972). 'On Sentence-Sense, Word-Sense, and Differences of Word-Sense.' In D. D. Steinberg and L. A. Jokobovits (eds.), *Semantics*. Cambridge: Cambridge University Press.

WINOGRAD, T., and FLORES, C. F. (1986). *Understanding Computers and Cognition*. Norwood, NJ: Ablex.

WITTGENSTEIN, L. (1961). *Tractatus Logico-Philosophicus*, ed. and trans. D. F. Pears and B. McGuiness. London: Routledge.

ZIFF, P. (1960). *Semantic Analysis*. Ithaca, NY: Cornell University Press.

—— (1966). 'On Understanding Understanding Utterances.' In his *Philosophic Turnings*. Ithaca, NY: Cornell University Press.

INDEX OF NAMES

INDEX OF SUBJECTS